African Histories and Modernities

Series Editors
Toyin Falola
University of Texas at Austin
Austin, TX, USA

Matthew M. Heaton
Virginia Tech
Blacksburg, USA

This book series serves as a scholarly forum on African contributions to and negotiations of diverse modernities over time and space, with a particular emphasis on historical developments. Specifically, it aims to refute the hegemonic conception of a singular modernity, Western in origin, spreading out to encompass the globe over the last several decades. Indeed, rather than reinforcing conceptual boundaries or parameters, the series instead looks to receive and respond to changing perspectives on an important but inherently nebulous idea, deliberately creating a space in which multiple modernities can interact, overlap, and conflict. While privileging works that emphasize historical change over time, the series will also feature scholarship that blurs the lines between the historical and the contemporary, recognizing the ways in which our changing understandings of modernity in the present have the capacity to affect the way we think about African and global histories.

Editorial Board
Aderonke Adesanya, Art History, James Madison University
Kwabena Akurang-Parry, History, Shippensburg University
Samuel O. Oloruntoba, History, University of North Carolina, Wilmington
Tyler Fleming, History, University of Louisville
Barbara Harlow, English and Comparative Literature, University of Texas at Austin
Emmanuel Mbah, History, College of Staten Island
Akin Ogundiran, Africana Studies, University of North Carolina, Charlotte

More information about this series at
http://www.springer.com/series/14758

John A. Marcum
Author

Edmund Burke III · Michael W. Clough
Editors

Conceiving Mozambique

palgrave
macmillan

Author
John A. Marcum
Santa Cruz, CA, USA

Editors
Edmund Burke III
University of California, Santa Cruz
Santa Cruz, CA, USA

Michael W. Clough
Oakland, CA, USA

African Histories and Modernities
ISBN 978-3-319-88144-7   ISBN 978-3-319-65987-9   (eBook)
https://doi.org/10.1007/978-3-319-65987-9

© The Editor(s) (if applicable) and The Author(s) 2018
Softcover re-print of the Hardcover 1st edition 2018
This work is subject to copyright. All rights are solely and exclusively licensed by the Publisher, whether the whole or part of the material is concerned, specifically the rights of translation, reprinting, reuse of illustrations, recitation, broadcasting, reproduction on microfilms or in any other physical way, and transmission or information storage and retrieval, electronic adaptation, computer software, or by similar or dissimilar methodology now known or hereafter developed.
The use of general descriptive names, registered names, trademarks, service marks, etc. in this publication does not imply, even in the absence of a specific statement, that such names are exempt from the relevant protective laws and regulations and therefore free for general use.
The publisher, the authors and the editors are safe to assume that the advice and information in this book are believed to be true and accurate at the date of publication. Neither the publisher nor the authors or the editors give a warranty, express or implied, with respect to the material contained herein or for any errors or omissions that may have been made. The publisher remains neutral with regard to jurisdictional claims in published maps and institutional affiliations.

Cover credit: © iStock/Getty Images Plus

Printed on acid-free paper

This Palgrave Macmillan imprint is published by Springer Nature
The registered company is Springer International Publishing AG
The registered company address is: Gewerbestrasse 11, 6330 Cham, Switzerland

Foreword

In the words of its author, John A. Marcum, the purpose of *Conceiving Mozambique* is to provide an "independent and probing review and understanding of the Mozambique struggle for independence." The book seeks to provide a necessary starting point for national reconciliation and the construction of a more just and democratic future for the country.

Marcum was the leading scholar on the liberation struggle in Portuguese Africa. His two volumes on Angola, *The Angolan Revolution*, Vol. 1, *The Anatomy of an Explosion* (1969), and Vol. 2, *Exile Politics and Guerrilla Warfare, 1962–1976* (1978), have since their appearance been widely recognized as the authoritative account of the protracted Angolan liberation struggle.

Conceiving Mozambique is in some respects the companion piece to these two works. It is based upon authoritative documentation of the gestation period of the Mozambique liberation struggle, including archival documents, abundant unpublished letters, diaries, and verbatim records of conversations with many of the principals. Part of a much larger work which he never got to complete, *Conceiving Mozambique* is a dispassionate look at the liberation struggle. It was completed by Marcum shortly before his death in 2013.

The book is clearly written in non-academic prose and takes the form of a detailed political history of the Mozambican liberation process, with particular attention to the early years. It is intended for those interested in the history of Mozambique, ex-Portuguese Africa, and African

vi FOREWORD

development. It introduces the major and many of the minor dramatis personae effectively.

For more on my role in the preparation of the manuscript, please see the Acknowledgements.

Michael Clough, the co-editor of this book, gave the manuscript its current shape, while remaining faithful to Marcum's original text. He also took the time to compare the footnotes with the materials in the John A. Marcum Papers in the Africa collection at Stanford University Library. For an overview of the Marcum Papers, please consult the website. https://searchworks.stanford.edu/view/8447318

Clough was a close friend and colleague of Marcum in the early 1980s, and is the author of "John Marcum and America's Missed Opportunities in Africa," with which this book begins. Mike was a Ph.D. candidate at the University of California, Berkeley and completing his dissertation on US Policy toward Revolutionary Change in Southern Africa when he and John first met. From 1980 to 1986, Mike taught at the Naval Postgraduate School in Monterey, California. In 1985–86 he served as the study director for the Secretary of State's Advisory Committee on South Africa. From 1987 to 1996 he directed the Council on Foreign Relations' African Studies Program. Before changing careers in 2001, Mike wrote extensively on US policy toward Africa, the domestic politics of American foreign policy, and globalization. He is the author of *Free At Last?: U.S. Policy toward Africa and the End of the Cold War* (New York: New York University Press, 1992). Mike is currently a criminal defense attorney and, among other clients, represents five inmates on California's death row.

Santa Cruz, USA   Edmund Burke III

PREFACE

Anti-colonial struggles in Africa during the 1960s fascinated me as a young academic and director of a scholarship program for African refugee students. One result was a two-volume study of the Angolan Revolution. The exigencies of an ensuing academic career delayed a similar account of the burst of nationalist awareness and activity that constituted the initial, conceptual phase of the struggle for independence in Portugal's other major African colony, Mozambique. From the fringes of that drama, I witnessed contesting ideas and conflicting ambitions within a conflict that ended in the collapse of Portuguese rule and a brief but bloody triumph of Marxist dogmatism, replete with forced collectivization, military dictatorship, and civil war.

Sequentially, a Eurafrican fantasy gave way to nationalist espousals of liberal nationalism, black populism, and orthodox Marxism. Drawing on ephemeral documents, personal interviews, and verbatim excerpts from the unpublished or buried words of key players, this historical narrative attempts to go beyond the myths, simplifications, doctrinal hyperbole, and hagiography that may accompany and obfuscate accounts of an anti-colonial insurgency. With divergent ethnic and regional identities, ambitions, ideologies, educational levels, and strategic priorities Mozambique's founders competed for political power. Their aspirations intertwined, combined, dissembled, hardened, and shaped the struggle. Much of the history of the early years of the independence struggle has been distorted, blurred, or buried by the dictates of political

vii

viii   PREFACE

convenience. My goal has been to recover, reconstruct, and reveal a more accurate account of what happened.

Today as a contemporary Mozambican polity fashions the country's future in a global digital age, the legacies of the formative period of conceptual clash, exile politics, and Cold War intrusion remain vital to an understanding of what caused a bloody civil war to follow independence yet ultimately to lead a war-weary society to a fragile political reconciliation and a corruption-flawed but increasingly democratic state.

Santa Cruz, CA, USA   John A. Marcum

Acknowledgements

John Marcum's Acknowledgements

I owe special thanks to former Mozambican students, among them nationalist pioneers such as Joao Nhambiu and Joseph Massinga, among others, for sharing their diverse experiences, insights and perspectives; to Janet Mondlane for making available personal archives housed at the University of Southern California; to Manuel de Araujo of the Centro de Estudos Moçambicanos e Internacionais (Maputo) for his encouragement; and to American actors and observers, notably J. Wayne Fredericks, George Houser, Douglas Wheeler, and Gerald Bender.

Edmund Burke's Acknowledgements

Although John Marcum left a completed manuscript of *Conceiving Mozambique* when he died, a great deal of work was required to produce a clean manuscript, given that the book was written over the last decades of Marcum's life on a variety of different word-processing systems. To produce the final version of the manuscript a host of unsuspected little problems, the result of the geological deposits of each generation of word-processing, had to be debugged. Let them all be thanked according to their contributions:

Former colleagues Peter Kenez and Will Vrolman each played important roles in the first phase of untangling the Marcum manuscript, and each is here abundantly thanked. Unfortunately the untangling process was only in its infancy.

x ACKNOWLEDGEMENTS

Had it not been for the amazing Candace Freiwald whose career as a typist and editor spanned the digital word-processing era, we would still be finalizing the manuscript. That Candace accomplished this with her usual combination of hard work, skill, and good humor is all the more amazing. In the process, she earned my undying gratitude and that of Gwen Marcum (as well as that of all of readers of this book).

Rachel Hohn assisted in the process of preparing the Marcum Collection for shipment to Stanford University Press. We are grateful to her as well.

Photo Acknowledgements

We'd like to thank the owners of the photos included here for their generosity
in authorizing their publication.

-The photo of John Marcum, George Houser, and others with Kwame Nkrumah at the 1958 All-African People's Congress was kindly supplied by the family of the late George Houser.

-The photo of John Marcum with some unknown African students was taken in 1960 on the occasion of a meeting of Crossroads Africa. It is supplied by Gwen Marcum, John's widow.

-We are grateful to Ambassador Lopez Tembe Ndelane for the group portrait of the founding members of UDENAMO.

-Shannon Moeser has made available the portrait of Leo Milas printed in this book, for which we are most thankful.

CONTENTS

1	Eduardo Mondlane	1
2	The Rise of Mozambican Nationalism	17
3	Frelimo	35
4	The Ravages of Exile Politics	55
5	OAU, UN, and USA	73
6	Mondlane in Dar es Salaam	85
7	New Contenders	101
8	Students vs. Soldiers	107
9	Mondlane's Assasination	129
10	The Collapse of Portugal	155
11	Independent Mozambique	171

xii CONTENTS

Bibliography   189

Index   197

About the Editors

Edmund ("Terry") Burke III is Research Professor of History Emeritus at the University of California at Santa Cruz. After John Marcum's death he undertook to bring the final manuscript into publishable form as a tribute to Marcum his friend and colleague of long standing.

Burke is the author and editor of numerous books and articles on Middle East and North African history, orientalism, and environmental history. His recent books include: *The Ethnographic State: France and Moroccan Islam* (Berkeley: University of California Press, 2014); *The Environment and World History, 1500–2000* (University of California Press, 2009); and *Genealogies of Orientalism: History, Theory, Politics* (University of Nebraska Press, 2008).

Michael ("Mike") Clough became a close friend and colleague of John in the early 1980s, when Mike was teaching at the Naval Postgraduate School in Monterey, California, and completing his dissertation on US Policy toward Revolutionary Change in Southern Africa. In 1985–86 Mike served as the study director for the Secretary of State's Advisory Committee on South Africa. From 1987 to 1996 he directed the Council on Foreign Relations' African Studies Program. Before changing careers in 2001, Mike wrote extensively on US policy toward Africa, the domestic politics of American foreign policy, and globalization. He is the author of *Free At Last: U.S. Policy toward Africa and the End of the Cold War*. Mike is now a criminal defense attorney and, among other clients, represents five inmates on California's death row.

ABBREVIATIONS

ACOA	American Committee on Africa
ANC	African National Congress
CEMO	Center for Mozambican and International Studies
CIMADE	Inter-Movement Committee to the Émigrés
CLM	Council for the Liberation of Mozambique
CONCP	Conference of Portuguese African Nationalist Movements
FRELIMO	Front for the Liberation of Mozambique
GRAE	Guinea Revolutionary Government in Exile
KANU	Kenya African National Union
MAC	Anti-Colonialist Movement
MANU	Mozambique African National Union
MONIREMO	Movement for Unity and Reconciliation
MPLA	National Movement for the Liberation of Angola
MRUPP	Mozambique Revolutionary United People's Party
NESAM	Central of African Secondary Students in Mozambique
NATO	North Atlantic Treaty Organization
OAU	Organization of African Unity
PAC	Pan Africanist Congress
PAFMECSA	Pan-African Movement of East, Central and Southern Africa
PAIGC	African Party of Guinea and Cape Verde
PCN	Coalition Party of Mozambique
PIDE	Portuguese secret police
RAWU	African Worker's Railways Union
RENAMO	Mozambican National Resistance Organization
SNASP	National Popular Security Service
SRANC	Southern Rhodesia African National Congress

xvi ABBREVIATIONS

TANU	Tanganyika African National Union
UDENAMO	Mozambican Democratic National Union
UGEAN	General Union of Black African Students Under Portuguese Colonial Domination
UNEMO	Union of National Mozambican Students

LIST OF FIGURES

Fig. 8.1   John Marcum, Kwame Nkrumah, and others at the
           1958 All-Africa People's Conference in Accra, Ghana   109

Fig. 8.2   John Marcum with African students at Lincoln
           University for Crossroads Africa Meeting in 1960   113

Fig. 8.3   Founding members of UDENAMO, date unknown. Right
           to left, among others: Seated: Daniel Malhalela, Lopez Tembe,
           Absalao Bahule, Lourenço Matola and Silverio Nungo;
           Standing: Eli Ndimene, Joao Munguambe, Diwas, Antonio
           Murrupa, Adelino Gumane, Urias Simango, Filipe Samuel
           Magaia and Fernando Mungaka   125

Fig. 8.4   Leo Milas (aka Leo Clinton Aldridge, Jr., aka
           Seifeddine Leo Milas)   126

xvii

Introduction: John Marcum and America's Missed Opportunities in Africa

"Knowledgeable, soft-spoken, fluent in French, and easy to get along with."[1] That is how George Houser, one of the pioneers of American efforts to support African liberation movements, described his reasons for asking John Marcum, a then young professor at Lincoln University, to accompany him on a long and dangerous hike into rebel territory in northern Angola in January 1962. Houser's description was remarkably apt. Language skills aside, the traits Houser listed explain, in part, why John was one of the very few prominent voices in the long and divisive debate over US policy toward southern Africa who was respected and warmly regarded by both activists like Houser and conservative policymakers like former US Assistant Secretary of State for Africa Chester Crocker. But the near-universal respect that John earned from diverse political and ideological quarters was due, most of all, to his ability to combine his unceasing commitment to ending Portuguese colonialism with hard-headed, fact-based analysis of Portuguese rule and the nationalist movements in Angola and Mozambique.

John completed this book in the final months of an exceptional life. He conceived it nearly a half-century earlier, in the early 1960s, as part of an ambitious project to document the struggle to end Portuguese rule in Angola and Mozambique. The first volume—*The Angolan Revolution: The Anatomy of an Explosion, 1950–1962*—was published in 1969.[2] It confirmed John's position as a preeminent member of the first generation of American political scientists to focus on post-colonial Africa. Nine

xix

years later, after the sudden collapse of Portuguese colonialism, volume 2—*The Angolan Revolution: Exile, Politics and Guerrilla Warfare, 1962–76*—was published.[3] John collected much of the material that this book is based on in the 1960s, but his plan for a book on Mozambique was interrupted as he was increasingly drawn into academic administration at the University of California, Santa Cruz, and, in 1990, became the director of the University of California's system-wide Education Abroad Program. In 2007, at the age of 80, he finally "retired," and, despite battling serious illnesses, completed *Conceiving Mozambique.*

Like everything else John wrote over the course of his extraordinarily long academic career, this book was written with a larger purpose. In the brief concluding section of the manuscript, which John emailed to his wife, Gwen, in May 2013, he wrote:

> By salving its wounds with an historical cleansing Mozambique can unburden its future, free itself from the straitjacket of historical mythology and dogma and enable its citizens to better comprehend how a long, harsh colonial rule negatively limited human perceptions and behavior, how centuries of educational deprivation and arbitrary rule inevitably warped views of race and ethnicity, and how the shortcomings of military intolerance and class determinism led to authoritarianism, impoverishment and unspeakable violence. The search for an unvarnished and compassionate understanding of Mozambique's past will be crucial over time to the construction of a more just and democratic future. Hopefully the narrative of the preceding pages may help to provoke such a liberating process.
>
> It is time for the country to clear the political deck and free young minds from the delimiting outcomes of cruel history. It is time for a new generation of Mozambicans to explore, think, question, challenge and commit themselves to the long, arduous step-by-step process of reconceiving and building a new Mozambique.

The values and hopes reflected in this conclusion are remarkably similar to those expressed in *The Challenge of Africa*, a long essay John published in February 1960.[4] Written after the first wave of decolonization and before Africa had become a Cold War battleground, that essay clearly distinguished John from other young political scientists who were flocking to Africa to begin their academic careers. At the time he wrote this essay, there were nine independent states in Africa and six more about to become independent, including the Belgian Congo. The civil war in the Congo, which arguably marked the beginning of the Cold War in Africa, had not begun. For most of those scholars, Africa offered a unique research opportunity—a chance to witness the birth of states firsthand, develop new theories of political development, and establish academic credentials. This group included, most notably, David Apter, James Coleman, Carl Rosberg, Richard Sklar, Immanuel Wallerstein, Ruth S. Morgenthau, and Crawford Young.[5] They all played leading roles in developing the study of African politics. But, with the exception of Morgenthau[6] and John A. Davis,[7] none of them became engaged in trying to shape US policy toward Africa in the ways that John did.

As he wrote in *The Challenge of Africa*, John viewed the emergence of independent Africa as part of "man's noble but desperate struggle to build a more humane, peaceful previous esthetic society."[8] His intended audience was not other Africanists. Instead, John sought to influence both "Western" policymakers and the "architects of tomorrow's Africa": the small educated African elite that was then in the forefront of the African independence movement.[9] In a passage that aptly reflected the perspective John would maintain throughout his life, he wrote:

> It is not for the West to try to force its behavioral patterns, values and institutions upon an unwilling Africa. The West's "democratic faith," however, dictates that it make a real effort to demonstrate the worth of such Western ideals as political tolerance, democratic process, cultural freedom, equal social opportunities and limited government. Not an unimportant part of this demonstration must come through the more perfect realization of these ideals in the West itself—in the American South and the Iberian Peninsula, for example.[10]

After detailing the challenges and opportunities facing Africa, John concluded: "With a little wisdom, compassion, good fortune and a measure of outside help, Africans can make their continent into a symbol of man's hopes for himself."[11]

In light of the developments that followed,[12] it is easy to read *The Challenge of Africa* as naive and hopelessly idealistic. But that would be a mistake. John was well aware of the hurdles that would have to be overcome in order to "construct a peaceful continent of new nations." It is only in retrospect that the possibilities that John tried to help Western policymakers and Africa's emerging leaders imagine and realize seem not to have existed.

xxii   INTRODUCTION: JOHN MARCUM AND AMERICA'S …

Conceiving Mozambique should be read first and foremost as part of the larger (and still largely untold) story of how US policymakers failed to meet the challenge of Africa in the early 1960s. As his conclusion reflects, it is also a testament to John's refusal to give up hope that, even if only in a future he would not live to see, Africa's political leaders would meet that challenge.

In the mid-1950s John had traveled to North Africa in conjunction with his doctoral dissertation research on French North Africa,[13] and his personal experiences in France during that country's bitter debate over its settler colony in Algeria informed John's understanding of the process of ending Portuguese rule in Angola, Guinea-Bissau, and Mozambique.[14] But John was not "introduced to Black Africa" until the summer of 1957, which he spent as a participant in an "Experiment in International Living" summer program in Nigeria.[15]

John's involvement in Portuguese Africa began in earnest in December 1958 at the All-African People's Conference in Accra, Ghana. The previous year Ghana became the first former colony in sub-Saharan African to become independent; and Kwame Nkrumah, Ghana's first President, became the leading proponent of a Pan-African vision of the continent's future. In 1958–59 he received a Ford Foundation grant that allowed him to travel to West Africa, and "being in neighboring Ivory Coast at the time," he flew to Accra, where he met the Belgian Congo's tragically fated first President, Patrice Lumumba. (Because of his fluency in French, John was asked to serve as an interpreter for Lumumba at the conference.) In Accra he was also introduced to Angolan nationalist leader Holden Roberto. Some weeks later John was in Brazzaville, the capital of the French Congo, and met with other Angolan nationalists, who described "a process of slow genocide going on inside Angola." Thus began John's personal connection with the nascent political movements that would shape the struggle for independence in Angola and Mozambique.

From 1955 until 1961 John taught at Colgate University.[16] In 1959 he introduced a course on Africa and, as a result of his friendship with Houser, was able to arrange for some of Africa's most prominent nationalist leaders including Kenneth Kaunda, the future president of Zambia (then Northern Rhodesia), to speak to his students. With money that came in part from a prize won by Colgate's "Quiz Bowl" team, John organized a scholarship program for students from Northern Rhodesia.

In the summer of 1960 John returned to Africa as a leader of a Crossroads Africa school-building projeçt in Senegal. Crossroads Africa was established in 1958 by Dr. James H. Robinson as a pioneering effort to "build bridges of friendship to Africa" and was called "the progenitor of the Peace Corps" by President John Kennedy. In 1961 Edward R. Murrow and Howard K. Smith of CBS News produced a film—*Crossroads Africa: Pilot for a Peace Corps*—that reflected the spirit of pragmatic idealism that motivated and influenced John's early involvement in Africa. While he was in Senegal, John received a call from the USA asking him to accompany former Governor of New York and Ambassador to the Soviet Union W. Averell Harriman on a fact-finding mission to West Africa on behalf of Democratic presidential c.andidate John Kennedy.

In 1961 John moved from Colgate to Lincoln University, the first degree-granting historically black university in the USA. Its alumni include Nkrumah and Nnamdi Azikwe, Nigeria's first president. When John arrived at Lincoln, the Kennedy administration seemed to be on the verge of embracing the winds of change that were sweeping across the African continent, identifying the USA with African nationalism and taking a strong stand at the United Nations against both Portuguese colonialism and apartheid in South Africa.

In July 1957, as a young Senator from Massachusetts, Kennedy sharply criticized the Eisenhower administration's "dismal" record on the Algerian issue and called for policies that would shape "a course toward political independence in Algeria."[17] After he was elected, Kennedy made three appointments that seemed to signal a dramatic change in the direction of US policy toward Africa. Former presidential nominee Adlai Stevenson, who was the leader of the liberal internationalist wing of the Democratic Party, was appointed to be the USA's Ambassador to the United Nations. Chester Bowles, another Democratic Party leader, who had served as Ambassador to India, was appointed to be Under Secretary of State, the number two position in the Department. (In 1956 Bowles, a prolific author, had written what is possibly the first major book on US policy toward independent Africa—*Africa's Challenge to America*.[18]) And G. Mennen ("Soapy") Williams, the former Governor of Michigan, was appointed to be Assistant Secretary of State for Africa.[19] Stevenson, Bowles, and Williams were fervent liberal internationalists in the tradition of Woodrow Wilson, Sumner Welles, and Eleanor Roosevelt. Unfortunately, Senator Kennedy's Algeria speech and the appointment of Stevenson, Bowles, and Williams raised hopes that were not realized.

When President Kennedy was inaugurated in January 1961, the USA was uniquely positioned to support and shape the emergence of the Africa John had imagined in his 1960 essay: a peaceful, democratic, and developing continent led by a new and growing generation of African leaders. The USA's advantages in post-colonial Africa included the leading role that Washington had played in championing self-determination at the end of the First World War and in creating the United Nations after the Second World War, the lack of direct association with Africa's colonial past, the international goodwill created by Kennedy's election, and the unparalleled economic and other resources at the disposal of American policymakers. Another important factor was the establishment of African studies programs at universities such as Northwestern University (1948), Howard University (1953), and UCLA (1959) that eagerly became involved in training future African leaders such as Eduardo Mondlane and supporting the development of colleges and universities in Africa. Finally, and not to be underestimated, was the enthusiasm of the Crossroads Africa volunteers John led in Senegal in 1960 and the young Americans who rushed to join the Peace Corps. US policy toward Africa was also inextricably tied to Africa by our country's history of slavery and the struggle for racial equality, which was becoming a powerful force in American society just as Africa was becoming independent.

Tragically, American policymakers failed to meet the challenges John identified in his 1960 essay. The opportunities that existed at the dawn of the African independence era were squandered as result of Washington's inability to see through the fog created by the Cold War. Instead of promoting peaceful transitions from colonial rule to independence, the USA intervened in Africa—politically and militarily, overtly and covertly—in ways that undermined movement toward democracy, exacerbated political and military conflicts, and promoted and entrenched some of the most dictatorial regimes that came to power in Africa, including, most prominently, Mobutu Sese Seko in Zaire (the Belgian Congo).[20] And, in an unfortunate twist of history, the USA came to be viewed by many Africans as an ally of Lisbon and the white rulers in Rhodesia and South Africa. The full story of the tragic failure of US policy in Africa in the early 1960s has yet to be told. But John's short book tells that story in microcosm.

In 1961 the State Department asked Lincoln University to create a program to support refugee students from Portuguese Africa. John became the director of that program. In that capacity, he became an advisor and friend to many Angolan and Mozambican students, including Joao Nhambiu. During this period he also developed a friendship with Mondlane. Those friendships provided much of the motivation for John to spend the last years of his life completing this book.

At the beginning of the Kennedy era John also developed a close working friendship with Wayne Fredericks, a businessman and Ford Foundation official who served as Deputy Assistant Secretary of State for Africa under Williams and was the single most important bridge between leading US politicians and policymakers, including Averell Harriman and Robert Kennedy and the leaders of the nationalist movements in Angola, Mozambique, Namibia, Rhodesia, and South Africa. Throughout the early 1960s Fredericks fought a valiant but ultimately losing battle against efforts by Portugal and its allies in the Kennedy and Johnson administrations to cut off American support for Mondlane and other southern Africa nationalists.[21] As John documents, by the mid-1960s Washington had abandoned efforts in the United Nations to pressure Portugal, bowed to pressure from Lisbon to cut off support for refugee educational programs for Mozambican students, and cut off lines of communication with Mondlane. (Because of John's hike into rebel territory in Angola with Houser in January 1962, the Portuguese government made his role at Lincoln University program part of negotiations to extend US basing rights in the Azores.)

In a paper presented at a conference in the spring of 1963, Mondlane frankly stated his concerns about the direction of US policy toward Mozambique:

> For some time we believed that the people of the world were committed to morality and the rule of law, but as we went forth to present our case to the United Nations, to governments within each country, and to the press of the world, we began to realize that interests other than morality and the merits of our case seem to be more important. For example, we know that the United States and her NATO allies are the paramount sources of military and economic power for Portugal. When we presented the facts at our disposal to the people of the United States, they seemed to fall on deaf ears.[22]

xxvi   INTRODUCTION: JOHN MARCUM AND AMERICA'S ...

As hopes that the USA would support the independence struggles in southern Africa faded, John began to warn of the likely consequences. In an essay published in 1966, John and Allard K. Lowenstein observed that, "[d]eprived of reasonable hope for peaceful change, Southern Africans are abandoning moral suasion as ineffective," and predicted that "the consequences of continued Portuguese refusal to agree to self-determination in Angola and Mozambique would be protracted and bitter conflict."[23] They also described how the policies of the apartheid regime in South Africa were forcing the leaders of the black opposition there to abandon non-violence.[24] They wrote:

> If there is an explosion [in southern Africa], it will be because the world outside, and especially the United States, permitted nonviolence to fail. If the thrust is anti-Western, it will be because the present white governments sustained themselves by Western indulgence. If it is anti-white, it will be because an official white racism has infected an entire society and because white men for so many years failed for so many years to oppose convincingly that which is antiblack.[25]

At the conference where this paper was presented, Mondlane emphasized, "if she wanted to, the United States could prevent Portugal from engaging in further violence against Africans" by cutting off the supply of American weapons to the Portuguese military. He also pointedly warned that Frelimo was "going to accept friendship from wherever it comes."[26]

In a November 1967 "conversation" with Helen Kitchen, the editor of *Africa Report*, Mondlane aptly summarized the evolution of US policy toward Africa:

> During the first three years of this decade, when John F. Kennedy was President, the United States went through a period of equivocation and seemed to be moving toward support for us. After the death of President Kennedy, the policy became equivocation without direction. More recently, U.S. policy has become one of support for the status quo.[27]

Mondlane added presciently that US policy toward Portugal and the prospects for negotiations to end Portuguese rule in Africa were tied to the outcome of the Vietnam War and predicted, "[a]s long as there is no peace in Vietnam, Portugal will never think of negotiating until she has been completely ruined in Africa."[28]

By the fall of 1967, John was deeply disappointed with US policy. In an essay he wrote in October 1967, the cautiously hopeful tone he expressed in 1960 was replaced by strong warnings that Washington's "complicity in the status quo of Southern Africa" was undermining the credibility of the United States as a model of democracy and "destroy[ing] confidence in American motives, which are seen as contaminated with racism."[29] John described US policy toward southern Africa as "a contradictory tandem of lamentation and laissez-faire," and wrote that Washington's diplomatic "importuning" and "advice" were being ignored and its diplomatic pressure had proved to be "totally ineffectual."[30] With regard to Portuguese Africa, he noted:

> In spite of the absence of any perceptible signs that Portugal is prepared to alter its policies, the United States has continued to provide direct and indirect financial and material assistance that shores up military efforts to suppress African nationalists seeking independence by the only means left open to them, i.e., violent action.[31]

And John quoted Mondlane as stating, after a visit by the US Ambassador in Lisbon, Admiral George Anderson, to Angola and Mozambique in March 1964, that "he expected that the United States 'like the Republic of South Africa will intervene against us in the forthcoming armed conflict with Portugal."[32]

John sadly noted, "we have become so detached from our own revolutionary origins and so unaware and unable to understand the needs and aspirations of the great bulk of mankind that we can only respond with moral clichés and irrelevant gestures," and he emphasized that, in considering policy alternatives, "it should be kept in mind that we have already intervened in Southern Africa—but on the wrong side."[33]

John proposed that the USA should adopt a policy of military, economic, cultural, and diplomatic "disengagement" with Portugal and South Africa. Specifically, he called for reducing US dependence on Portuguese bases in the Azores, strictly limiting defense cooperation with Lisbon, withdrawing economic support from Portugal, levying a "selective anti-apartheid tax upon profits, incomes and trade with South Africa," applying the policies governing cultural and scientific cooperation with the Soviet Union to cultural and scientific cooperation with

South Africa, "politely but unequivocally" repeating US objections to apartheid "publicly and at every opportunity," insisting on reciprocity in the granting of visas, and increasing the number of black foreign service officer in the US embassy in South Africa.[34] These policies are very similar to the kinds of policies that the USA eventually adopted in South Africa, but instead of coming before the escalating conflicts and increased violence that John had predicted in the essay he wrote with Lowenstein, they came after a civil war in Angola that drew in the USA, the Soviet Union, Cuba, and South Africa, an escalating war in Rhodesia, and substantial and sustained unrest and violence in South Africa.

The turning point in southern Africa finally came on April 25, 1974, when army rebels staged a coup in Lisbon. As John documented in detail in the second volume of his history of the Angolan revolution, the new Portuguese regime moved quickly to give independence to its African colonies. In Mozambique, power was handed over to Frelimo. In Angola, independence sparked a civil war between the three rival nationalist movements. As the civil war unfolded in late 1975, John was thrust into the national spotlight. He was called to testify before the Senate Foreign Relations Committee and made a widely hailed appearance on *Meet the Press.*

By the time Frelimo came to power in 1974, a new generation of Africanists was in the forefront of research on Mozambique. In the wake of the Vietnam War and the Nixon administration's adoption of a policy that abandoned all pretense of opposition to white rule in southern Africa, Africanists in the USA were politically marginalized. With few exceptions, the young scholars and journalists who became engaged in research on Mozambique saw the struggles that had shaped Frelimo as a battle between "narrow" and racist nationalists, who sought to replace white colonialists with an educated black elite, and progressive socialists.[35] This group, which included academics and journalists such as Allen Isaacman and Barbara Isaacman, James Mittelman,[36] John Saul,[37] and Barry Munslow,[38] hailed Frelimo's triumph as part of a broader transition to a new model of socialism in Africa. In 1982 the Isaacmans wrote that political independence in Mozambique "was only the first step in the larger struggle to transform basic economic and social relations" and declared that Frelimo's effort to create "Socialism with a Mozambican Face" carried "important ideological implications for the continent as a whole."[39] But, as the final brief sections of this book document, the dream that Mozambique would usher in a new socialist era in Africa proved to be short-lived.[40]

By the time that Frelimo came to power, John's personal involvement with Mozambique was limited. He did not join the debate over the prospects for socialism with a Mozambican face, but he remained deeply interested in the country's future. And he made the completion of this book his final project. He did so out of a modest hope that, as he wrote in conclusion, it would encourage the kind of honest reflection on the past that he believed will help to solidify the foundations for lasting democracy and respect for human rights in Mozambique.

Michael W. Clough

NOTES

1. George M. Houser, *No One Can Stop The Rain* (Pilgrim Press 1989), p. 155.
2. John Marcum, *The Angolan Revolution* Volume I (1950–1962) (MIT Press 1969).
3. John Marcum, *The Angolan Revolution* Volume II (1962–1976) (MIT Press 1978).
4. John Marcum, "The Challenge of Africa," *The New Leader*, February 8, 1960.
5. David Apter, *The Gold Coast in Transition* (Princeton University Press, 1955); James Coleman, *Nigeria: Background to Nationalism* (University of California Press, 1958); Carl Rosberg, *Political Parties And National Integration In Tropical Africa*, with James Coleman (University of California Press, 1964); Richard Sklar, *Nigerian Political Parties: Power in an Emergent African Nation* (Princeton University Press, 1963); Immanuel Wallerstein, *Africa: The Politics of Independence* (Vintage Books, 1961); Ruth Morgenthau, *Political Parties in French-Speaking West Africa* (Calendon Press, 1965); Crawford Young, *Politics in the Congo: Decolonization and Independence* (Princeton University Press, 1965).
6. Morgenthau taught international politics at Brandeis University from 1963 to 2003. During her long career she was an Africa advisor to Presidents John F. Kennedy, Lyndon B. Johnson, and Jimmy Carter, and served as a US representative to the UN Commission for Social Development.

xxx INTRODUCTION: JOHN MARCUM AND AMERICA'S ...

7. Davis was an important early leader of the civil rights movement and probably the most significant African-American academic to become involved in the debate over US policy toward Africa in the early 1960s. He taught political science at Howard University, Lincoln University, and City College of New York, and, as President of the American Society of African Culture, organized a series of conferences in the early 1960s that brought together American and African writers, scholars, and policymakers, including Marcum and Mondlane. See *Pan-Africanism Reconsidered* (University of California Press, 1962) and *Southern Africa in Transition* (Praeger, 1966).
8. Marcum, "The Challenge of Africa", 6.
9. *Id.*, 5–6.
10. *Id.*, 37.
11. *Id.*, 43.
12. See Aristide Zolberg, Creating Political Order: The Party States of West Africa (Rand McNally, 1967).
13. "French North Africa in the Atlantic Community," Stanford University, 1955.
14. See, for example, John Marcum, "Three Revolutions," *Africa Report*, November 1967.
15. Letter from John Marcum to Danny Schechter, February 25, 1969.
16. One of John's students at Colgate was Peter Tarnoff, who joined the foreign service after graduating in 1958, and served as one of Secretary of State Cyrus Vance's top deputies when President Jimmy Carter became the first US President since John Kennedy to support the kinds of policies toward Africa that John had long advocated.
17. This speech is reprinted in John F. Kennedy, *The Strategy for Peace* (Harper & Row, 1960).
18. *Africa's Challenge to America* (University of California Press, 1956).
19. See Thomas Noer, *Soapy: A Biography of G. Mennen Williams* (University of Michigan 2006).
20. See Michael Clough, *Free At Last? U.S. Policy Toward Africa and the End of the Cold War* (Council on Foreign Relations, 1992).
21. Fredericks's efforts with regard to Mozambique and Mondlane's contacts with the USA are described in Joao M. Cabrita, *Mozambique: The Tortuous Road To Democracy* (Palgrave, 2000), pp. 11, 17–18, 42–43.
22. *Southern Africa in Transition*, p. 209.
23. "Force: its thrust and prognosis," *Southern Africa in Transition*, p. 247
24. *Id.* 258–60.
25. *Id.* 277.
26. *Id.* 279.

27. "A Conversation with Eduardo Mondlane," *Africa Report*, (November 1967), 51.
28. *Id.*
29. John Marcum, "Southern Africa and United States Policy: A Consideration of Alternatives," *Africa Today*, October 1967.
30. *Id.*
31. *Id.*
32. *Id.*
33. *Id.*
34. *Id.*
35. Allen Isaacman, *A Luta Continua: Creating A New Society In Mozambique* (Fernand Braudel Center, 1978), p. 23.
36. James Mittelman, *Underdevelopment and the Transition to Socialism: Mozambique and Tanzania* (Academic, 1981).
37. John Saul, *The State and Revolution in Eastern Africa* (Heinemann, 1979).
38. Barry Munslow, *Mozambique: The Revolution and Its Origin* (Longman, 1983).
39. Allen and Barbara Isaacman, *Mozambique: From Colonialism to Revolution, 1900–1982* (Westview, 1983), pp. 3, 1.
40. See William Finnegan, *A Complicated War: The Harrowing of Mozambique* (University of California, 1992), and Cabrita, *Mozambique: The Tortuous Road to Democracy* (Palgrave, 2000).

Fig. 1 Map of Mozambique. Courtesy of Kimberly Hwe

CHAPTER 1

Eduardo Mondlane

AUGUST 1962: A TIME FOR OPTIMISM

Our car arrived at the home of Syracuse University social anthropologist Eduardo Chivambo Mondlane at mid-afternoon on Saturday, August 4, 1962. It was stuffed with students and sleeping bags. I had recently learned from one of the Mozambican participants in the scholarship program for African refugee students that I directed at Lincoln University that Mondlane had returned from Dar es Salaam, where he had just been elected president of the newly formed Frente de Libertação de Moçambique (Frelimo). I wrote to congratulate him and volunteered to drive a group of students from Portuguese Africa up to Syracuse to meet with him. The students were studying English and preparing to be placed at various American colleges and universities. They were eager to learn firsthand about the creation of Frelimo from its designated leader. Mondlane enthused at the opportunity to recount the drama of Dar es Salaam. With characteristic verve, he played the dual role of didactic professor and visionary nationalist.

It was a warm summer weekend when we barged into the accommodating hospitality of the Mondlane household, which include Dr. Mondlane's American wife, Janet, and their three young children. In an atmosphere of optimism, Mondlane provided a blow-by-blow account

© The Author(s) 2018
J.A. Marcum, *Conceiving Mozambique*, African Histories and Modernities, https://doi.org/10.1007/978-3-319-65987-9_1

1

of how he had outmaneuvered competitors and claimed leadership of Frelimo in a lopsided vote (116 to 19) of Mozambican exiles in Dar es Salaam. The newly independent government of Tanganyika had assembled and prodded representatives from fledgling, quarrelsome nationalist movements in exile to merge within a common front. Our two-day meeting in Syracuse provided a megaphone through which Mondlane could broadcast his aspirations and expectations via a group from the first wave of what would develop into several hundred students from Portugal's African colonies studying at US institutions.

Acutely aware of his status as the sole African with a doctoral degree in a country where illiteracy persisted at over ninety five percent, Mondlane viewed the expansion of educational opportunity at all levels as the most critical need facing the future of Mozambique. And in the immediate term, he confronted a paucity of educated persons among the approximately 800,000 Mozambican exiles living and laboring in neighboring African countries and elsewhere from which to draw and build the cadres of an effective independence movement. The educational deficit would persist as a treacherous issue for Mondlane as he moved from academia into the turbulence of exile politics, the cauldron of Cold War rivalry, and finally anti-colonial insurgency.

There appeared to be solid reasons for Mondlane to exude optimism at our informal weekend palaver in the summer of 1962. Portugal's colonial authority had swiftly crumbled in December 1961, when India's army invaded and annexed Goa. An anti-colonial insurgency that had erupted in Angola in early 1961 was continuing at a low level with support from neighboring Congo-Leopoldville despite Lisbon's efforts to wipe it out. And, although internal political and economic problems preoccupied newly independent African states and dampened their commitment to Pan-African outreach, the specter of colonial rule and white supremacy in southern Africa continued to generate fervent calls for collective action. Mondlane was also encouraged by developments in Washington. The very presence of the African students at his home in Syracuse seemed to signal a major shift in American policy toward Africa.

In August 1960, as I was nearing the end of a summer stint directing a student work program, a Crossroads Africa project to build a one-room school house in Rufisque, Senegal, I received a phone call from New York. Averell Harriman was making an exploratory trip to Africa on behalf of Senator John Kennedy's presidential campaign. I was asked if I would like to join as an advisor? And I answered, "Of course."

Our small team traveled by private plane down the West African coast that September listening to the hopes and aspirations of the leaders and people of colonies emerging into independence.[1] Sometimes Harriman's Cold War instincts took hold, as, for example, when he tried to sway Ghana's President Kwame Nkrumah with accounts of how the Soviets bugged the seal in the American embassy in Moscow. But mostly he listened and learned. He reported back to Kennedy that the USA needed to appreciate the anti-colonial sentiment of Africa and give the continent a higher level of attention.

The first appointment to the new Kennedy Administration was Assistant Secretary of State for African Affairs, Governor G. Mennen Williams of Michigan, a leading figure in the liberal internationalist wing of the Democratic Party. As his deputy, Williams chose J. Wayne Fredericks, a former Ford Motor Company executive and Ford Foundation official with substantial experience and contacts in Africa.

In the early days of the Kennedy administration, Fredericks initiated a new approach to African policy. He took the unprecedented action of appointing a non-governmental advisory body on African affairs that incorporated a wide range of academic and financial perspectives.[2] As the former Belgian Congo struggled toward independence, the new administration took a strong stand against the secession of the Congo's Katanga region. And Washington seemed ready to take on the unyielding colonial policy of Portugal, a small NATO ally.

In March 1961 the American ambassador in Lisbon was instructed to inform Prime Minister Antonio Salazar that he should not expect support during the forthcoming United Nations Security Council debate on self-determination for Angola. The American government believed that "step by step actions were now imperative" for "political, economic and social advancement" toward self-determination in Portugal's African territories "within a realistic timetable."[3]

Motivated by a combination of anti-colonial sentiment, political vision, and Cold War competition, the Kennedy administration also authorized the State Department's Bureau of Educational and Cultural Affairs to launch a scholarship program for students fleeing the repression of Portugal's colonies. That program was based at Lincoln University, and I was chosen to direct it. Mondlane lent his support to the program by helping to persuade refugee students arriving in Europe to opt for scholarships in the USA over rival Communist bloc educational grants. The program soon expanded to include students from white-minority-ruled Rhodesia, South Africa and South West Africa and even southern Sudan and Spanish Guinea, as well as all the Portuguese territories.

All of this encouraged Mondlane to expect American support in the struggles that lay ahead. And, after being elected president of Frelimo, one of the Americans Mondlane was most eager to see was Deputy Assistant Secretary of State Fredericks.

Mondlane's Personal Journey

Born on June 20, 1920, in a small village (Machecahomie, Chibuto) in the Gaza District of southern Mozambique, Eduardo Mondlane was the son of a Tsonga chief and his third wife. At age ten he was still illiterate, herding livestock with his brothers in the Limpopo Valley bush. But in 1931, at age eleven, thanks to what he later described as the decision of a "very determined and persistent" mother that he should be educated, Mondlane entered a government school at Manjacaze in southern Mozambique, a ten-mile hike from his village. He was the only member of his family to embark on the path of formal education.

> You see my father had fifteen children. My father and mother and all my brothers were illiterate. I was the youngest. My mother died when I was 13. She was dying of cancer and had to go away to hospital. I wanted to stay with her but she wouldn't let me. She said I must get an education. I must learn the white man's magic.[4]

From this late beginning in life, Mondlane mounted the rungs of a narrow and rickety ladder of educational opportunity provided by the few foreign Protestant missions permitted in the country. From the Manjacaze government school, Mondlane proceeded to the Swiss Presbyterian mission school of Mauzes, Manjacaze, where Calvinists took an interest in him and arranged for him to complete a primary school certificate in Lourenco Marques. At that time, this was the highest level of general education open to Africans within the Portuguese colonial system. But Mondlane was not willing to settle for that. He "snatched at the straw" of a training opportunity at an American Methodist mission agricultural school at Kambine (Cambine), gained admission, and completed a course in dry farming. Importantly, he also seized the opportunity there to learn English. He followed this with two years teaching dry farming techniques to peasant farmers in the Manjacaze region. Then, buttressed by his English and a new scholarship, and with the support of a Swiss missionary, André Clerc, who tutored him, he proceeded across the border with South Africa to a Swiss Presbyterian secondary school at Lemana in the Northern Transvaal. He had become a protégé of Clerq, for whom he wrote the preface and inspired the "childhood notebooks" of a book edited, fictionalized, and published by Clerc as *Chitlangou: Son of a Chief* (Butterworth Press, 1950).[5] This was followed with a year at the Jan H. Hofmeyr School for Social Work in Johannesburg, and in 1948 Mondlane enrolled at the University of Witwatersrand. He was the first African Mozambican to be admitted to a South African university.[6]

Just days before final examinations in 1949, Mondlane's quest for a "Wits" degree crashed. The newly installed National Party government in Pretoria declared him under apartheid law to be an illegal "foreign native" in a white university. His student permit was revoked and he was deported. After returning to Lourenco Marques, Mondlane directed his energy into efforts to organize a local student association, Núcleo dos Estudantes Secundários Africanos de Moçambique (NESAM). This led to his arrest and interrogation, but did not end his educational journey.[7]

Mondlane later recounted that the Portuguese authorities concluded that his "embryonic spirit of black nationalism might be cured by sending [him] to a university in Portugal." Seizing the opportunity with a scholarship from the Phelps Stokes Fund in New York, Mondlane sailed in mid-1950 to Lisbon, where he enrolled at the University of Lisbon. There he socialized with a handful of other "African intellectuals" (some twenty-five out of a student body of approximately three thousand). They included future leaders of Angola (Agostinho Neto and Mario de Andrade), Cape Verde/Guinea-Bissau (Amílcar Cabral), and Mozambique (Marcelino dos Santos). But, after a year of harassment by the Policia Internacional e da Defesa do Estado (PIDE)—the Portugal's secret police unit—Mondlane prevailed upon the Phelps-Stokes Fund to transfer his scholarship to the USA.

In the fall of 1951, Mondlane entered Oberlin College as an undergraduate (junior) at age 31.[8] He swiftly adjusted and thrived at Oberlin. With a supplemental college scholarship and summer work at a cement works in Elyria, an industrial suburb of Cleveland, he graduated in

6   J.A. MARCUM

1953 and moved straight on to graduate work in sociology and anthropology at Northwestern University. There he studied with Professors Kimball Young and the celebrated anthropologist and Africanist Melville J. Herskovits. He earned an M.A. in 1956 and then pushed on to complete a Ph.D. in 1960. He capped his doctoral studies with a year as a visiting scholar at Harvard, where he worked under the mentorship of Professors Samuel Stouffer and Gordon Allport.[9]

To appreciate what he had achieved in the improbable journey on which his mother had launched him two decades earlier, one needs to consider that, as of 1955, in a Mozambique population then approaching six million, there were as few as ten Africans attending academic high schools (*liceus*) and just over 200 enrolled in technical schools and seminaries. Colonial rule was rooted in and assured by a system of educational deprivation. Mondlane's graduate school mentor, Herskovits, underscored the deliberately exclusionary nature of the colonial education system. It kept the number of Africans in Mozambique's few secondary schools at a negligible level by capping entry eligibility at age thirteen. At that age Africans had not yet completed primary school, so they were blocked from educational advancement. Herskovits also cited statistics indicating the fact that, as of 1950, in the Sul do Save district, the location of the capital, Lourenco Marques, after centuries of imperial claim, 1% of the male population could speak Portuguese and 1% of that cohort could read and write it. The comparable figures for women were 0.1%.[10]

Were it not for the presence of the few Protestant mission stations permitted by Portuguese authorities and resented by a local Portuguese Catholic hierarchy that enjoyed a privileged educational role in the colonies under the terms of a 1940 concordat between Portugal and the Vatican, Mondlane could not have propelled himself beyond the confines of rural poverty. And it was as a workshop leader at a summer Christian youth conference in 1951 that he met a high school participant born in Downers Grove, Illinois, whose ambition was to become a missionary doctor in Africa. Over time, they fell in love, and after she graduated from Northwestern in 1956, despite initial opposition from her white, middle-class Indianapolis family and his Swiss Calvinist mentors in Mozambique, Janet Rae Johnson and Eduardo Mondlane defied racial prejudice in their respective countries and married.

Although his education was made possible by Protestant institutions and he considered himself a Christian, Mondlane was critical of what he described as the hypocrisy of most Christian missions. Writing in 1952, as an Oberlin student, he noted that Protestant missions in Mozambique relegated to remote areas far from white Portuguese influence tended to divide the world into artificially separate spiritual and material realms. He saw some hope, however, in the decision by the Methodists to begin sending missionaries to Mozambique in fields such as engineering and agriculture, signifying an awareness of the need to respond to African material circumstances.[11]

A decade later, as he prepared to assume a political career, Mondlane took a more critical stance. Western missions had cooperated intimately with the techniques of economic and political control by European whites. In doing so, they had failed to follow the "Christian Way," the essence of which was "Love thy neighbor as thyself" and "be prepared to suffer for it": to bear the cross. Too often Christian missionaries worked hand in hand with the colonial administration. Only a very few were prepared to stand up against injustices perpetrated against Africans. "The Western Christian proclaims the brotherhood of man under the fatherhood of one God but," he declared, "at the same time assiduously fights for the maintenance of separate communities based on every conceivable human characteristic, including race, language and even Christian denomination."[12]

In a 1962 talk to a group of Protestant mission organizations, Mondlane observed: "If Western Christians could not find their way through the maze of national and cultural interests involved during the period of the rise of independence movements in Africa, a new opportunity is [now] being offered to them." The road to redemption could reside, he said, in the creation and maintenance of Christian institutions of higher learning in Africa. Many American Churches already supported colleges and universities in Asia. "We Christian Africans, he continued, "have some difficulties in understanding why you should concentrate on helping Asians at the exclusion of our people." He then emphasized,

> On the personal level, the same spirit that drove thousands of young men and women over the last century into Africa as missionaries should inspire new generations of Christians into going to Africa, not necessarily as missionaries attached to specific boards of missions, but as technicians, educators, and co-workers with many Africans in the development of the new Africa.

8   J.A. MARCUM

In this age of "corps" and "brigades," he continued, it would be only fitting that the Christian community should play its part. And in a country such as Mozambique where Western (Catholic) Christians exercise direct political control there can be no meaning to Christian protestations of brotherhood without "temporal expression." The growth of Islam in Africa, he argued, was related to the way in which its missionaries identified with the African people "in every respect." And the influence of Communism derived from the failure of Western political and economic systems to stand up against exploitive economic interests. Consequently, the Western Christian needed to reevaluate rationalizations for inaction.

> It is not sufficient to hide behind the theology of dilemmas, or neo-existentialist excuses. Christ demands that you love your neighbor as you love yourselves. And if it has to be admitted, as it must be, that to truly love one's neighbor is not easy, a Christian has to remember that Christ also admonished: 'If any man would come after me, let him deny himself and take up his cross daily and follow me.' (Luke 9:23)[13]

Implementation of Mondlane's call for building religion-based institutions of higher education, however, would have to await political independence. As of 1962, beleaguered Protestant missionaries in Mozambique were finding that years of efforts to assuage Portuguese paranoia and resentment of their presence had led nowhere. Reporting to headquarters in New York, the local Methodist mission complained that, although it had ostensibly been given the right to establish schools and training centers in Mozambique since 1883, there had followed "years and countless instances of discrimination, harassment, intimidation, suppression of worship." This extended "even to private meetings in homes for prayer, head beatings, imprisonment and exile." On one occasion in the Zavala area all pastors were beaten just for attending an annual church conference. "Now," he lamented, "we face an official and determined decision to eliminate our mission schools."[14]

If Christianity and education were of central importance to Mondlane's conceptions of a future Mozambique, for others material well-being and socio-political status were the first and primary motivations for a struggle that had episodic but persistent historical roots. The forces of inchoate yet mounting nationalism focused on escape from socio-economic exploitation and accession to political power.

HOPES FOR REFORM

As an idealistic graduate student in 1954 Mondlane wrote an article in which he saw potential in the Portuguese system, despite his own unhappy experience of it. He saw hope in Lisbon's constitutional pledge that all those living under its flag would henceforth be considered and treated as Portuguese citizens, "one and indivisible." To achieve this, he said, Portugal would need to do three things. First, it had to improve educational conditions, which lagged behind even those of racially segregated bordering countries. For this the Catholic Church would be responsible. Next, it had to eliminate disease and continue to improve the health of the population. In the health arena, he said, Portugal was already doing "everything within its power." Lastly, it had to renegotiate the terms under which Mozambicans labored in Southern Rhodesia and South Africa and address issues related to the impact on workers' family lives of the standard two-year contracts. Reflecting his own bitter experience of South Africa, Mondlane deplored the influence of race relations in Southern Rhodesia and South Africa on Mozambican workers and questioned whether white colonial Portuguese could resist succumbing to their racist influence. Would "Portuguese Africans" who work in South Africa be able on their return to Mozambique and to "identify themselves with Portuguese co-citizens?" Would they be able to live together constructively with whites "after experiencing segregation that causes hatred?" On their return to Mozambique would Africans be able to "identify themselves with Portuguese co-citizens?" Would Africans be able to appreciate what good the Portuguese had been doing and were going to do? Or would they be consumed by resentment? The answer, he said, would depend upon whether the high ideals of the Portuguese constitution were "implemented by the European Portuguese working in harmony with [...] indigenous peoples in [such] a way that Africans will feel that their cultural values are appreciated and that nothing stands in the way of the advancement of the African peoples."[15]

About the same time, writing to the *New York Times* with the security of a pseudonym, "Vincent Robinson," a questioning Mondlane expressed skepticism. Portugal had been allowed to join the United

10   J.A. MARCUM

Nations and simultaneously "avoid scrutiny" of its rule in Africa "by virtue of declaring it African colonies to be "provinces." This exemption from international accountability, "Robinson" wrote, called for an international commission to study the economic, political and social conditions" of these "provinces" and to report on them to "world opinion."[16] But the idea of a study commission failed to gain traction. So did any idea of implementing constitutional ideals. Political and social conditions in Mozambique deteriorated. By 1961 Mondlane was describing it as a country "full of tension and fear." A paranoid threat perception of "communist" subversion had become the rationale for repressive rule under a "ubiquitous secret police."[17]

When Portugal joined the United Nations in 1955, it claimed not to possess any *non*-self-governing territories. This absolved it of the international responsibilities that came with transitional governance under the Trusteeship System. But Mondlane was dedicated to the obligations and accountability incorporated within the UN Trusteeship System, with which he worked upon completing his doctorate. A variant of the short-lived French Union, which incorporated France's African and other overseas territories into a single polity, Lisbon's own Eurafrican myth merged Portugal's colonies with a metropole that would, in Mondlane's words: pursue a policy of "slow, unforced assimilation of [a presumed] weak or inferior" community into a "strong or more highly developed" one. However, he concluded, Portugal would come to "regret" that it did not "opt" for the Trusteeship System in time to avert the "catastrophe" that would befall it.[18]

In 1957, while working on his Northwestern dissertation at Harvard, Mondlane initiated correspondence with Adriano Moreira, one of Portugal's leading scholars, seeking a research position in Lisbon. In a letter written on March 18, 1957, Mondlane accepted Moreira's offer of a professorship at the Instituto de Ciensias, Sociais e Politica Ultramarina in Lisbon. After settling on terms, including his teaching curriculum, social research agenda, pay, and a research post for his wife, Mondlane sought and obtained permission to delay assumption of the professorship. It was agreed that Mondlane would first gain the experience of a brief period with the trusteeship section of the United Nations secretariat.[19] Mondlane never took up the post.

Shortly after earning his Ph.D., Mondlane took the position with the UN Trusteeship Council. During four and half years there he established a relationship with Tanganyika petitioner Julius Nyerere, who promised

Mondlane personal support when Tanganyika gained independence. In the fall of 1960 Mondlane went to British Cameroons as a member of a UN team to observe preparations for a plebiscite on the future of the territory. Tanganyika had gained independence the previous December. It was time to make a move.

The relationship of mutual respect between Moreira and Mondlane ended after Mondlane made an exploratory visit to Mozambique in early 1961. That visit revealed the dire circumstances prevailing there and that the "reforms" put in place by Moreira, who became Portugal's Overseas Minister in 1961, had been reinterpreted to render them consistent with the Salazarist doctrine and intent to solder the "overseas provinces" ever more securely to the Portuguese body politic. Mondlane responded to the rising nationalist discontent that he found sweeping the urban centers of Lourenco Marques and Beira. It was time to act.

FEBRUARY 1961: MONDLANE RETURNS TO MOZAMBIQUE

In February 1961 Mondlane joined his wife, who had preceded him by two months, on a visit to Mozambique. In the words of George Houser, in whom Mondlane confided, "hundreds of people came to see him singly or in small groups." Whenever he appeared in the streets after church, he attracted large crowds. Africans sought his advice on how to leave the country to join nationalist organizations abroad. He responded with circumspection since some inquiries were surely from government informers. He was spied on by the police day and night and returned to New York ready to throw in his lot with the independence cause. The Portuguese watched him closely. Houser wrote:

> I recall stopping by his office one day just as two men were leaving. With a quiet laugh Mondlane explained that they had just offered him a teaching position in Portugal. 'I have been offered many jobs. I just keep them guessing but maintain cordiality. They don't want me back in Mozambique'.[20]

During his visit to Mozambique, Mondlane focused intensively on educational issues. He had discussions with the Director of Education and with the head of the largest government high school. He was told there were no funds for a major expansion of the school system. "Out of a total of over $6 million from the total of individual African head tax[es] collected, only some $1 million is given to the Roman Catholic missions, which monopolize African education in Mozambique." With a per capita expenditure of less than $3.00 a year per African child of school age, it was not surprising the rate of illiteracy in Mozambique remained at "over 99 percent." On visits to schools in Lourenco Marques and Beira, Mondlane was confronted with evasive answers about the number of African students. He heard from students in Beira that out of an estimated 500 students in the official high school there were no more than five Africans. Aside from education, he confirmed a disastrous absence of economic reform. South African mines continued to suck away the male population of the south, while African cotton concessionary companies elsewhere profited handsomely by exploiting grossly underpaid African agricultural workers. For those in charge there was no incentive for change.[21]

Mondlane gave a report of his visit to the US Department of State and expressed concern about the possibility of a war: "one shudders at the consequences of such an eventuality, judging by Portugal's reaction to a similar situation in Angola." He urged the USA to encourage Portugal to accept the principle of self-determination and set a target date for self-government leading to independence.[22] Mondlane continued to believe that Portugal could be persuaded to accept the inevitable.

After returning to the USA, Mondlane resigned from his UN position, thus freeing himself from the apolitical strictures of international civil service. In May 1961 he produced a report on his two-month visit to Mozambique entitled "Present Conditions in Mozambique," a preface to his entry into the political arena. In Mozambique, he reported, he had been accorded a "gracious interview by the Governor General," who conceded that the government lacked the resources for expansion of educational opportunity and economic development. The Governor General acknowledged "it might be possible to get economic and technical aid from friendly nations among Portugal's Western allies, but added that Portugal was a proud nation. "We prefer to be poor [rather] than to accept aid and be told what to do by foreigners," he concluded.

Mondlane traveled to rural areas and Protestant missions and spoke openly about how the ability of Africans to advance socially was due to the paucity of cultural advantages allowed to them. The American Consul General in Lourenco Marques cited a missionary report that "many

Africans operated as informers" during the progress of Mondlane's trip and many others went

> to jail as an aftermath of his association with them. At the same time, the government officials in several posts and especially in Vila de Joao Belo area entertained him as an example of the Africans' progress within Portuguese culture. Governor Ruas of the Gaza District gave him a large open-air luncheon which was widely publicized.

During the event the "Governor emphasized several times that no such activity would be permitted to Mondlane or other Negroes in the United States."[23] Portuguese authorities were confused, conflicted, and suspicious. What were the real intentions of this itinerant black Mozambican with a US doctorate and a UN passport?

Mondlane concluded from his trip that it was almost impossible for Africans to progress under existing circumstances of political repression, lack of educational facilities, and economic subservience. Since his departure in 1950, the living standards of white and Asian minorities had risen, stoking black African discontent. And Africans working in South Africa and Rhodesia observed "the difference in the educational standards achieved by the Africans of those countries in spite of segregation."

Mondlane noted that, "thus far," Lisbon had reacted to internal and foreign pressures with "more imprisonments, more secret police, more European armed soldiers, more mass rallies and more speeches against any changes." He added that the war in Angola had made the situation worse. There were fears "that as soon as Tanganyika is independent, the Mocambicans who are in Tanganyika will begin to attack from the north and the Portuguese Government will punish those Africans who are now under suspicions in the south." Mondlane observed that many southern Mozambicans wanted "to leave the country and join any force that is against Portugal, but they are hemmed in between the Indian Ocean and the Union of South Africa and British Central Africa." (From Lourenco Marques to the border with Tanganyika was approximately 1500 miles.) "Yet the tension is mounting every day."[24]

In the summer of 1962, Mondlane joined the faculty of the Maxwell School at Syracuse University, which left him free to plunge into active politics. On June 7, 1962, he flew into Dar es Salaam to begin his new role as the leader of a newly formed nationalist party.

14 J.A. MARCUM

Notes

1. The other team members were Ulric Haynes, Jr. (Ford Foundation, US Ambassador to Algeria [1977–1981]), and Ernest Dunbar (*Look* magazine).
2. Membership of the African Advisory Council changed over time, and the citizens' advisory council experiment ended with the conclusion of Frederick's incumbency in 1969. It was a novel initiative never to be repeated in the State Department. The initial members were: David E. Apter, University of California Berkeley; William H. Beatty, Chase Manhattan Bank; Gwendolen Carter, Northwestern University; Rufus E. Clement, president, Atlanta University; Gray Cowan, Columbia University; John A. Davis, American Society for African Culture; C.W. du Kieweit, American Council of Education; Edward R. Dudley, Supreme Court of New York; Frank E. Ferrari, African American Institute; George M. Houser, American Committee on Africa; Helen Kitchen, editor, *Africa Report*; George N. Lindsay, lawyer; John A. Marcum, Lincoln Univ.; Vernon McKay, Johns Hopkins University; William E. Moran, Georgetown University; Ruth S. Morgenthau, Brandeis University; Frederick Patterson, Phelps–Stokes Fund; Christopher H. Phillips, International Chamber of Commerce; James H. Robinson, Crossroads Africa; Mrs. Oscar Ruebhausen, Women's Africa Committee; Harvey Russell, Pepsi Cola and African American Institute; Ruth Sloan, Ruth Sloan Associates; Kenneth Spang, First City National Bank, New York; Immanuel Wallerstein, Columbia University.
3. Richard D. Mahoney, *JFK: Ordeal in Africa*, Oxford University Press, 1983, p. 189.
4. *Egyptian Gazette*, Cairo, January 20, 1969.
5. Herbert Shore, "Mondlane and Mozambique," mimeo. Delany Library, special collections, Mondlane archives, USC, Los Angeles.
6. Helen Kitchen, "Conversation with Eduardo Mondlane," *Africa Report*, November 1967. Also George M. Houser, *No One Can Stop the Rain*, New York: Pilgrim Press, 1989, p. 17.
7. For a discussion of the importance of NESAM and how it "nourished the preparation of a community of interest within the educated Mocambique population" and transmitted "some of the ideas of the foreign [South African] experience acquired by a few to a larger, though still quite small, elite," see Brendan F. Jundanian, "The Mozambique Liberation Front. Mémoire présenté pour le Diplôme de l'Institut," Lausanne, Switzerland, July 1970, p. 17; Barry Munslow, *Mozambique: The Revolution and its Origins*, New York, Longman, 1983, p. 66.
8. Kitchen, "Conversations with Eduardo …"; Eduardo Mondlane, "Dissent on Mocambique," in Ronald H. Cbilcote, *Emerging Nationalism in*

1 EDUARDO MONDLANE 15

Portuguese Africa: Documents, Stanford: Hoover Institution Press, 1972, pp. 411–426.

9. Eduardo Mondlane, "The Struggle for Independence in Mozambique," April 11–13, 1963. Marcum Papers, Box 36/7. Mondlane's M.A. thesis research as well as his Northwestern, doctoral dissertation, "Role Conflict, Reference Group and Race," led him to postulate that, in general, commitment to national or ethnic identity and ideology overshadows or outweighs people's commitment to factors of race.

10. Melville J. Herskovits, *The Human Factor in Changing Africa,* New York: Alfred A. Knopf, 1962, pp. 238–239. See also Eduardo C. and Janet Rae Mondlane, "Education in Portuguese Africa," in Ruth Sloan, ed., *The Educated African,* New York: Praeger, 1962.

11. Eduardo Mondlane, "Christian Missions under Test," *Archways,* YMCA/YWCA press, Oberlin, December 24, 1952, p. 18.

12. Eduardo C. Mondlane, "African Nationalism and the Christian Way," mimeo, Marcum Papers, Box 36/7.

13. Ibid.

14. Max V. Kemling, "A Chronicle of Events in the Life of Methodist Missions: Mozambique," typescript, 1962, Marcum Papers, Box 40/3. Legal recourse having failed, Kemling lamented that the government's decision would result in the closing of well-equipped primary Methodist schools and medical facilities in the province of Inhambane.

15. Mondlane, "Mozambique," in Calvin W. Stillman, *Africa in the Modern World,* University of Chicago Press, 1955, p. 233.

16. *New York Times,* August 14, 1955.

17. Mondlane, "Present Conditions in Mozambique," typescript, May 1, 1961, Marcum Papers, Box 36/7.

18. Mondlane, *The Trusteeship System of the United Nations Conference on South West Africa,* Oxford, March 1968, Mondlane Archives, USC.

19. Mondlane letters to Moreira, March 18 and 30, 1957, Mondlane Archives, USC.

20. Houser, *No One Can Stop the Rain,* pp. 179–180.

21. Eduardo Mondlane, "Dissent on Mocambique"; and Mondlane, "Present Conditions in Mozambique," mimeo, May 1, 1961, Marcum Papers Box 36/7, in which he noted that "many Africans own radio sets and can listen to important radio stations such as Radio Brazzaville which has a Portuguese news service twice a day giving details of African news."

22. As quoted in Joao M. Cabrita, *Mozambique: The Tortuous Road to Democracy.* London: Palgrave, 1988, p. 6. Drawing upon a trove of State Department dispatches obtained under the Freedom of Information Act (FOIA), Cabrita documented a long sequence of Mondlane's exchanges

16 J.A. MARCUM

with US foreign service personnel, confidential meetings that continued for years even as American support for his cause waned.

23. Report by Consul General William H. Taft, III, May 1, 1961. Marcum Papers, Box 39/3.
24. Mondlane, "Dissent on Mocambique."

CHAPTER 2

The Rise of Mozambican Nationalism

HISTORY, THE MUEDA MYTH AND THE FORMATION OF MANU

Portuguese penetration into sub-Saharan Africa dated back five centuries. After taking the coastal training post of Sofala in 1505 and then pushing up the Zambezi Valley, where they made profitable contact with the gold-producing Monomatapa kingdom and its tributaries, the Portuguese began trafficking in East African slaves for sale in India and elsewhere. The number of Mozambicans enslaved never reached the proportions of those of Angola, but as many as 25,000 per year were taken in the years immediately before the end of the slave trade in 1850.

The first three centuries of Portuguese rule were "almost wholly injurious to the African societies with which they [came] into direct contact."[1] In Angola, for example, "the criminal classes of Portugal were employed in inciting the native peoples to make war on each other in the interests of slave labour for Brazil."[2] In Mozambique, despite the destruction they caused, as of the 1870s the Portuguese did not control much beyond a few towns along the country's 1500-mile coast. "As late as 1890 most of Mocambique was almost completely innocent of Portuguese authority, and in 1894 Lourenco Marques suffered serious assault by African warriors from the outlying area."[3] The vast northern districts bordering on Tanzania were progressively occupied for the first time between 1906 and 1912. Portugal was still engaged in campaigns of conquest and pacification up through the First World War. In the

© The Author(s) 2018   17
J.A. Marcum, *Conceiving Mozambique*, African Histories
and Modernities, https://doi.org/10.1007/978-3-319-65987-9_2

18   J.A. MARCUM

Barue region of the Zambezi Valley the revolt against the Portuguese did not end until 1920.[4]

One development of enduring significance was the failure of the Portuguese to build a north–south transit system, road or rail, bridging large rivers such as the Zambezi and Sabe. These rivers flowed from the interior to the Indian Ocean, dividing the country into separate geographic and ethnic layers. Without a strong, unifying educational and political system the country was left physically, culturally, and socially divided.

When slavery was finally abolished in 1850, it was replaced by a system of conscript labor for European farms and mines that persisted into the 1960s. It was embellished with an official policy of assimilation in the 1930s. But "the grinding abuse of African labor, the poverty of Portugal itself, the economic backwardness of the colonies, the lack of minimal educational or medical facilities, and the absence of technical personnel all made the goal of assimilation in the 1930s and 1940s a legislative dream."[5] The 1950 Mozambique census listed just 4300 out of approximately 5.7 million Africans as having qualified as *assimilados*.[6] It would require the seepage of incendiary nationalist ideas through sealed colonial boundaries, airborne news via Radio Brazzaville, and "bush telegraph" accounts of social and political achievements elsewhere in Africa to give rise to explosive demands for African self-determination and independence.

In 1957, after years of legal political protest by Africans, colonial reforms including moves toward self-government, Ghana became the first colonized territory in sub-Saharan Africa to gain its independence. The stirrings of contemporary African nationalism began to register on Mozambique's political seismograph. In southern coastal centers of maximal Portuguese impact, most notably Lourenco Marques, grievances festered and surfaced within the ranks of port workers, students, local administrators, and others with connections to the outside world. But over time their efforts to organize were snuffed out or taken over by colonial authorities. Portugal's divide-and-rule strategy was reflected in a 1950s policy that deliberatively kept social and racial groups apart. Accordingly, there was an official Associacao Africana with its iconoclastic journal, *O Brado Africano*, designated mainly for *mestiços* and a Centro Associativo dos Negros de Mocambique for blacks, in particular for African *assimilados*.

Exceptional was the case of one 1950s urban reformist organization in Lourenco Marques, a multiracial Associacao dos Naturais de Mocambique. An essentially white social organization that evolved into a movement favoring racial integration, it organized a scholarship program to aid young Africans seeking secondary, technical, and commercial education. As the Associacao's tendency to favor political autonomy progressed toward "a more genuine nationalism," however, the government became alarmed, reversed its earlier support, arrested the top leadership, and replaced it with pro-Salazarists. In Mondlane's view, Mozambique's Portuguese population of some 120,000 would come to "regret the emasculation of this organization, for with its demise as a multi-racial nucleus may have gone all the hopes for a racially tolerant Mozambique."[7]

According to one African activist who fled to Rhodesia, by late 1957 most nationalist oriented Africans in Mozambique's largest cities—Lourenco Marques and Beira—were either in prison or out of the country. Whether members of soccer clubs, carpenters' associations, burial societies, or the numerous other social and cultural organizations "where plans were made and hopes entertained," a "clandestine outflow" of Mozambican nationalists swelled, sometimes with "disastrous results" at the hands of border police.[8]

However, it was not in the southern part of the colony, where most of the schools and the white minority of 1 in 70 lived, that African nationalism first emerged in Mozambique. Instead, it was among the more than half a million Mozambicans laboring in the mines and fields of neighboring South Africa and the British colonies of Northern and Southern Rhodesia, Nyasaland, and Tanganyika. There were an estimated 65,000–80,000 Mozambican men working in the gold and other mines of South Africa under contracts entailing per capita payments to the Portuguese government. Hundreds of Mozambicans who migrated to the relatively better economic conditions and educational opportunities of neighboring countries were exposed to and caught up in the ideas and activities of local African nationalist movements.

Perhaps the most celebrated, iconic, and ironic case of influence from outside took place in the town of Mueda, in Mozambique's northernmost province, Cabo Delgado. The people of Mueda were Maconde (or Makonde). The rural Maconde straddled the Ruvuma River border with Tanganyika, which merged with Zanzibar in April 1964 to

20 J.A. MARCUM

become Tanzania. In June 1960, two pro-Portuguese Macondes living in Tanganyika got an idea for an entrepreneurial venture. They decided to persuade fellow Mozambican émigrés to leave British East Africa, which was in an economic downturn at the time, and return back across the border and resettle in what seemed to them at that time economically more promising opportunities in northern Mozambique. Their plans ran counter to a long history of Maconde migration to British East Africa[9] and, therefore, to normal political expectations—and they may have aroused Portuguese suspicion of outside influence.

What happened next, according to Michael Cahen, a prominent French research scholar, demonstrates how impervious Portuguese authority was to changing African realities and how political myths are created. Interviewing extensively in Africa and Portugal, Cahen separated what he concluded to be fact from fiction within what became known as the Mueda Massacre.[10] A nervous local colonial administrator misconstrued the actions of the two Tanzania-based Maconde organizers of the project, who had been ensnarled in the dilatory red tape of Portugal's visa services and out of frustration traveled to Mueda without proper papers. Viewing them as hostile, he ordered their arrest. The hapless organizers had meant to break through bureaucratic barriers and facilitate the relocation of émigré Macondes in the province of Cabo Delgado. On June 16, 1960, the same panicked official overreacted to a spontaneous gathering of several thousand protesting against the organizers' arrest, confronted the crowd, and compounded his problem. A fracas ensued. The official called in eight nearby soldiers driving two jeeps equipped with a single functioning machine gun. Between 9 and 36 people were reportedly killed, many more wounded, there was a general panic, and a thousand bicycles were abandoned.[11] This event convinced the Maconde people that "war against Portugal" was the only answer. In this way, "Portugal's obsolescent dictatorship transformed an ethnic movement which could still have been treated as a social problem into a political" one.[12]

The June 16, 1960, incident was subsequently portrayed by a Frelimo military leader and purported witness of the event, Alberto Joaquim Chipande, as a "massacre" in which demonstrators who had denounced forced labor and demanded independence were attacked by a well-armed platoon of soldiers and more than 500 Mozambicans were killed. In fact there were almost no Portuguese military forces in Cabo Delgado at the time. And the Maconde had not yet developed an independence agenda. Thus, Chipande's report lacked credence. However, the event did prompt Macondes to coalesce into a new nationalist movement, the Mozambique African National Union (MANU).[13] Later Mondlane, as well as outside observers and academics, would routinely cite the Mueda debacle as a massacre of over 500 and a critical precursor to the Mozambique Revolution.[14]

On February 19, 1961, some fifty delegates from Dar es Salaam, Tanga, Pemba, and other Maconde émigré communities in British East Africa met in Mombasa, Kenya, and formed MANU. MANU's cautious platform sought to "rais[e] the political consciousness" of Mozambicans living and working in the sisal fields and ports of East Africa. The conference was organized by a Kenyan MP, C. Chokwe, and received a promise of support from Tom Mboya, a prominent leader of Kenya's governing Kenya African National Union (KANU).[15]

In early 1961 reports surfaced of a MANU underground operating within northern Mozambique and there were rumors that it was receiving Ghanaian assistance.[16] MANU became a member of a new regional grouping of nationalist organizations, the Pan-African Freedom Movement of East, Central and Southern Africa (PAFMECSA), and its leaders were invited to participate at an April 1961 meeting in Casablanca, Morocco, to create an alliance of Portuguese African nationalist movements, a Conferencia das Organizacoes Nacionalistas das Colonias Portuguesas (CONCP). MANU's leader, Matthew (Mateos) Mmole, was a second-generation English-speaker from Dar es Salaam. Given his linguistic limitation, he suggested that Adelino Gwambe, a Portuguese-speaking émigré recently arrived in Dar es Salaam, accept the invitation and represent both MANU and Gwambe's own exile organization, the Uniao Democratico Nacional de Mocambique (UDENAMO), at the Casablanca meeting. Gwambe accepted. In Casablanca, however, Gwambe obtained exclusive Mozambican membership for UDENAMO. Thus, Mozambican nationalism was recognized as an institutionalized reality, but at the cost of divisive personal enmity resulting from Gwambe's double-cross of Mmole.

Adelino Gwambe

In January 1961, shortly before the Casablanca conference, three Mozambican political activists in the Southern Rhodesian town of Bulawayo—Aurelio Bucuane, David Chambale, and Adelino Gwambe—traveled to Salisbury, the capital of the British white settler colony, to consult with Joshua Nkomo, the leader of the Southern Rhodesia National Democratic Party (NDP), the colony's leading African nationalist party, about how to further their political objectives in Mozambique. They told the local press that they were on their way to Lisbon, Portugal, where they intended to meet with Antonio Salazar and "unveil the evils of their Portuguese brothers in Mozambique."[17] They said they would tell Salazar they were seeking independence through peaceful negotiations, interim representation in the Portuguese National Assembly or the Mozambique Legislative Council, and an end to all forms of discrimination. According to Bucuane, a 23-year-old former schoolteacher who was the group's spokesman, in September 1960, with the permission of a local official, he and friends had formed a short-lived Partido da Unidade (PUN) in a rural area some 200 miles north of Lourenco Marques. Two months later, however, the government declared a "State of Emergency," and arrested and imprisoned him and other PUN members without trial. He escaped prison in Lourenco Marques and made his way to Southern Rhodesia. Now he, Chambale and Gwambe, like Dorothy and her companions making their way along the Yellow Brick Road to quiz the Wizard of Oz, were on their way via African countries to quiz the Wizard of Lisbon.

Hlomulo Jani Chitofo (Adelino) Gwambe, a garrulous 22-year-old Mozambican nationalist, was introduced to the public in an interview with Lusaka's *African Mail*.[18] He had begun working as a émigré in Bulawayo in 1954 at age 15. In November 1960 he decided to return to his "home country, Mozambique, and fight for the liberation of my people," but, he told the paper, "[i]t is still an offense in our country to speak of freedom or say anything contrary to the Salazar Regime." And he was arrested.

Gwambe described his experiences in jail. He shared "a cell with two African political prisoners who complained of stomach trouble." A "friendly African prison official or 'spy' in plain clothes" advised Gwambe not to eat prison food because it was being poisoned. Thirty minutes after the other two prisoners were removed from his cell, Gwambe said they were reported dead. By the time a Portuguese prison official brought Gwambe some food, he had become so hungry he was tempted to eat a "spoonful," but he "felt" the food had "a suspicious taste" and gave it up. After he told the "spy" that he had taken some of the food and his stomach had begun aching, the "spy" gave Gwambe some tablets. Later, Gwambe offered the friendly spy a bribe. The spy accepted and Gwambe escaped back into Rhodesia. Now, he told a journalist, "my friends and I must go to Portugal where we intend to present our case." With this tale, Gwambe introduced himself and his gift for storytelling to the world.[19]

Instead of going to Lisbon, Nkomo recommended that the three Mozambicans go to Dar es Salaam. The independence of Tanganyika, which was slated for December 1961, promised a new opportunity for Mozambicans to organize in a bordering country. Gwambe followed Nkomo's advice.

In many ways Gwambe was the polar opposite of Eduardo Mondlane. The product of a third-grade Catholic primary schooling, he was untouched by Protestant teaching and ethics and was left to live by his wits, raw ambition, and gift for imaginative narrative. His political career combined a frenetic mixture of ambition and guile. He defied critics who denounced him as an opportunist who had worked with PIDE in Rhodesia before shifting his to the nationalist cause.[20]

In 1966 Gwambe offered his version of the formation of UDENAMO in what he called "My Concise Autobiography."[21] It describes Gwambe's rise from rural obscurity to political prominence. His prose reveals a penchant for mixing fact and fiction and portrays a life of frenetic behavior. He began by explaining the correct spelling and meaning of his name, "HLUMULU JANI CHITOFU GWAMBI." He wrote, "*Hlumulu* means (depression)" and was given to him by his mother because "I was born when my father was at South Africa on forced labour and my mother had no means to support the children including the new comer (myself)." The name Jani was "requested" by his grandfather, who, "although [...] dead by that time [...] could still communicate with my parents and relatives for this purpose." It was the name his grandfather had used "during the time he was on forced labour at South Africa and its origin is French JEAN." Chitofu was his father's name, "which has also some influence of South Africa *stove* and this name [was used] while in the mines." Gwambi "is used by all Gwambi family for hundreds of years and is never changed."

Gwambe was born in the village of Chimbutsa in the rural district of Vilanculos or Bilankulu, Inhambane district, Sul do Save Province, on

April 4, 1939. He "was born from proletarian class" and his "parents lived only on petty agriculture." His father was Lakeni Chitofu Gwambi. His mother was Petani Wanisawu Ngilazi Sumbi. They were from the same district and were married traditionally. Gwambe's father and grandfather were often arrested and sentenced to forced labor in South African mines. His mother manufactured and sold a local African gin known as "nipa" to support the family. Gwambe was the "third born" of five children, three male and two female, from the same father and mother. Of the five, he was the only one who was "reasonably educated" and "directly engaged in politics."

Gwambe was educated at the Missao de Sao Jose de Vilanculos em Maphinhane from 1947 to 1951 and left after obtaining a third class diploma in Primary Education. He continued educating himself in Portuguese and English and in 1966 was "still continuing educating [him]self in many languages and many subjects including military theory and application specially guerrilla warfare for application in Mozambique."

From 1952 to 1953 Gwambe worked in Beira as a forced laborer at Mocambique Industrial, Ltda., Manga. During this period, he "organized secret night school for other youths at the compound of this company." When the company authorities discovered his night school, he was detained and tortured for a month, then released. He also worked at the Emporium (Grandes Armazens da Beira). According to Gwambe, after a popular uprising in the Sofala rural district in 1953, he wrote a petition to the United Nations, which was discovered by the PIDE. He was arrested, tortured, and sentenced to five years' imprisonment. He was sent to work at the Urban Administrative Council of Beira as "a clerk and interpreter reserved for special assignments." Gwambe wrote that it sounded like a "good job," but he was not paid. In the first four months of 1954 Gwambe described being detained four times on suspicion he was "continuing with anti-Government activities" and "warned that the fifth time meant" he would be deported to work at the cocoa plantations on Sao Tome e Principe, Portugal's island colony off the West Coast of Africa.

In May 1954, after analyzing "the threats by the Portuguese authorities" and because he "could have failed to serve the interests of my country and people from the islands on the Atlantic ocean," Gwambe forged a travel document and fled to Southern Rhodesia, where there were many Mozambicans. There Gwambe worked at the Pioneer Steam Laundry & Ninety Minutes Dry Cleaning in Salisbury from June to September 1954. In October, he left for Bulawayo and worked as a domestic servant. In 1955 he worked at the Rhodesian Timber Ltd and Laing & Roberts construction company.

In October 1955 Gwambe "went back to Mozambique at CHIKWALAKWALA to start an underground movement against Portuguese foreign domination," but "stayed only one month and [...] was instructed by other comrades to go and organize other Mozambicans in Shabani and on Saturdays and Sundays [...] oftenly went to Shabani Mines to organize other Mozambicans." At this time, he was working for Rhodesia Railways, but he resigned in December 1955 and "went to organize fully at Shabani Asbestos mines and then to Rutenga, Fort Victoria and Rhodesia/Mozambique border Malvernia." He described his activities as being "done underground and amongst few dedicated patriots."

Between 1956 and 1960, Gwambe wrote that he organized "other Mozambicans" at Gwelo and Que Que," went back to Bulawayo and worked at the Consolidated Textiles Ltd, "joined the Rhodesia Railways-Bulawayo as office Messenger [with] the Chief Accountant and Finance Officer," resigned in 1959, and worked as a cashier/storekeeper at Madeira Fish & Chips "for a while," and then went back to Chikwalakwala to report the work he had done to his comrades. In 1960 he returned to Southern Rhodesia, worked at the Portuguese Association-Bulawayo and Madeira Fish & Chips again, but resigned after a while to establish his own business as a professional photographer at Luveve. He "used this business to organise many Mozambicans in Bulawayo under the cover of door-to-door photographer."

In Rhodesia, Gwambe joined the Southern Rhodesia African National Congress and then the NDP. While working on the Rhodesian Railways, he joined the Railways African Workers' Union. During this period Gwambe wrote that he "organize[d] other youths during the 1956 railway strike in order to blockade the roads leading to all railways departments so that all the workers should be forced back home in order to ensure the success of the strike," and "led squads of youth during the September 1960 Uprising in Bulawayo and took a very active part in many actions throughout the city and suburbs." After what he called "the September People's Uprising," Gwambe "decided to convene a

26 J.A. MARCUM

secret conference of all Mozambican patriots." The "secret conference" took place on October 2, 1960, at Luveve village, about 10 miles out of Bulawayo. According to Gwambe, activists from all over Mozambique attended and elected him to be National President of the new party— the Uniao Democratica Nacional. Mozambique was added to the party's name in March 1961, and it became UDENAMO. Gwambe identified this as point at which he and other Mozambican activists "started to work fully for the liberation of Mozambique and made many contacts by correspondence to governments and organizations and of all peace loving nations and peoples of entire world." As a result of those communications, the PIDE tried to arrest all of those who attended the October 1960 conference. In January 1961, Gwambe went underground and, as described above, visited Salisbury to consult with Joshua Nkomo and the leaders of the NDP, who advised Gwambe, Bucame and Chambale to go to Northern Rhodesia and Tanganyika.

In Lusaka, the capital of Northern Rhodesia, Gwambe tried but failed to gain support from Kenneth Kaunda, the country's leading African nationalist. In his autobiography, Gwambe described in detail how he got from Lusaka to Dar es Salaam in Tanganyika:

> I was given a lift by a Portuguese Roman Catholic Priest who was going to Angola and I sold him a Parker 51 pen at 10/- (ten shillings) and I used this amount to pay a lorry which took me to Kanona [...] From Kanona I walked to Mpika where I was assisted by the Welfare Department after I claimed to be an orphan from Tanganyikan parents and I was given a warrant to travel free on the account of the Welfare Department to Mbeya in Tanzania. From Mbeya I went to Dar es Salaam and my fare was paid by the Provincial Headquarters of the *Tanganyika African National Union* [TANU] and at Dar es Salaam I was accommodated at a private residence of TANU which was allocated for Freedom Fighters from Southern Africa.

Shortly after arriving in Dar es Salaam, Gwambe met with MANU's Matthew Mmole, who, as described above, offered him an invitation to attend the founding conference of CONCP.

In June 1961, at the "invitation of the OSAGEYFO the President Dr. Kwame Nkrumah," Gwambe and UDENAMO vice-president Fanuel Guideon Mahluza went to Ghana. On their way there from Dar es Salaam, they were arrested at the Usumburu (Burundi) airport, held for 24 hours and sent back to Nairobi. But, drawing on his formidable powers of persuasion, Gwambe was able to convince Ethiopian Airlines to carry the two to Ghana without travel documents. In Ghana, Gwambe found the lasting financial and ideological sustenance he needed to fuel his ambitions. He developed solid support within the orbit of Nkrumah's Bureau of African Affairs and its director, A.K. Barden. This included military training for twenty to thirty young UDENAMO militants. By this time, mention of dialogue with Salazar was long gone.

Gwambe adopted a tough anti-colonial posture compatible with the Africanist militancy of *The Voice of Africa*, published by Nkrumah's African Affairs bureau. Lashing out with a harsh racial and class critique of the situation in Mozambique, Gwambe charged that a small group of privileged mulattos and *assimilados* were operating at the bidding of Portuguese "slave" owners. "From my own experience," he declared, "I have realized that what the oppressed people of Mozambique want is not a highly educated leader but just a determined and dedicated leader armed with the principles of Pan African Nationalism, because the political leadership of the mulatto-assimilado groups will never be accepted." (In other words, the people want a Gwambe, not a Mondlane.) "Nothing can shake us from the conviction that the policy of multi-racialism would lead Mozambique to a new form of colonialism, i.e. neo-colonialism." We want straightforward majority rule and "will deal with [those] who oppose it."[22]

After returning to Dar es Salaam on July 12, 1961, with his Ghanaian boost, Gwambe went for broke. He called for a mass rally and declared that UDENAMO had decided to fight for the independence of Mozambique through a people's armed struggle. Gwambe dismissed the idea of non-violence and "so-called peaceful co-existence." Without alerting, let alone consulting, Julius Nyerere and his Tanganyikan hosts, Gwambe boasted that, with the help of Ghana and a military force of 70,000, UDENAMO was preparing to launch an armed struggle from Tanganyika for Mozambican independence.[23]

Militarily vulnerable, Nyerere's nascent government feared Portuguese retaliation. Nyerere also resented Nkrumah's transcontinental ambitions. Accordingly, Tanganyika quickly declared Gwambe a Prohibited Immigrant and sent him packing. The Ghanaian High Commissioner to Tanganyika in turn denied Gwambe's claims and declared that Ghana had obtained its independence without bloodshed and expected other countries to follow its example.[24]

DAVID MABUNDA

David Joseph Maurice Mabunda, born of Mozambican parents in Witbank, South Africa, on August 24, 1934, was educated and acculturated in the country's rigorously segregated school system. He earned a 15-year matriculation certificate at the Pax Training College in Petersburg, Transvaal, in 1954, in a region where white supremacy was especially rigid. Mabunda then moved to Lourenco Marques, where he worked as a tally clerk until 1957, when the exposure of his political activities obliged him to flee to Rhodesia.

Writing as a participant in one of the small, ephemeral nationalist groups that emerged inside Mozambique in the late 1950s, Mabunda attributed "the relatively late emergence of widespread and organized opposition" to Portuguese rule to the absence of educational opportunity for the vast majority of the Africans, which "minimized the amount of contacts the African community could have with the ideas of freedom and independence taking hold in the rest of Africa." Mabunda also credited the "highly efficient Portuguese security police—PIDE," which "operated concertedly to put down the least semblance of nationalist sentiment among the Africans."[25] In 1959, two anti-Salazarist Portuguese expelled from Mozambique, Dr. Alvaro Fernando Peres do Carmo Vaz and Antonio Jose Simoes de Figueiredo, reported that there were only "isolated instances" of African protest in Mozambique.[26] They confirmed the existence of a police state in the colony and attributed "the non-existence of an African nationalist movement" to "the changeless rigors of a colonial system that has persisted for 450 years."

According to Mabunda, the early stages of nationalism in Mozambique took "the form of social and cultural clubs and associations" in which "young men of all walks of life gathered for social activities and in the process were able to exchange free words on national as well as international affairs."[27] "Indeed," he asserted, "the famous conspiracy of 1958 in which eminent African employees of the government-owned and operated Mozambique Railways and Harbors at Lourenco Marques and several Portuguese and African officers were involved, was the direct result of the work and influence of these social and cultural organizations."[28]

Mabunda described the events of 1958 as an "attempt to overthrow" the colonial government "through a series of mutinies." The mutinies were supposed to begin at the Namaaona barracks outside Lourenco

Marques and to be followed by another at the Malhangalene barracks inside Lourenco Marques and consequently others. Many of the young men involved were members of cultural clubs and, if not directly involved personally, managed to persuade their fathers "to engage in clandestine political activities." Clubs such as the Associacao dos Carpenteirias Indigenas and Centro Associativo dos Negros de Mocambique enjoyed legal status and "had access to information which was useful to the young militants." However, army informers infiltrated the operation and leaked news of it to government authorities. Its leaders were arrested, and the plan was crushed.[29]

In a handwritten letter, Mabunda described the *modus operandi* of the dissident social groups centered in Lourenco Marques and Beira. They took different forms, from soccer clubs to burial societies.

> The Associacao dos Carpenterias Indigenas organized weekly dances with admission open to all (members and non-members) and [this provided] an opportunity for political discussions for the politically involved. An underground wing of the [Associacao], the JOVENS MILITANTES, sprang out of these meetings and later became strong enough to attack police patrols at night.[30]

The Portuguese called these groups "Bandidos." The Jovens Militantes held picnics in order to organize meetings on the side. Mabunda wrote:

> [T]he most popular meeting method was that of organizing a dance. I was one of the seven founders of the *Jovens Militantes*. The interests behind the founding of this group was to seek means to advocate the uprisings [by] the forced laborers among whom we worked at the port of Lourenco Marques. In time our field of interest widened as many others joined. Our meetings were conducted in small groups during the dance and word would be passed from group to group or table to table by member waiters. Usually unanimity was reached on important issues. No written records were kept. In 1954 we drafted a petition to the UN reporting on the condition of the forced labourers among other issues. Mistakenly, the petition was mailed in Lourenco Marques and because of our signatures, I was arrested together with other members.[31]

In 1957, fearing arrest, Mabunda fled to Southern Rhodesia, where he worked as a supervisor/storeman and a wages clerk in Salisbury from

30   J.A. MARCUM

1957 to 1961 and remained politically active. In Rhodesia, Mozambican nationalists organized surreptitiously under the cover of the Portuguese East African Association. Social clubs and burial societies mobilized émigré opinion.

Mabunda also described the formation of UDENAMO beginning with the October 2, 1960, meeting in Bulawayo as the genesis of Mozambique's liberation movement. Other UDENAMO founders present at the October 1960 meeting in Bulawayo were Fanuel Mahluza and Calvin Mahlayeye. But Mabunda's chronology differed slightly from Gwambe's chronology. According to Mabunda, the Uniao Democratica Nacional was founded on February 11, 1961, after a preparation period during which Gwambe, Bucane and Chabane traveled to Salisbury to meet Nkomo with a plan to go on to Lisbon to meet Salazar. He described his early involvement in UDENAMO as follows:

> I worked in Salisbury and about the time that preparations for the formation of UDENAMO [were] going on in Bulawayo, I was together with Poles Ndelane, Alifa Speke, Joaquim Vilanculos and others working out plans for the formation of a liberation movement. When [we got] the news of the establishment of a UDENAMO office in Dar es Salaam, [some of us] decided to go and join the others. [In Dar es Salaam] the workday started at sunrise and ended late at night. Organizing Mozambicans working in Tanzania, receiving refugees from home, establishing foreign contacts, growing contacts with the interior. Work was hard but rewarding. Sometimes we spent days without food or baths for lack of funds.[32]

Mabunda rose in the movement ranks to become Deputy Secretary General and head of UDENAMO's Accra office, where he linked up with Nkrumah's Bureau of African Affairs. He traveled to Moscow in quest of Soviet assistance and described UDENAMO as "a movement with a Pan-Africanist orientation, a democratic-socialistic basis and an Africanist outlook" with an outreach to Mozambicans working in South Africa.

By early 1962, UDENAMO was led by what Mabunda described as two groups: "organizers"—Gwambe, Mahlayeye, Mahluza and Paulo Gumane—and "political orienteers"—Marcelino dos Santos, Jaime Sigauke, Joao Mungwambe, and Mabunda. Mondlane viewed Sigauke, who was arrested in early 1962 inside southern Rhodesia and imprisoned in Mozambique, as the most formidable of UDENAMO's leaders.

Mabunda wrote that UDENAMO "bore the brunt of political battle throughout its short period of life 1960–62." During those two years, it spearheaded African nationalism until it began peeping through the curtain of darkness long hung around Mozambique by the Portuguese. It was the first to establish effective underground cells and maintain contact with the interior, the first to begin military preparation for its militants, the first in grouping Mozambicans of all tribal groupings under one leadership, and it was instrumental in mobilizing public opinion against Portuguese colonialism.[33] Mabunda acknowledged that the organization "had weaknesses," but its successor, Frelimo, "was built on a foundation long laid by UDENAMO."[34]

"While the UDENAMO appeared to flourish in its external policies," Mabunda later wrote, "internally it was plagued by conflict arising mainly from the carelessness of its president, Adelino Gwambe." Gwambe's "dramatic announcement to the press in 1961 that arrangements had been made for UDENAMO to start the liberation of Mozambique with the aid of several African states and some 70,000 soldiers, prompted his expulsion from Tanganyika." Gwambe's "arbitrary expulsion" of Marcelino dos Santos ("a dedicated nationalist") from UDENAMO and his apparent "desire to turn the party into his household tool, turned many members of the party against him." The party began to lose the support of the "somewhat educated Africans who had come from Mozambique" to work with it. Gwambe also gained the description of "anti-intellectual" by attempting to stop a group of students who had been offered scholarships for study in the USA from going there.[35] In contrast with Mondlane, who had helped to arrange the scholarships, Gwambe denounced the USA as evil and Christian missionaries as "propagandists for the United States spreading neo-colonialist mentality" and attempted to steer the students to Eastern Europe.[36]

Internal feuding in UDENAMO came to a head as a result of external pressure on it to merge with MANU. In early June 1962, representatives of the two movements sketched out a preliminary agreement at Nkrumah's Ideological Institute in Winneba, Ghana. But, before it could be implemented, Mondlane arrived in Dar es Salaam. Gwambe was admitted back in Tanzania for unity talks and the two began a no-holds-barred duel for leadership of the Mozambican independence movement.

NOTES

1. Roland Oliver and J.D. Page, *A Short History of Africa*. Baltimore: Penguin, 1962, 128. For an analysis of Portuguese rule, its rationale, and its consequences in Angola, see Gerald L. Bender, *Angola Under the Portuguese: The Myth and the Reality*. Berkeley: UC Press, 1978.
2. Ibid.
3. James Duffy, *Portugal in Africa*. Cambridge, MA: Harvard University Press, 1952, p. 119; see also Allen F. Isaacman, "The Tradition of Resistance in Mozambique," *Africa Today*, July–September 1975, pp. 37–50; and A.J. Williams-Myers, "Regional Aspects of a Historical Legacy of Resistance," *Journal of Southern African Affairs*, University of Maryland, January 1977, pp. 43–60.
4. Malyn Newt, *A History of Mozambique*. London: Hurst & Col, 1995, pp. 415–419.
5. Duffy, *Portugal in Africa*, p. 164.
6. Ibid.
7. Eduardo Mondlane, "The Struggle for Independence in Mozambique," *Presence Africaine*, Paris, vol. 20, no. 48, 1963, p. 35.
8. David J.M. Mabunda, "The UDENAMO and Nationalism in Mozambique," typescript, San Diego, May 16, 1966, Marcum Papers, Box 36/3. Mabunda detailed the fates of three would-be escapees shot to death at the Rhodesian border by Portuguese soldiers.
9. Edward A. Alpers, "To Seek a Better Life: The Implications of Migration from Northern Mozambique to Colonial and Independent Tanzania for Class Formation and Political Behavior in the Struggle to Liberate Mozambique," University of Minnesota, Conference on Class Basis of Nationalist Movements in Angola, Guinea-Bissau and Mozambique, May 25–27, 1983.
10. Michel Cahen, "The Mueda Case and Maconde Political Ethnicity," *Africana Studia* (Porto, Portugal), no. 2, November 1999, pp. 29–46.
11. Ibid.
12. Ibid.
13. Chipande presented himself as a survivor, the link between the event and Frelimo. But according to Cahen's research, it is unlikely that Chipande was personally present at the time in Mueda-sede (chief town), because he was a member of Linguilanilo, a cooperative movement organized by a local Maconde leader, Lazaro N'Kavandame, which had nothing to do with the arrested organizers of the ill-fated Tanganyika delegation, Faustino Vanomba and Kibirite Diwane. (For a disparaging description of N'Kavandame's Linguilanilo movement see *Centro de Estudos, "Africanos, Nao Vamos Esquecer!"* Universidade Eduardo Mondlane, Maputo, February, 1983.)

14. Eduardo Mondlane, *The Struggle for Mozambique*. Baltimore: Penguin Books, pp. 117–118; Munslow, *Mozambique*, p. 11; and George Houser and Herb Shore, *Mozambique: Dream the Size of Freedom*. The Africa Fund, 1975, pp. 22–23.
15. *East African Standard* (Nairobi), February 20, 1961; Anders E. Per Wastberg, *Angola and Mozambique: The Case Against Portugal*, New York: Roy Publishers, 1963.
16. Edwin C. Munger, "Mozambique: Uneasy Today, Uncertain Tomorrow," *African Field Reports*, Cape Town, South Africa, C. Struik, 1961, p. 392.
17. *African Mail*, Lusaka, January 31, 1961.
18. Ibid.
19. Ibid.
20. Mondlane portrayed Gwambe as a duplicitous former PIDE agent. See Mondlane, "The Mozambique Liberation Front," mimeo, 1962; Marcum Papers, Box 36/7. Gwambe may have worked for PIDE, but it seems likely that he slipped into Rhodesia with a mission to report back to PIDE on the activities of Mozambican émigrés then cut short his collaboration when he saw the opportunity for a leadership role within burgeoning African nationalism.
21. "Hlomulo Jani Chitofo Gwambe: My Concise Autobiography," typescript, Lusaka, June 13, 1966. Marcum Papers, 36/1. Written during a period when he and Paulo Gumane were collaborating, the script was sent to the author by Gumane. Gwambe signed each page. The autobiography ends with the statement: "This was typed by me personally and any alteration or addition is false. All the contents are type written by one make of typewriter and anything by hand or otherwise is not mine and correction or omission is forgery. Documents, pictures and additions to this Concise Autobiography to support the substance can be applied directly to me with specific purpose and consideration shall be made to release them or not."
22. *The Voice of Africa*, Accra, November 1961. On March 30, 1962, UDENAMO distributed leaflets to a group of Goan refugees aboard an ocean liner that had arrived in Dar es Salaam harbor from India, warning that there would be no place for them as "stooges" of the Portuguese in the future of Mozambique. "African people would not tolerate such people when independence was won." Dar es Salaam Radio, domestic, 1600 GMT, March 30, 1962.
23. *Daily Nation*, Nairobi, July 18, 1961.
24. *The Times*, London, July 22, 1962.
25. Ibid.
26. *New York Times*, April 11, 1959.
27. Mabunda, "The UDENAMO and Nationalism…".

34 J.A. MARCUM

28. Ibid.
29. Prominent among the many involved and arrested in the 1958 affair were Narciso Mbule (later UDENAMO foreign secretary), Mohamed Hussein, Tomas de Almeida, and Joao Baptista.
30. Mabunda, "The UDENAMO and Nationalism...".
31. Letter to author dated, June 12, 1966, Marcum Papers, Box 36/3.
32. Ibid.
33. Mabunda, "The UDENAMO and Nationalism...".
34. Ibid.
35. Ibid.
36. Gwambe's anti-American view were reflected in an UDENAMO statement "America the Country Responsible for the Colonial Wars in Africa," mimeo, Dar es Salaam, October 8, 1962, Marcum Papers, Box 36/1.

CHAPTER 3

Frelimo

FOUNDING FRELIMO

In the summer of 1962, Mondlane left the United Nations and joined the faculty of the Maxwell School at Syracuse University. That freed him to plunge into active politics. On June 7, 1962, he flew into Dar es Salaam.

Because he belonged to neither UDENAMO nor MANU, Mondlane was at an initial disadvantage. After Gwambe was permitted back into Tanzania for the unity talks, he had a brief meeting with Mondlane. Gwambe sought to gain time by explaining that UDENAMO and MANU had already agreed to "work together in the same office" and (under his leadership) to prepare a conference to establish a common organization. Mondlane rejected Gwambe's delaying tactic and insisted on acting immediately to create a single Mozambican independence front. They argued. Sensing that the momentum was with Mondlane, Gwambe reacted with a scheme to block him.

Gwambe refused to deal with Mondlane, whom he dismissed as an American agent, and he left Tanganyika after only a day back in the country for a "secret" trip to India, hoping the talks would stall until Mondlane had left the country. Gwambe ignored internal UDENAMO and Tanganyikan requests that he postpone his trip to India until the issue of unity had been settled. Mondlane and American diplomats suspected that the real motive for Gwambe's trip to India was a prospective

© The Author(s) 2018
J.A. Marcum, *Conceiving Mozambique*, African Histories and Modernities, https://doi.org/10.1007/978-3-319-65987-9_3

deal with India's Defense Minister, Krishna Menon, to obtain the release of Mozambican solders captured during India's invasion of Goa. Those soldiers were to be flown to Ghana to receive ideological training and form the nucleus of a Gwambe-led liberation army.

Gwambe's petulant departure created an opening for Mondlane. Gwambe had left, but not before being pressured into setting up a special UDENAMO committee to negotiate the merger. When negotiations began on June 20, 1962, the participants quickly agreed on a draft constitution, and, as Mondlane later described, "All of us signed it." Next came the selection of candidates for the Central Committee. MANU's Mmole evened the score with Gwambe for his betrayal at the CONCP meeting in Casablanca by agreeing that presidents neither of UDENAMO nor of MANU should be allowed to stand for president.

According to Mondlane: "Just before we had finished selecting our candidates, Gwambe came back from his secret mission. He immediately set out a machinery to destroy the new unity." But Gwambe was unable to prevail against growing pressure from Tanganyika's foreign minister, Oscar Kambona, who was a Maconde, and Peter Koinange, the head of PAFMECSA, who presided over the talks and elections. Before Gwambe returned, UDENAMO 's secretary general, Calvino Mahleyeye, invited Mondlane to join UDENAMO, which made it possible for Mondlane to participate in the unity talks and stand for office.[1] In a political obituary for Gwambe's UDENAMO, David Mabunda credited it with spearheading the independence struggle during its two years of existence, "establishing effective underground cells, sending militants to Ghana for military training, [...] exposing the real nature of Portuguese rule, [and] laying the groundwork for its successor, Frelimo."[2] But it was time to move on.

Before Gwambe returned from India, Mondlane lobbied for support, promising alternative sources of support to those dependent on Gwambe's funds (which came principally from Ghana and the Soviet bloc). Three candidates were put forward to lead the new organization: Mondlane; Reverend Uria T. Simango, of UDENAMO, who came from Beira and had served as a Protestant minister for some years in Highfield, Salisbury, Southern Rhodesia; and Jose Balthazar da Costa Chagonga, president of a small party of Mozambican exiles, from the Tete area of Mozambique, living in Nyasaland (Malawi). (Chagonga among others had written to Mondlane while the latter was at the UN urging him to come to Dar es Salaam to promote unity among the ranks of Mozambican nationalists.[3])

On June 25, 1962, at the Arnautoglu Community Center in Dar es Salaam, the delegates elected an interim Supreme Council of Frelimo, pending a national congress. Mondlane was elected as President and Reverend Simango was elected as Vice-President. Mabunda was elected as Secretary General, and MANU's Mmole was elected Treasurer. The others elected to the Supreme Council were: Deputy Secretary General Paulo Gumane; Deputy Treasurer John Mavenda; Deputy Publicity Secretary Ali Mouhamed; and, at Mondlane's urging, Leo E. Milas, elected *in absentia* to be the new organization's Publicity Secretary. A special Scholarship Committee was also set up to "help the many refugee students who need to be placed at colleges and universities," abroad with Lawrence Millinga as its executive secretary.[4] The slate of officials balanced former UDENAMO and MANU personalities.

Before returning to the USA, Mondlane visited the American chargé d'affaires in Dar es Salaam, Thomas Byrne. Mondlane signaled an urgent need for funds and urged Byrne to alert Assistant Secretary of State Fredericks to this need. He also met with the Ghanaian High Commissioner, explained Gwambe's leadership flaws, and received an invitation, including air tickets to Accra. Mondlane also complained to Tanganyika's Foreign Minister Kambona that Gwambe had posted spies to track his personal movements and had informed the Portuguese of his travel plans leaving him open to abduction.

On July 10, 1962, Byrne cabled Washington:

> Dr. Mondlane's position as leader of the Mozambique Liberation Front appears at the moment to be strong. His future prospects will depend to a great extent upon how successful he is in obtaining money to carry on the party's activities here. Another as yet unclear factor is the sincerity of Kambona of support. If Ghana is now shifting its support from Gwambe to Mondlane, the latter's position should be secure.[5]

But Ghana's support had not shifted.

Shortly after his return to the USA, Mondlane issued a joint fundraising appeal with Mabunda, his young (age 28) Secretary General. It underscored the dicey nature of the financial base for Mondlane's leadership. They presented a brief history of events leading to the creation of Frelimo, and then wrote: "A few days after the election [Gwambe] was found selling some of the office equipment of the UDENAMO which by signed agreement, should have been handed over to the new party. He

38 J.A. MARCUM

also refused to hand over the funds which had been deposited in his name for the UDENAMO party." Former associates estimated that Gwambe had recently received some $20,000 from supportive governments, had deposited these funds in his own personal account, then departed for Moscow, where "he is now working hard to reestablish himself amongst Mozambican nationalists." They added: "The great advantage [Gwambe] has over the rest of the leaders of the united front is that he can more easily acquire large amounts of money from governments sympathetic to his position." Such funds have been the basis of his power, and we "cannot count him out from creating some difficulties in the future."

Gwambe, accompanied by Marcelino dos Santos, had first visited Moscow in September 1961. He was reportedly viewed with skepticism by the Soviet Union's main conduit with African liberation movements, Petr Yevsyukov.[6] Gwambe was seen as a man of "extremes and limited world view," a "petty political adventurer, whose main aim was to misinform us and to receive more money." He was reported to have arrived in Moscow "from the USA," but there is no evidence Gwambe ever visited the USA. He presented himself as the single true representative of Mozambique freedom fighters. Touring the Soviet Armory Museum in the Kremlin, Gwambe was reportedly captivated by a display of medieval hauberks, swords, and maces. Gwambe commented, "it would be good to arm all our fighters with these weapons." Although Gwambe's "inadequacy was evident," Moscow agreed to assist UDENAMO with $3000 dollars. (It disguised additional funding by passing it through the Ghanaians.)

After the Frelimo election, the Tanganyikan government promised needed assistance for Mondlane's initial organizational costs. "The party's immediate financial needs amount[ed] to a minimum of $30,000" for office rental, support of eight fulltime officers, travel to "crucial international conferences." In their fundraising appeal, Mondlane and Mabunda revealed that Mondlane viewed his presidency as a part-time responsibility. Wedded to the efficacy of a political reform process within Mozambique, "Dr. Mondlane is making plans to teach in Dar es Salaam in September 1963. This would eliminate a large proportion of the costs of the party." Appealing for financial help for what would be a "long struggle to come," Mondlane and Mabunda stressed the need for the resources essential to bring effective "political pressure on the Portuguese government to relinquish its power in Mozambique."[7]

Frelimo Deputy Secretary General Gumane and National Representative John Zarica Sakupwanya (soon to leave for study in the USA) also embarked on an intense and systematic effort to organize Mozambican Maconde sisal, port, and other workers in communities throughout Tanganyika. The resulting membership dues were meant to provide Frelimo with a source of sustained financial support.

Faced with the loss of his leadership role after Mondlane's election, Gwambe obtained information on his rival's flight plans with the intention of passing it on to Portuguese agents so that they could arrest Mondlane at stops along the way. Gwambe also brought 20 members of his Ghana-trained "army" to Dar es Salaam and barracked them in an apartment building. As he gathered information on Mondlane's flight plans, some of the 20 members of Gwambe's army were to get rid of Simango and Gumane. But the would-be assassins balked, Mondlane changed his flight plans, and Tanganyika's Minister Kambona resisted Ghanaian pressure and blocked Gwambe from returning to Dar es Salaam after his planned visit to Moscow and, with Nyerere's backing, promised urgently needed financial help to Mondlane. Gwambe's plotting was, at least temporarily, foiled.

In July 1962, Gwambe visited Moscow to attend the World Congress for General Disarmament and Peace. He used the occasion to assail Mondlane for allegedly acting under the direction of the US embassy in Dar es Salaam and sought more funds.[8] After his visit to Moscow and a period in Cairo, Gwambe continued his assault on Mondlane. Writing to A.K. Barden, of Ghana's Bureau of African Affairs, on July 23, 1962, he spelled out a plan for a coup to take over Frelimo. With Mondlane back in the USA and Simango scheduled to travel to the USA for study, Gwambe's plan depended on Ghana funneling funds to Mabunda while feigning loyalty to Frelimo. Mabunda would receive and use the funds to buy allegiances and gain control of the movement for Gwambe and Ghana.

But vigorous organizational efforts by Deputy Secretary General Gumane had markedly strengthened Frelimo's internal structure. And Mabunda, whom Gwambe had earlier placed as UDENAMO representative in Accra to insure against potential leadership competition,

40   J.A. MARCUM

collected the funds ($10,000) but delivered them to Frelimo. The money proved crucial, enabling Frelimo to organize its congress and pay its bills.

Coincidentally, Mondlane traveled with Mabunda from Cairo, where he received the Ghanaian money, in a shared flight on September 22 to the Congress in Dar es Salaam. En route and in Dar es Salaam, Mabunda got to know [Mondlane] for the first time and concluded that he was a "loyal African" and willing to amend his "racist" views, which derived from his experience as a youth in South Africa. Gumane and Mondlane agreed that Mabunda's international contacts and potential as an effective leader constituted an important asset.[9] Frelimo seemed to be emerging on a sound footing.

Organizing Frelimo

Mondlane faced a difficult choice between his new academic position at Syracuse's Maxwell School and his new role as leader of an African nationalist movement. Weighing the difficulties of relocating and supporting a family only just ensconced in Syracuse and a perceived need to mobilize American support to persuade Portugal to negotiate and seek to raise funds in the USA, Mondlane decided to stay at the university and teach through the fall semester. However, he delayed and then proceeded with plans to organize and attend a formal Frelimo Congress in Dar es Salaam. The Congress would choose a new and expanded slate of candidates to head up the party he planned to head for some time *in absentia*.

On September 23–28, 1962, 80 some representatives and an estimated 500 observers from all regions but mostly the north of the country met in Dar es Salaam, reviewed the political, military, and economic situation in Mozambique, and chose a new slate of officers for Frelimo. A constitution was drawn up by Marcelino dos Santos along Marxist-Leninist lines. It was to feature elections up the line from cell, area, district, and province to Central Committee, all functioning within the discipline of "democratic centralism." It set forth a nationalist philosophy that Mondlane described as blending Catholic heritage, Anglo-Saxon and Protestant ideals, and socialist concepts and called for political independence along with gender, racial, and ethnic equality. In this fashion, dos Santos deftly prepared Frelimo structurally for an eventual injection of Marxist dogma.

The new Central Committee of 11 members included just three former members of MANU (both Treasurer Mmole and Scholarship Secretary Millinga were eliminated for alleged transgressions). This signaled the predominance of former UDENAMO members from the south of the country. Mondlane, Simango, Mabunda, and Gumane retained their previous positions as President, Vice-President, Secretary General and Deputy Secretary General, respectively. Silverio Nungo was elected as Administrative Secretary, Marcelino dos Santos as Secretary for External Relations, and Joao Mungwambe as Organizing Secretary. Three former MANU members were elected: Johannes Mtschembelesi as Treasurer; James Msadala as Deputy Treasurer; and Paulo Bayete as Deputy Secretary for Information. And Leo Milas was elected Secretary for Information and Culture.

The Congress opened in Arnautoglu Hall with congratulatory speeches by Tanganyikan Prime Minister Rashidi Kawawa and Minister of Home Affairs Kambona hailing Frelimo unity. It featured a stem-winding speech by John Sakupwana, which brought participants to their feet pledging to shed their blood. And it set a timetable for independence: September 1964.

At the end of the Congress, Mondlane demonstrated his personal sway by announcing his appointment of dos Santos as secretary for foreign affairs. He then rushed off to catch his plane back to the USA without answering protests from anti-*mestiço* members, who claimed that dos Santos was really a Cape Verdean. Dos Santos's appointment would prove to be a matter of major long-term ideological significance and political controversy.

Mabunda and Gumane were reportedly among those who questioned dos Santos's bona fides and protested against his appointment. They saw him as mounting a long-term, Marxist challenge to Mondlane's leadership. A former UDENAMO official, Narciso Mbule, who in years to come would become a frequent source of caustic anti-Frelimo polemics, publicly denounced dos Santos's selection. Mbule later described the end of the Congress as follows:

> In his closing speech, Dr. Mondlane read out the list of names of new members of the Central Committee. It should be noted that these members were not submitted to the appreciation of the Congress, including the President himself. When the name of Mr. dos Santos was read there

42   J.A. MARCUM

were reportedly cries of shame. But Mr. Mondlane refused to acknowledge the anger of various delegates and after his speech left the Conference Hall straightaway to a taxi, which was already waiting and drove to the airport where he was booked for a flight to the United States.[10]

Mondlane returned to Syracuse and spent the next months teaching, writing, attending conferences, testifying to United Nations committees, raising money, and lobbying the US government and other possible sources for support. One of the private benefactors he contacted was the Brazilian head of a New York-based mining shipping and marketing company, J.E. de Sousa, with interests in rare ores found in Mozambique.

Mondlane displayed his self-assured academic bite in a paper he prepared for an American Negro Leadership Conference on Africa at a conference in Harriman, New York, on November 23–25, 1962. Entitled "The American Negro and the Struggle for Independence in Portuguese Africa," the paper attacked the pro-Portuguese lobbying of Max Yergan and George S. Schuyler, journalists with the African-American *Pittsburgh Courier*. Responding to their claim that the Portuguese system was racially non-discriminatory and actually designed "to foster and promote interracial marriage," Mondlane retorted:

> In all my life in Mozambique I have never known or heard of any white or black person marrying a person of the other race [...] in the last 75 years of direct Portuguese control of our country there has never been a marriage of a white Portuguese person with a black African.

Schuyler and Yergan, he said, were probably referring to "illicit sexual relations between white Portuguese men and black African women, which is resulting in the development of a new class of people known as 'mixts,' or the so-called mulatto." Mondlane concluded by bluntly telling the mostly black conference audience: "Africans from Portuguese colonies would be heartened to see at least one American Negro of the stature of Yergan and Schuyler, work on their behalf to influence public opinion in favor of freedom."

MILAS

While Mondlane was back in the USA, the dysfunctional foibles of exile politics were taking hold in Dar es Salaam. Increasingly, Mondlane found containing fractious egos, paranoias, ambitions, and delusions from afar extremely difficult. Frelimo was a collection of individuals with different experiences and persuasions, some looking to war, some to a socialist revolution, some preferring the pursuit of negotiated reform. There were regional and ethnic tensions among and between northerners and southerners. There had been no time to solder together and meld a coherent movement—and Mondlane was not in Dar es Salaam to mediate.

In late 1962 Mondlane responded to the cacophony of communications from Dar es Salaam by sending Leo Milas, who had been elected *in absentia* as Frelimo's publicity secretary in June of that year, to Dar es Salaam as his personal representative and troubleshooter. Milas's mandate was to contain and channel exile ambitions into political unity pending Mondlane's return to the scene.

I met Milas in April 1962, when I was invited to lecture at UCLA's African Studies Program on the findings of an exploratory trek that George Houser, the director of the American Committee on Africa (ACOA), and I made in January 1962 into a nationalist-held area of northern Angola.[11] At the end of the lecture, a flamboyant young woman wearing a flaring broad-brimmed hat came up to the podium, presented herself as Sarah D. Archdeacon, and asked if I knew her boyfriend. She said he was a Mozambican teaching Romance languages at the University of Southern California (USC), had an M.A. from UCLA, and was from a prominent chief's family. She went on to say that she intended to visit his family in Mozambique at a location just north of Lourenco Marques and to write an article for *Vogue* magazine. According to Archdeacon, her boyfriend was eager to work for Mozambique's independence. I had not heard of him, but I told her I would pass along his contact information and interest in working in Mozambique to Mondlane.

After I returned to Lincoln University, I called Mondlane and related the incident to him. He, too, had no previous knowledge of her boyfriend. A few weeks later, Mondlane called me back and posed a series of questions. Contextually, he explained, there were few well-educated Mozambicans that he could turn to. What again were this man's

44   J.A. MARCUM

academic degrees? Where exactly was he from in Mozambique? How long had he been in the USA? What more did I know? I explained that I had told him everything I knew, and urged him to use the contact information Archdeacon had given me.

The next time I heard of Milas was when I read the list of names chosen for interim Frelimo leadership positions. Leo Milas had been made Publicity Secretary. Apparently Mondlane, attracted by Milas's educational credentials, had met him in New York and was persuaded of his *bona fides* and sophistication. Therewith began a bizarre and critical chapter in the early history of the Mozambique independence movement.

On January 14, 1963, I received a telephone call from Eduardo. He had just received a report from Milas in Dar es Salaam that he had fired Mabunda and Gumane. The same day, Mondlane received a letter from Mabunda and Gumane professing their loyalty. The next day Mondlane called me again. He asked if I thought Sarah Archdeacon, who had broken off her relationship with Milas, might be a Portuguese spy. He suspected her of mischievous involvement. Milas claimed he had acted against Mabunda and Gumane based on a Tanganyikan police report that revealed serious Portuguese-linked duplicity. Milas, with the support of a majority of other Central Committee members, thus orchestrated the ousting of key party leaders. All of those who had questioned or challenged his identity and authority were singled out and purged.

Joseph Massinga, Mondlane's representative in New York at the time, later noted that it was conspicuous to all that Milas spoke Spanish but no Portuguese, fueling skepticism about his real identity.[12] But Milas insisted he was Mozambican born and had acquired Spanish during military training in Mexico.

Milas had initially begun correspondence from California with UDENAMO. Mondlane argued that Gwambe had become concerned that he, Mondlane, would prove more difficult to control than poorly educated and ill-informed UDENAMO and MANU leaders. Therefore Gwambe conferred with the Ghanaian High Commissioner in Dar es Salaam, Joe-Fio Meyer, phoned Milas in California, and offered him a position as educational coordinator for Mozambique refugees in East Africa. The idea was to secure the services of a Western-educated exile to counter balance Mondlane. Milas was to receive a Ghanaian passport and air ticket to Dar es Salaam from Ghana's UN ambassador in New York. The African-American Institute reportedly contacted Milas and proposed a position connected with a proposed educational institution for Mozambique refugees to be established in Dar es Salaam. Mondlane, impressed with Milas's academic background, then intervened. He met Milas and persuaded him to join Frelimo.[13]

Confirmed *in absentia* at Mondlane's insistence as a member of Frelimo's Central Committee, Milas arrived in Dar es Salaam as Mondlane's emissary on November 14, 1962, and immediately called a meeting of the Central Committee armed with what he represented as "full powers by the President to act on his behalf." (This authority was confirmed in a letter from Mondlane to Kambona asking him to help Milas "settle the dispute among the leaders of Frelimo.") Milas explained to the Central Committee that he had left Mozambique at age 19 to study in the USA. Mabunda challenged him, noting that: "Even Kamuzu Banda [president of Malawi] who lived in England and America for forty-eight years could still say words like Kwacha in Nyanja, his mother tongue, yet this Milas who may be twenty-nine years old cannot greet me in any Mozambican language." Milas, Mabunda alleged, "repeatedly complained of not having any money but could hire cars, pay for a body guard and 5 henchmen," never had to borrow but was able to lend money to others and to reside in the Splendid Hotel at 45 shillings a day. For Milas, the likes of Mabunda had to go.[14] Suspicions were spreading that Milas had "connections with some [foreign] intelligence [agency] which was financing him."

According to Massinga, at the time of Tanganyikan independence in December 1962, the Algerian delegation to the ceremony offered Frelimo 100 military scholarships. It was agreed that the trainees would be sent in two initial batches of 25 each via commercial charter flight so as to avoid undue attention. "Milas opposed this idea. He wanted to send the fifty in one single plane." Joao Munguambe, a Milas critic who was in charge of military affairs at the time, opposed this. But Milas insisted and called a meeting of the Central Committee to condemn Munguambe, whom he denounced as a Portuguese agent. The Committee balked, but the local police subsequently detained Munguambe.

According to Massinga, in December 1962, Milas instructed Vasco Matabela, a Frelimo militant, to steal travel documents of students who had been offered scholarships and reported to the police that Munguambe was the culprit. Matabela later confessed to stealing the documents on the instructions of Milas. After this incident, Milas

46 J.A. MARCUM

accused Munguambe of spending Frelimo's money for his personal enjoyment. Munguambe denied the accusation, but could not produce the receipts that would have exonerated him, because Milas had stolen them. Munguambe was expelled from Frelimo.

On January 5, 1963, the Central Committee and several other refugees met and during their discussions Narciso Mbule accused Milas of being a CIA agent who had been sent to disrupt the Mozambican organization. Mbule ordered the exiles to beat up Milas. On January 13, Milas, Simango, and their supporters issued expulsion orders against General Secretary Mabunda, Deputy General Secretary Gumane, Defense Secretary Munguambe, Deputy Organizing Secretary Joel Guduane, and Fanuel Gideon Mahluza, the representative of Frelimo in Cairo. Twenty other refugees accused of having planned the attack on Milas were also expelled from Frelimo and from Tanganyika. The group fled to Kenya.

The Central Committee supported Milas, in part, because Mabunda and Gumane had alienated foreign affairs secretary dos Santos by accusing him of nepotism. The fact that most of those expelled were from the south helped to explain the vote of Simango, an Ndau from Beira. When he learned of the expellees' attempt to regroup in Kenya, Simango persuaded Kenyan President Jomo Kenyatta to expel them to Egypt, where they were given political asylum. Milas, soon to be elevated and placed in charge of military training, "found" and brandished a letter showing that Mabunda and Gumane worked for PIDE. From distant Syracuse, Mondlane accepted Milas's "coup."

Remember Sarah Archdeacon?

The widely circulated narrative is that she did indeed travel to Mozambique to meet her boyfriend's family. She found no family. She then traveled up the coast to Dar es Salaam, where she socialized intimately with members of the Tanzanian government. Milas, she spitefully declaimed, was an imposter.

By 1964, Milas occupied the key Frelimo post of Secretary for Defense and Security. In June 1963, Mondlane confirmed that Milas was in overall charge of planned military operations in Mozambique. Mondlane had retracted the scholarship of a young militant, Filipe Magaia, who was accepted for study at Lincoln University. Instead he sent Magaia to Algeria to obtain critical military training in guerilla warfare. There was an urgent need for Frelimo to develop a military option.

3 FRELIMO 47

Magaia would now serve as the field commander inside Mozambique. Meanwhile an Algerian general had arrived in Dar es Salaam to supervise local military training. But Mondlane placed Milas in overall charge of military operations in the eventuality of Portugal's continued rejection of a negotiated political solution.

Indicative of his close relationship with Milas, Mondlane took the former USC Romance language instructor with him to meet with the American Ambassador to Tanganyika, William K. Leonhart, in March 1964. In a meeting that lasted over an hour, Leonhart reported that Mondlane expressed hope that the USA would use its influence to avert a tragedy of "irreversible violence" that would result if efforts to find a diplomatic solution failed. He declared that Frelimo had unified in the wake of the expulsion of potential dissidents and averred that a "complete understanding exists between himself and Milas." He described plans "to strengthen the present six-man Dar es Salaam headquarters by bringing back about five Mozambicans now in U.S. schools who he knows. Milas nodded agreement to all this." Ambassador Leonhart ended his report on the meeting by expressing the opinion that "internal Frelimo strains still exist." But, he said, Mondlane had a chance to "try his diplomacy in [the] West. What he is able to accomplish may well determine not only leadership in Frelimo and [the] character [of] that organization but [also the] question [of] how long violence can be staved off in Mozambique."[15]

Less than two months later, Milas presented a different, less Western-oriented image in Cairo, where leaders of African independence movements had gathered after the founding of the Organization of African Unity (OAU) in Addis Ababa. Milas was "viewed by many as an agent infiltrated into Frelimo." To counter this perception, according to the head of Frelimo security, he "used to go around the hotels with a book by Marx and various Leninist writings under his arm."[16]

Despite Mondlane's expressions of confidence, Milas's outsize ambition provoked persistent and intense controversy. Mondlane finally bowed to pressure from within and without and authorized an investigation into Milas's background. According to some reports, with the help of a detective agency this led to a fateful telephone call to San Pedro, California, during one of Mondlane's visits to New York. Together with Frelimo's representative in New York, Joseph Massinga, Mondlane located and talked with Milas's parents by phone. The conversation

48 J.A. MARCUM

convinced Mondlane of Milas's real identity, and, in Massinga's words, he "took immediate if belated steps against the impostor who had by then almost shattered the organization." Frelimo "had lost many of its founders."[17]

On August 25, 1964, the Central Committee issued a circular in which it announced that Leo Clinton Aldridge, Jr., alias Leo Milas, born in Pittsburgh, Texas, was the son of Leo Clinton Aldridge, Sr., and Catherine Bell Miles of San Pedro, California. The Committee charged Milas with "identity falsification," activities against Frelimo's "cohesion and unity," and "false accusations against certain members of Frelimo which resulted in expulsions engineered by him." "For quite a long time," it said, "the Central Committee had been carrying out investigations into the activities of Leo Aldridge Milas" and "attempts by the president to convince him to change his behavior" had failed. On August 14, 1964, the Central Committee expelled Milas.[18] Dodging self-incrimination, the Central Committee did not explain why it had taken two years, or "quite a long time," of investigating to unveil the Milas scam. The revelation was an embarrassment and a severe blow to Mondlane's authority.

According to George Houser, Milas contrived to have Mabunda and Gumane expelled from Frelimo and Tanganyika on the basis of a letter identifying them as Portuguese agents, "a letter, which, it was later discovered, he had not 'found' but had himself forged."[19] As late as Frelimo's second congress, in 1968, Mondlane attempted to dissociate himself from the Milas debacle. He attributed Milas's role to "interference by foreign elements in the central structure of the movement" and to the "introduction [of Milas] into the organization by his friend Adelino Gwambe." Mondlane said Milas had managed "to deceive some members of the Central Committee and passed himself off as Mozambican." Mondlane, Milas's former champion and obstinate defender, went on to blame David Mabunda, rather than Milas, for the factionalism that arose in 1962. He said Mabunda had "decided to obstruct the participation" of other members in the Central Committee. "The result was the expulsion of the Secretary General himself, who had to leave Tanganyika, accompanied by a handful of dissident allies, such as Paulo Gumane and Joao Mungwambe," the latter of whom was later persuaded to return.[20] In short, Mondlane rewrote history. Conveniently for him, Mabunda was long gone and unavailable to defend himself.

Milas Redux

Without losing a beat, Milas produced his own historical rewrite. He turned the narrative upside down. It was Mondlane who had stacked the Central Committee with personal supporters (e.g., Marcelino dos Santos, Silverio Nungu, Joao Mungwambe, etc.), and Mondlane who had made false allegations against Mabunda and Gumane based on fake documents. Having discovered they were false, he, Milas, had begun to observe Mondlane "much more carefully," including his connections with the American embassy, lavish lifestyle, "lack of interest in beginning armed action, receipt of a $200 monthly stipend from the Israeli Embassy" and his "bribing" or sending of those opposed to him "on long missions outside Africa, or in some cases to study outside Africa." Mondlane, he wrote, "planned to send me on a long mission and then expel me when it would be safe to do so."[21] Milas claimed to have anticipated Frelimo's action. He claimed to have immediately activated a prepared option in consultation with military personnel "formerly under [his] charge." He formed a Conselho de Libertacao de Mozambique (CLM), which he said was based on "the former Frelimo organization in northern Mozambique."

Next, Milas donned a MANU mantle.

MANU had reorganized after Mmole was expelled from Frelimo, and had named Lucas Fernandes, who had left Frelimo in the wake of Mmole's expulsion, military commander of a Maconde group exiled from Tanzania and now based in Mombasa, Kenya. On June 18, 1964, Fernandes reportedly infiltrated the Maconde region of Cabo Delgado via the border town of Lindi with some 150 MANU Youth League militants. However, Fernandes "made the huge mistake of killing a popular Dutch missionary, Daniel Boorman." He did so because Boorman's Catholic mission was "helping Frelimo." The mission denounced the slaying and responded by helping Portuguese authorities pummel MANU, which Lisbon considered to be a greater danger than Frelimo. The Portuguese mounted a campaign of repression and completely destroyed MANU implantation on the plateau. This left Frelimo to become "the first to genuinely wage war."[22]

Milas's connection with the Fernandes initiative is unclear. But in his attempt to regain political power he attacked Frelimo for "discriminating against the people of Northern Mozambique" and against coastal Moslems "who [together] constituted 35% of Mozambique's

50 J.A. MARCUM

population." Then, in 1965, MANU claimed credit for Fernandes's attack of August 28, 1964, on Nangololo. A lengthy document denounced Frelimo for allegedly sending Mozambicans to Israel for military training, condemned American imperialism, called for a merger with Malawi-based UNAMI, and scheduled a MANU Congress in Mombasa. The same document then declared the "Congress" or conference to have been successfully held. Published in English and Maconde the document was signed by "Bwana Seif Al-Aziz L. Milas, MANU president."[23]

Over time, Milas's activities became obscure and marginal. In June 1987, *Africa Confidential*, a London newsletter, reported he was working in Nairobi for the United Nations Environment Programme and also was a founding member of RENAMO, which launched an armed rebellion against Frelimo in the 1980s. Milas's last words as "president of MANU" were issued from Khartoum. Having sided with the Chinese in their competition with the Soviets for influence in Africa, he wrote a series of communiqués for the Chinese press agency, Hsinhua. Hailing Chairman Mao as "the greatest revolutionary genius of our time," he congratulated China on its third successful nuclear test and condemned Soviet "splitists" for holding a conference outside the purview of the pro-Chinese African-Asian Writers' Bureau.[24]

While attending the Third International Conference of Africanists as president-elect of the African Studies Association of the USA, I visited the University of Addis Ababa. There, a visiting academic and friend from the University of Wisconsin chided me for having upset one of his local university colleagues. I had accused that colleague of having been expelled from Frelimo as an impostor and author of "pro-Chinese communiqués from Khartoum in the name of a "phantom Mozambique African National Union." The reference was to an article I had written for *Africa Report* ("Three Revolutions," November 1967). The affronted colleague was Seifik Aziz Milas.

In an interview with an enterprising University of Colorado doctoral student, Milas later claimed to have been born in Inhambane in 1934, the son of a Shangan woman named Milasi and a Zulu father. He laid claim to a primary school education in Mozambique and secondary education in Swaziland. But gave no reason for his lack of rudimentary Portuguese.

After expulsion from Frelimo and his brief military venture with MANU in Cabo Delgado, followed by a period in Khartoum and a teaching position at the University of Addis Ababa, he said he had become news editor of the *Ethiopian Herald*.[25] He also worked as program organizer for the "Voice of Addis" Gospel radio station.[26] The ambition that had fueled lies and half-truths enabled Milas to create a fictitious persona. He played this role with a remarkable talent for persuasion and manipulation. An extraordinary phenomenon, he was nevertheless doomed to eventual exposure. Because of his preoccupation with educational status and his streak of academic bias, Mondlane had been especially vulnerable to Milas's wiles and was victimized on the strength of an M.A. degree from UCLA!

Frelimo long persisted in burying the Milas matter as seen in the quasi-official history of Frelimo published in 1983 by the Centro de Estudos Africanos at Eduardo Mondlane University in Maputo. Disingenuously, it stated that as a result of a critical analysis of internal contradictions "soon after Frelimo was formed many leaders of [its] former [founding] organizations abandoned Frelimo and tried without success to recreate their old political basis."[27] For Frelimo, Milas slipped quietly down the memory hatch.

But Milas used this slippage as an opportunity to reinvent himself. Under a readjusted name, Seifulaziz Leo Milas, he emerged once again in the 1990s with a new persona, that of a respected East African researcher. He published *Causes and Consequences of the Somalia Conflict* for UNICEF in 1997 and a major 248-page work, *Sharing the Nile, Egypt, Ethiopia and the Geo-Politics of Water* (Pluto Press, London, 2013). The latter was reviewed by Fantu Cheru, a Senior Research Fellow of the Nordic Africa Institute, Uppsala, Sweden, in the following terms: "Essential reading for those interested in the hydro-politics of the Nile waters, and in the attempt to establish acceptable legal rules for managing water utilization by the riparian countries. A brilliant book by one of the best observers of the complex politics of the Horn of Africa." The Amazon blurb on Milas described him as a research specialist on the countries, peoples, conflicts, and development issues of the Nile Basin and the Horn of Africa who had worked with the United Nations Environment Programme, UNICEF, the African Union (on Darfur), and the International Planned Parenthood Federation African Region. Absent from the laudatory description of the specialist on the Horn of Africa, Seifulaziz Leo Milas, was any reference to Leo Clinton Aldrich, Jr., or to Mozambique.

NOTES

1. Mondlane, Frelimo, "Memorandum" to the African Liberation Committee of the Heads of State Conference, mimeo, Summer 1963, Marcum Papers, Box 34/7.
2. Mabunda, "The UDENAMO and Nationalism …".
3. A medical orderly from Zambue, Mozambique, Chagonga had organized a social group at Moatize (Tete) known as the Associacao Nacional Africana de Mocambique, was briefly arrested in 1960 for criticizing government repression of students and workers, then sought asylum in Nyasaland (Malawi).
4. Frelimo, Press Release, "Mozambique Political Parties Fuse," Dar es Salaam, June 26, 1962, Marcum Papers, Box 34/7.
5. Cabrita, *Mozambique*, pp. 12–13.
6. Vladimir Shubin, *The Hot Cold War: The USSR in Southern Africa*, Pluto Press, University of Kwa-Zulu-Natal, 2008.
7. Mondlane and Mabunda, "The Mozambique Liberation Front (Frelimo)", mimeo, Marcum Papers, Box 34/7.
8. Shubin, *The Hot Cold War*, pp. 120–121.
9. Report by John D. Blacken, 3rd Secretary, US Embassy, Dar es Salaam, October 22, 1962, Marcum Papers, Box 39/3. Blacken concurred with Gumane and Mondlane that the real origin of the funds was the Soviet Union and that the Ghanaian motive was intended to undermine, not strengthen, Mondlane's hold on Frelimo.
10. Frente Unida de Mocambique (FUMO), "Memorandum to Heads of African States and Governments," mimeo, Nairobi, Kenya, June 21, 1971, Marcum Papers, Box 37/1. This rejection of the dos Santos appointment became a common theme of Frelimo critics. See Fanuel G. Mahluza, *Patriota* (Cairo), No. 1, 1962 special edition.
11. We delivered medical supplies to villagers and ascertained that rebel forces in fact controlled a swath of territory in the north of the country. See Houser, "Journey to Rebel Angola," *Africa Today*, March 1962, pp. 4–9.
12. Joseph Massinga, "United Nations and Decolonization of Angola, Mozambique and Rhodesia," doctoral dissertation, Geneva, 1971, mimeo, 376 pp., Marcum Papers, Box 36/3. Massinga, who studied in the USA, earned a B.A. from Manhattan College and an M.A. from Fordham University and wrote his dissertation for the Graduate Institute of International Studies, Geneva, Switzerland.
13. Mondlane interview with US diplomat Thomas R. Byrne, US Embassy dispatch, June 19, 1962, Dar es Salaam, Marcum Papers, Box 39/3.
14. Mabunda, "Special Report on the Present Disturbances within Frelimo," Dar es Salaam, January 7, 1963, Marcum Papers, Box 36/3.

15. William K. Leonhart, Dar es Salaam, Dispatch to Secretary of State, March 21, 1963, Marcum Papers, Box 39/3.
16. Jacinto Veloso, *Memories at Low Altitude*. Cape Town, Zed Press, 2012, p. 28.
17. Massinga, "*United Nations and Decolonization...*" p. 288.
18. Frelimo, Department of Information, *Mozambique Revolution*, Dar es Salaam, no. 9, August 1964, Marcum Papers, Box 35/1.
19. Houser, *No One Can Stop The Rain*, p. 184.
20. Eduardo Mondlane, "Report of the Central Committee," Frelimo: Documents of the 2nd Congress, Niassa, Mozambique, July 1968, pp. 7–8, Marcum Papers, Box 38/8.
21. Milas, "O.A.U. Must Probe Frelimo," *Voice of Africa*, Accra, January 1965, pp. 39–40.
22. UDENAMO (Gumane), not to be left out of the picture, later claimed that Lucas Fernandes had actually led a UDENAMO military patrol of ten men that launched an attack on September 25. UDENAMO, *Resolute Combat* (Lusaka), December 1964.
23. Marcum Papers, Box 36/6.
24. Hsinhua Bulletins printed in London, occasional issues from September 1966 into early 1967, for which the Chinese probably paid a pittance.
25. Milas, "Portugal's African Vietnam," *Ethiopian Herald*, February 25, 1972.
26. Walter C. Opello, Jr., "Internal War in Mozambique: A Social-Psychological Analysis of a Nationalist Revolution," Ph.D. dissertation, Boulder, Colo., 1973, n. 49, pp. 242–243.
27. *Centro de Estudos Africanos*, "Frelimo from Front to Party: Revolutionary Transformations," Maputo, 1983.

CHAPTER 4

The Ravages of Exile Politics

In March 1963, six months after Frelimo's founding Congress, Mondlane returned to Dar es Salaam. In the interim, the ravages of exile politics had taken their toll. Frelimo had fallen from its wall of unity and the challenge was how to put the pieces back together. Expelled from Tanganyika after Mondlane was elected president of Frelimo, Gwambe led a "UDENAMO delegation" to the World Congress for General Disarmament and Peace in Moscow. In keeping with his peripatetic impulses, he next flew to Accra, attended a Youth Festival in Helsinki, and then made his way to Cairo, where he held a press conference denouncing Frelimo leadership for its "failure to carry on the struggle as it was planned by UDENAMO." In Cairo, Gwambe took a short course in economics and history at the Jesuit El-Nasr College, and then headed to Kampala, Uganda. In Uganda he proclaimed the resurrection of UDENAMO.

UDENAMO's rebirth was pursuant to what Gwambe claimed was the analytical work of a Comite Secreto da Restauracao do UDENAMO that allegedly spent five months investigating and verifying the take-over of Frelimo by "a clique of USA hired stooges and traitors."[1] On May 2, 1963, Gwambe met with former MANU head Mmole, who had recently been expelled from Frelimo along with a dozen others. Together, they pronounced Frelimo "dissolved," resurrected their respective movements, and promptly rejoined them to create a Frente

© The Author(s) 2018
J.A. Marcum, *Conceiving Mozambique*, African Histories
and Modernities, https://doi.org/10.1007/978-3-319-65987-9_4

55

56 J.A. MARCUM

Unida Anti-Imperialista Popular Africana (FUNIPAMO) with Gwambe as president. Explaining their return to Gwambe, MANU defectors complained:

> Frequently police stations in Southern Tanganyika received telegrammed instructions, signed by Frelimo Publicity Secretary, Leo Millas [*sic*] to the effect that the president of MANU, Mr. Mmole, and his vice-president, Mr. Kalomba, be arrested and kept under police custody. Because the police were not satisfied by Frelimo's reasons, Messrs. Mmole and Kalomba were released.

On April 15 the same charges were repeated, and Mmole and the same 12 others were again arrested, yet again released for lack of evidence.

When former UDENAMO and MANU members of Frelimo committees pressed an allegedly haughty Mondlane with questions, he was irritated and made disparaging remarks about uneducated northerners (Maconde) opening a "gap between the people from northern and southern Mozambique." Charges against Mondlane's leadership included: his "secret" relations with the American Committee on Africa; his failure to quash internal infighting between Administrative Secretary Silverio Nungu and the Vice-Treasurer, James Msadala, and Milas's refusal to reconsider his firing of top Frelimo executives, giving education a higher priority than independence; his failure to "step down from the American way of living"; his failure to "cooperate with the African masses"; and his failure to abandon his overall pro-American stance. Mondlane's pro-American "stance" was said to have been "evidenced" by a Milas speech at an Afro-Asian Conference in Moshi, Tanzania. The speech was rumored to have been written by the American consulate and to have been visibly passed to Milas to read.[2] Such was the prevailing level of exile gossip and obfuscation.

Gwambe replayed the unity theme on his own terms. FUNIPAMO, whose draft constitution limited membership to "indigenous Mozambican Africans" (no Americans, Asians or *mestiços*), lasted just a few weeks. In June 1963, Gwambe disbanded FUNIPAMO and replaced it with a resurrected UDENAMO, substituting Monomotapa for Mozambique. Then it was off again for fundraising, a journalist conference in pro-Gwambe Accra, Nigeria, Tunisia, Algeria, and Egypt, and back to Kenya, where he began organizing within a growing ex-Frelimo community. According to Gwambe, "I mobilized many people and instructed them to infiltrate through the NORTH while I led [another] detachment through the CENTRAL provinces."[3] Indefatigable, Gwambe persisted in mounting an incessant anti-Frelimo campaign that became a distraction for the latter's fundraising. Mondlane reported that three times during 1963 the director of Ghana's Bureau of African affairs had supported the "dissolution" of Frelimo and sent a staff member to Dar es Salaam to support the rebirth of UDENAMO. The Bureau representative "scooped together a number or refugees" and declared Frelimo dissolved. But, Mondlane said, the result was "nothing."[4] Keeping his options open, in March 1964 Nkrumah received Mondlane and his information chief, Pascoal Mocumbi, in Accra for what were described as "cordial talks."[5] Publicly, the meeting smoothed over the acrimony of Nkrumah–Mondlane relations. But mistrust persisted.

It was, however, the expulsion of Mabunda and Gumane and their colleagues that hurt most. On his return to Africa in March 1964, Mondlane stopped in Cairo to meet Mabunda and Gumane and seek a resolution. Mabunda and Gumane had resurrected their own version of UDENAMO, and maintained their innocence of the charges that had led to their expulsion. They held to their assertion that Milas was an American impostor and demanded he be removed from office. After two days of negotiations, the parties reached an impasse. Mondlane held firm to his support of Milas and flew on to Dar es Salaam.

Mondlane blamed Mabunda for the schism.

> While I was finishing my contract as a professor at an American university, preparing to return to East Africa as president of Frelimo, the gentleman who had been elected secretary general became involved in a number of quarrels with other members of the organization. On being disciplined for his part in the disturbances that followed, he and a small number of his supporters were asked to leave Tanganyika.[6]

GUMANE

It was at this point that Paulo Gumane emerged as a soft-spoken, politically seasoned contender in the Mozambique nationalist drama. He and Mabunda reversed the order of their Frelimo status, with Gumane as UDENAMO's president and Mabunda as vice-president.

Mabunda had been the first Frelimo official to seek military training and armaments from the Soviets, during a visit to Moscow in August

58   J.A. MARCUM

1962.[7] By early 1965, Mabunda was leaning westward. He sent a memo to John Blacken in the State Department's Bureau of Educational and Cultural Affairs entitled, "What Should the U.S. Do?" He decried the overreliance of liberation movements on communist "slogans" and their failure to develop independent political philosophies. He urged American support for training programs that stressed democratic values. In 1963 Mabunda went off to New York, where he testified at the United Nations with a student colleague, John Sakupwana.[8] In November, he presented a brief "history" of Portuguese rule to the UN's Committee on Non-Self-Governing Territories and set up a short-lived New York Rescue Committee for Mozambique in conjunction with UDENAMO. Eventually, discouraged and disenchanted with the turmoil of exile politics that had severed his connection within Frelimo, Mabunda departed the political scene and enrolled as an undergraduate at California Western University in San Diego.

Gumane dug in. Conveniently, Fanuel Mahluza, an early UDENAMO militant and Frelimo's representative in Cairo, turned his office over to the dissidents. Born at Xai Xai in the southern province of Gaza and one of the many who had labored in South Africa, Gumane moved to Rhodesia at age 28. There he joined other Mozambican exiles gaining political experience in Joshua Nkomo's National Democratic Party. In 1962 he helped to create Frelimo but was expelled as part of the Milas upheaval and subsequently served for years in various anti-Frelimo movements.[9]

With the advent of Zambian independence in 1964, Gumane moved his UDENAMO headquarters from Cairo to Lusaka. His personal biography, written in 1966, emphasized the political preparation of his South African trade union experience.[10] Gumane was born in 1918 in the district of Inhambane, the son of a Methodist deacon converted to Catholicism. He began school in 1924 in a Catholic mission called Saint Francis of Assisi of Mocumbi-Inhambane. After completing his primary education in 1932, he was admitted to the Escola de Habilitacao de Alvores in Manhica, which was the only teacher training college in Mozambique at that time. In 1936 Gumane completed school; he subsequently taught for six years in government and mission schools. He resigned from the teaching "as a protest against the injustice and discrimination done to African teachers all over Mozambique."[11]

In his autobiography, Gumane wrote:

4 THE RAVAGES OF EXILE POLITICS 59

> After resigning, I decided to go to South Africa in 1943 where I was shocked by the segregation and oppression [...] but I decided to stay and get myself employment in Johannesburg. And in 1944 I joined the Laundry and Dry Cleaner Trade Union Movement, this of course was the beginning of my Political career. And I began to attend the Trade Union and political meetings and the more I attended these meetings the more I became committed on African nationalism. As result, in 1946 I joined the African National Congress (ANC) of South Africa of which I remained a member and till after the formation of the Pan-Africanist Congress (PAC) in 1958. In 1959 I resigned my membership from the (ANC) South Africa, and I joined the PAC. And my resignation from ANC happened after attending several meetings of PAC, addressed by many leaders including their great leader Robert Mangaliso Sobukwe, who inspired me so much on Pan-Africanism.

Gumane devoted himself to trade union activities. He became the Cape Town Branch Secretary of the Laundry and Dry Cleaner Workers' Union, a position that he held for twelve years. Gumane returned to Mozambique in 1960. Gumane "found that the African peasants and farmers were the most exploited group in all the country." He "decided to organize the African Farmers Trade Union as a first step towards helping [his] people." When the Portuguese authorities heard of the union, they issued an arrest warrant accusing Gumane of "organising an unlawful Societe." Alerted by "a friend" in the government, Gumane escaped from Inhambane to Lourenco Marques and stowed away on a ship to Cape Town, where he rejoined his family.

Gumane joined UDENAMO when it was formed in October 1960, became its National Organizing Secretary, and began organizing and mobilizing Mozambicans in South Africa. When the South African police became aware of his activity, they arrested him. He spent three months in jail pending deportation back to Mozambique. Out on bail, Gumane escaped to Bechuanaland (Botswana) in September 1961.

In November 1961 Gumane went to Dar es Salaam, where he became part of the quest for nationalist unity. He was rewarded with the post of deputy secretary general of Frelimo. He "worked hard to maintain the hardly won unity" within Frelimo, but, in Gumane's view, the "forces of reaction and enemies of independence had already infiltrated." He "could not do anything and [...] was compelled to resign from Frelimo."

In January 1965, along with ten others who had resigned from Frelimo, Gumane left Dar es Salaam for Nairobi. They proceeded to

60   J.A. MARCUM

Kampala-Uganda and from there left for Cairo. On May 1, 1965, they reformed UDENAMO with Gumane as President. But, Gumane later wrote, he "was still not happy with the disunity which was again taking place in the Mozambican struggle."[12] In his view, PIDE infiltration of nationalist movements had helped to create a widespread and infectious climate of suspicion. Expulsions, resignations, reunifications, bribes, personal tirades, and above all allegations of links to foreign intelligence became destabilizing and pervasive.

Thus, by 1965, there were two competing UDENAMOs: one led by Gwambe, the other by Gumane. Given Gwambe's ambitions, the resurrection of UDENAMO-Gwambe was unavoidable, but the creation of UDENAMO-Gumane was not. It was primarily the consequence of Mondlane's misplaced confidence in an "educated" impostor—Milas—and in the long run, more costly than the resurrection of UDENAMO-Gumane.

FAILED ATTEMPTS TO MEDIATE

Despite salvoes of angry, accusatory hyperbole, there were several attempts to reconcile Frelimo and Gumane's UDENAMO. The first was the March 7, 1963, meeting with the expelled group at the Atlas Hotel in Cairo. Later that year, on November 23, Mondlane and Mabunda met at the New York apartment of Thomas Patrick Melady, the president of the Catholic Africa Service Institute. Melady had befriended both men. As in Cairo, Milas was the core of contention. Mondlane again rejected proposals that Milas be removed from Tanganyika and Frelimo. In December, Mondlane re-opened negotiations with the UDENAMO group in Dar es Salaam with Sebastian Chale, Executive Secretary of the OAU's new Africa Liberation Committee, acting as conciliator.

> Again Gumane and the others demanded the dismissal of Milas but also asked that the posts of the Vice President and Secretary of Defense be given to them. Of course, this demand was [unacceptable] to Simango and Milas, who adamantly refused to receive the group back. After this failure at reconciliation, Gumane and his men left Dar es Salaam to settle in Lusaka.[13]

In August 1963, African expectations for a newly formed government in exile (GRAE, Govêrno revolucionário de Angola no exílio) in Angola, led by Holden Roberto, were high. Roberto's "government," based in Léopoldville, was officially recognized by the hosting border state administration of Cyrille Adoula. Roberto took the occasion of the OAU meeting in Addis Ababa to negotiate the formation of a Congo Alliance of liberation movements. Meeting on the edges of conference deliberations with select southern Africa liberation movements, Roberto advised Adoula to invite one group from each country to establish a politico-military presence in Léopoldville.

With the threat of Katanga secession having been eliminated, Adoula sought to assume a new pan-African role. It was designed, among other things, to boost his credentials among the more radical Casablanca states that had previously supported Lumumbist rebels. At the end of the conference, Adoula invited the leaders of liberation groups Roberto had a natural affinity with to fly from Addis Ababa to Léopoldville on his private plane. Those movements were: (1) uniracial, vocally suspicious of multiracialism; and (2) wary of ideologically inclined intellectuals. Based on these criteria, Gumane was invited to set up a UDENAMO branch office in Léopoldville.[14]

The Congo Alliance was conceived partly as a counter to the avowedly multiracial and socialist-leaning CONCP grouping of Portuguese African movements. Mondlane had a nominally friendly if ambivalent relationship with Roberto, who had only recently publicly recognized him as the principal spokesman for Mozambican nationalism.[15] But Frelimo was allied with Roberto's MPLA [Movimento Popular de Libertaçao de Angola] adversaries within CONCP, and though Mondlane was no less angry for the reasoning, Roberto established formal relations with UDENAMO.

UDENAMO's strategy was to use Léopoldville as a rear base of operations. Fanuel Mahluza and Anibal Chilenge, former residents of Lourenco Marques and laborers in South Africa, were put in charge. Because they were blocked from Tanganyika, their new line of infiltration was to be through Katanga across Zambia into the Tete region of Mozambique. Adoula promised funds and arms—and Roberto opened his Kinkuzu military base in the Lower Congo for the training of UDENAMO's military units.

Gumane still yearned for a reconciliation with Mondlane and argued that "people don't understand why he puts his white American wife to the fore, fails to realize that people like Simango are not loyal to him, or why Marcelino dos Santos bitterly opposed his idea of calling for a meeting of Portuguese African movements to unite outside of CONCP" [and thus outside the influence of Marxist-leaning associates].[16]

62   J.A. MARCUM

Gumane had returned to Kampala in July 1963 only to find that Gwambe's rants against American imperialism had troubled the Uganda government to the point that it closed both UDENAMO offices, Gwambe's and Gumane's. Joining Gumane and others in rejecting Gwambe for the UDENAMO presidency, vice-president Mahluza reported the defection of Mmole (ex-MANU) from Gwambe's group and welcomed his imminent arrival at the UDENAMO office in Léopoldville. He said that Mmole underscored the UDENAMO-Gumane view that it was Portuguese colonialism rather than American imperialism that constituted the enemy. UDENAMO-Gumane also rejected Gwambe's financial ties with China and his parroting of Maoist dogma. By mid-August, 1963, Gumane was making his way from Stanleyville by riverboat with an initial group of 20 young men for military training at Kinkuzu and harboring schemes to attract Frelimo fighters in Algeria to defect to his Congo-based group. The deadline projected for a military intrusion into the Tete region of Mozambique via Katanga and Zambia was "early 1964."[17]

The Congo Alliance proved ephemeral. By late 1964, Roberto's GRAE had lost momentum under a hunker-down, insecure, and paranoid leadership. Chaotic conditions at the GRAE's Kinkuzu military base were too crude and chaotic for forces from UDENAMO and the Pan-Africanist Congress (PAC). The Alliance collapsed. Military trainees reboarded riverboats and made their way back up the Congo River and on into East Africa and southward to new headquarters in newly independent Zambia. In Dar es Salaam, under the auspices of Foreign Minister Kambona and then in Lusaka at the initiative of Zambian Foreign Minister Simon Kapwepwe, unity talks were reconvened. But Frelimo took a hard line. It enjoyed privileged recognition by the OAU and claimed to be the only truly representative organization. It demanded that other groups or preferably individuals within them join Frelimo on its terms as individuals.

MALAWI AND UNAMI

In late 1963, Frelimo suspended Jose Balthazar de Costa Chagonga from his position as head of health and social affairs. Kwame Nkrumah, always ready to undercut Nyerere and Mondlane, had his High Commissioner in Dar es Salaam urge Chagonga to pull his movement out of Frelimo and visit Accra. Chagonga visited the Ghanaian capital, where he confronted pressure to join Gwambe's FUNIPAMO. Wary of Gwambe's behavioral record, however, he resisted and returned to Malawi and his original Uniao Nacional Africana de Mocambique Independente (UNAMI). Even though he had served in a senior Frelimo position, thanks to Mondlane's permissiveness, Chagonga had never dissolved his movement.

In leaving Frelimo, Chagonga cited the growing dominance of southerners and the disrespectful and dismissive way in which they treated northerners as fit only for low-level military service. In particular, he faulted Mondlane, with whom he had fallen out. Chagonga was disillusioned with the man he had urged to return to Africa and create a united movement. In his view, Mondlane had become too "conscious of his educational achievements" and acted with the arrogance of a Portuguese official toward the uneducated peoples of north and central Mozambique. In interviews and in an autobiographical statement and collection of petitions to Portuguese and UN authorities, Chagonga set forth views that were widespread among black Mozambicans. His views on race were antithetical to those held by Frelimo's core. If quirky in the extreme, they nevertheless reflected the perceptions of an African who was embittered by the falsity of Portuguese pretentions to *luso-tropicalismo*, or assimilation. In Chagonga's view, the Portuguese were determined to obliterate African cultural identity.

Born in 1905 at Zumbo in the Tete district, Chagonga was the son of a goldsmith who worked for some time in the South African mines. In 1917, at age 12, he was arrested on suspicion of sympathy for groups responsible for a local tribal revolt. The experience of being placed in a concentration camp at Cachomba at an impressionable age was searing. He described being "an eye witness to monstrous massacres," the enslavement of women, and being forced to carry white troops with heavy gear for long distances through the waters of the Zambezi. Despite these and other scarring experiences, Chagogna was able to make his way through what there was of an African educational system to complete studies at a nursing technical school and obtain a diploma in "technical competence." Yet, over time, he became so alienated by the harshness of the colonial system that in 1944, while working in health posts at Mueda and Mocimboa da Praia, he later claimed he had created a short-lived, clandestine nationalist movement, the African Congress of Mocimboa da Praia.

64   J.A. MARCUM

Chagonga broke ties with his family in order to devote himself totally to his political quest. In 1957 he went to work for a coal company in Tete, where he developed a local following and began sending petitions to Portuguese and international authorities demanding reform. The futility of Chagonga's petitions was dramatized by a letter to him from the United Nations Undersecretary for Trusteeship and Non-Self-Governing Territories, Godfrey Amachree, on April 14, 1964: "Dear Sir, I wish to acknowledge your letter of 13 March 1964 and to inform you that the Secretary General is not aware of any reply to your letter of 4 September 1963 addressed to the Prime Minister of Portugal concerning [proposals for] a round table conference with the Mozambique nationalists."[18]

Faced with the prospect of being flown to Lisbon to face court action for his persistent petitioning, Chagonga winced at the thought of a Portuguese aircraft dropping him into "the immensity of the atmosphere over the high seas of the Indian Ocean" and fled to Nyasaland and the protection of the "fearless Malawi people and the valorous leader of Nyasaland, Dr. Ngwazi Kamuzu Banda."[19]

Chagonga's petitions ranged from warnings about an impending Portuguese invasion of Nyasaland in cooperation with South Africa to the dangers of "NATO, which was formed specially to defend the Portuguese Colonies" and preserve "Western supremacy in Africa." His conspiracy theory concerning race warrants highlighting because it reflected the reality of African experience and therefore enjoyed an aura of plausibility in the eyes of many Africans: in an example of his jaundiced imagination, he once wrote, "There are over five thousand white girls in Mocambique from Portugal with the only aim of getting themselves married to Africans [so that] in the course of their time there may not be any traces of the African race in Mocambique, there being only the so called multiracial."[20]

In the past, he said, the Portuguese had not permitted black men to marry white women. Now in the village of Guija

> many African boys are forcibly married to white girls by the church ministers who persuaded them that white and black are equal. Only now and why? We do not want to marry a white girl since later on their grandchildren will come again to colonise Africa. So enough with the hundreds of millions of half castes created by the white man who enslaved the African ...

Chagonga signed off his petitions and speeches with: "Portugal for the Portuguese!! Mozambique for the genuine Africans!"

Physically, Malawi points like a dagger at the Indian Ocean, nearly severing Mozambique in two. Like the leaders of other landlocked countries, President Banda was intrigued with the idea of acquiring a land corridor to the sea at the port of Nacala. He watched the unfolding Mozambique conflict with a mixture of caution and ambition. Banda tolerated UNAMI so long as it did not threaten violence. But the limits of Malawian assistance to the nationalist cause were underscored when, after I interviewed him in Blantyre, Chagonga requested £1 10 shillings to pay for his trip back from town to his home near Chileka airport.[21]

Fate was unkind. A few weeks after my interview, a forlorn UNAMI vice-president, G.E.N.T. Saylah, circulated a memorandum in Blantyre announcing that a PIDE agent had kidnapped Chagonga. He now resided in a Mozambican prison.[22]

Meanwhile, Malawi's wily, strong-willed president kept a range of options open. In response to Portuguese threats to close Nacala port facilities, Banda negotiated with Dar es Salaam for the possibility of back-up free port usage of the southern Tanzanian port of Mtwara.[23] Later, Banda hosted a breakaway movement that proposed to split off the northern half of Mozambique and create a state of Rumbezia linked to, if not absorbed into, Malawi. The Uniao Nacional Africana de Rumbezia (UNAR) appealed for support among Macua, Nianja, Yao, Maconde, and other northern ethnicities who resented the dominance of Frelimo's southern-dominated leadership. Created in 1968 at Limbe, Malawi, and led by Amos M. Sumane, the UNAR denounced Mondlane and argued for peaceful negotiations with Portugal.[24] However, it failed to attract either Portuguese interlocutors or African followers and soon faded from the scene.

ZAMBIA AND COREMO

Bordering the Tete district of Mozambique, Kenneth Kaunda's Zambia became independent in October 1964 and entered the Mozambique drama the following year. It was in Lusaka that the last, major effort to re-solder the pieces of the Humpty Dumpty breakage of 1962 took place. Milas was gone. His divisive deeds had been acknowledged, and denounced. But concrete amends had not been forthcoming.

66   J.A. MARCUM

On July 20, 1964, in Cairo, Frelimo and UDENAMO delegations headed by Mondlane and Gumane met and signed a document declaring that unity was essential. They gave their organizations one to two months to consult their members on how to proceed with reunification before resuming negotiations.[25] There was no follow-up. The logic of bringing an end to the fracturing that Milas had provoked nonetheless seemed compelling to Zambia's new rulers. President Kenneth Kaunda and his foreign minister, Simon Kapwepwe, dove in. They summoned the Mozambicans to unity talks in Lusaka with the expectation that they could facilitate the creation of a united Mozambican independence movement.

With high hopes, Gumane and Zarica (John) Sakupwana of UDENAMO led off the discussions. But the climate quickly soured due at least in part to the unsettling participation of Mondlane's long time *bête noire*, Gwambe. Gumane began by asking for eight of the fifteen positions on the Frelimo Central Committee along with the vice-presidency (Gumane), foreign affairs and defense. Mondlane countered with the offer of the vice-presidency and "supervisory responsibility" over foreign affairs, publicity and information, education, and health and welfare. Gumane rejected "supervisory responsibility" as not carrying real authority over those actually holding the positions of administrative secretary. As bargaining intensified, Gumane reduced his request to five members of the Central Committee, leaving Frelimo with a two-thirds majority. Haggling continued. Finally, Gumane abandoned all claims to positions and proposed instead that an act of unity be submitted to a party Congress and a new Central Committee be elected by that Congress. According to Gumane, Mondlane reacted with an "incoherent [...] rejection of this demand."[26] For Mondlane, already threatened by military and political defections and festering northern resentment of the predominance of southerners within Frelimo political and military leadership, a Frelimo Congress ostensibly to be held in Tanzania where Maconde and other dissidents could be mobilized against him, was an unacceptable risk.

Exasperated by what he viewed as intransigence, the Zambian chair of the conference, A.J.K. Kangwa, Under-Secretary for Pan-African Affairs, declared the negotiations a failure. It had proved impossible, he said, to persuade the Frelimo delegation to meet the demands of the other parties "in one way or another." Frelimo members were asked to leave the conference "since they had refused UNITY on conditions agreed by the three [other] organizations."[27] The "other" three were the two versions of UDENAMO (those of Gumane and Gwambe) and the Mozambique African National Congress (MANC). Not an impressive coalition. UNAMI and MANU did not participate. Earlier UDENAMO (Gumane) had held MANC suspect given the "cordial treatment" it received "at the hands of the Smith regime" in Southern Rhodesia, where it was the only movement not banned. This cast doubt on the value of its credentials as a participant. And, above all, Gwambe's history of duplicity undercut chances for an accord.[28]

The collapse of the talks with Frelimo left the way open for the formation of a new but disparate Zambia-based movement, a Comite Revolutionario de Mocambique (COREMO). Gwambe's ability to maneuver himself into its presidency instantly undermined its credibility and lent credence to Mondlane's wariness of an accord that went beyond an UDENAMO–Gumane/Frelimo agreement. Founded in Lusaka in June 1965, COREMO faced multiple defections and leadership quarrels from its outset.[29]

In September 1965, John Blacken of the US State Department visited Dar es Salaam and reported that Frelimo was taking full advantage of the "break-up" of COREMO. Gumane was in China desperately seeking support; the MANC official who was left in charge of COREMO's Lusaka office, had naively invited Milas in Khartoum to come to help (he did not); and Mondlane, feeling vindicated for refusing unity with these ne'er-do-wells was pressing the US Embassy for more American scholarships.[30]

Faulty military planning led COREMO into ill-advised November 1965 military action close to the Zambian border. During the fighting at least one Portuguese policeman was killed. The Zambian government was embarrassed, and in the view of one seasoned observer, the hit-and-run raid was "almost fatal for the party." "Savage" reprisals by the Portuguese followed, and by the end of December some 5,000 refugees had streamed across the border into Zambia.[31] In the aftermath of this incident, COREMO suffered top-level resignations. Its national chairman, Joseph Nyakhombe, and the Secretary for Cultural and Social Services and Dar es Salaam representative, Vasco C. M. Alfazema, defected to Frelimo.[32] John Sakupwana, COREMO national secretary, who was implicated in the Zambia border military fiasco, fled to Southern Rhodesia and a job at the Salisbury Plate Glass Beveling and Silvering Co.[33]

68   J.A. MARCUM

Finally, returning to Zambia after spending a period with COREMO forces inside Mozambique and contemplating COREMO's leadership disarray, Gumane called an emergency party conference for May 12–16, 1966. Gwambe was demoted, and then ousted for gross financial and administrative malfeasance. Gumane assumed the COREMO presidency and undertook to rescue and reorganize it.

The veteran of at least five previous political affiliations, Gwambe responded by creating a new paper party, the Partido Popular de Mocambique (PAPOMA). But it evaporated into the haze of exile fantasy along with UNAR and MANC, all of which Mondlane disparaged as "office organizations." The episode marked the end of the pioneering but hugely destructive political career of Adelino Gwambe.

COREMO changed policies as well as leaders. Influenced by Maoist military doctrine, its guerrilla activity was henceforth to take place only deep inside Mozambique, far from the Zambian border. At any given time, 10 of its 15-member party executive were to be inside Mozambique. Most military and political training was to take place in-country. Communiqués were to be kept relatively modest in comparison to Frelimo's arguably exaggerated claims of Portuguese casualties. And an in-country headquarters accommodating some 5000 militants was projected to contrast with Frelimo leadership, which, in Gumane's words remained mired in exile in the midst of the "fleshpots of Dar es Salaam."[34]

Gumane positioned COREMO as a champion of Africanist populism. There would be no school for its leaders' children (a misleading dig at Frelimo's Mozambique Institute), no white members, and only a few, low-profile external offices—Cairo (at that time the United Arab Republic, UAR), a steady supporter; Nairobi (locus of many Frelimo dissidents); and Dar es Salaam (an office headed by COREMO recruiter, Valentino R. Sithole). Assessing COREMO's new leadership, investigative journalist John St. Jorre described Gumane as "an impressive man [...] who appears to have formulated a sensible, if modest, plan of action."[35] External admirers such as the African-American journalist Richard Gibson praised COREMO for its "realistic" battlefield communiqués, its stress on internal versus exile leadership and its black Africanist values.[36] And for a while, the COREMO strategy seemed to be working.

However, after a major military victory deep within Tete, the movement was torn by more schisms. Replacing Mazunzo Bobo as Secretary

4 THE RAVAGES OF EXILE POLITICS   69

for Foreign Affairs with Fanuel Mahluza, COREMO announced that Bobo had been killed in a clash with Portuguese forces. This led to charges from dissidents that he had been killed by a compatriot, Matias Tenda, who shortly afterward joined ex-vice-president Sumane in creating the Rumbezia (UNAR) splinter movement in Malawi.[37]

Months later, Portuguese intelligence detected an effort by five Comite Revolutionario de Mozambique (COREMO) soldiers, led by Julio Dzonzi, to escort twelve PAC soldiers through Mozambique to South Africa via Swaziland. Christened "Operation Crusade," its progress was plotted for weeks by the Portuguese, who ultimately attacked, captured, or killed its members near Vila Pery in central Mozambique. The infiltrators left behind Chinese weapons and documents indicating that, if successful, their mission would be followed by a second group of some 50 PAC soldiers on hold in Lusaka.[38] The blow to COREMO and PAC was fateful. COREMO never regained its earlier momentum and, in the words of one scholar, was reduced militarily to "nuisance status."

NOTES

1. COSERU, Press Communiqué, Kampala, May 14, 1963. Marcum Papers Box.
2. "FUNIPAMO Memorandum Supporting the Dissolution of Frelimo," Kampala, May 27, 1963, in Ronald Chilcote, *Emerging Nationalism in Portuguese Africa*, Stanford: Stanford University Press, 1973, pp. 470–475. The "dissolution" of Frelimo was signed by the same four persons that had signed the June 26, 1962, transfer of UDENAMO and MANU properties to Frelimo: Gwambe, Mmole, Millinga, and Mahleyeye. They were joined by an ethnically Chimonica (Umtali area) group based in Rhodesia, the Mozambique African National Congress (MANC), whose president, Peter Balamanja, the Portuguese managed to spirit away to a Lourenco Marques prison later that year.
3. Gwambe, "Autobiography," Marcum Papers, Box 36/1.
4. Mondane, "The Mozambique Liberation Front: the Crystalization of a Struggle for Freedom," Dar es Salaam, January 1964, Marcum Papers, Box 36/7.
5. *The Mozambican Revolution*, no. 14, Dar es Salaam, March 1964.
6. Mondlane, "Crystalization of a Struggle…".
7. Shubin, *The Hot Cold War*, p. 123.
8. Mabunda and Sakupwanya, "The UDENAMO at the United Nations," November 7, 1963," Cairo, 1963, Marcum Papers, Box 36/7. They

70   J.A. MARCUM

called upon the UN to press for the "complete and unconditional independence" of Mozambique.

9. "Who is Fanuel Mahluza," RENAMO, A Luta Continua! Cacais, Portugal, no. 3 June 1982, Marcum Papers, Box 37/6.

10. Paulo Jose Gumane, "Biography," typescript, Lusaka, June 3, 1966, Marcum Papers, Box 34/3.

11. Ibid.

12. Ibid.

13. Massinga, "United Nations and Decolonization ..." pp. 286–287.

14. Other representatives of the Congo Alliance invited to Léopoldville: Nana Mahomo, London representative of the Pan Africanist Congress (PAC) of South Africa; Sam Nujoma, president of the South West Africa Peoples' Organization (SWAPO); and Reverend Ndabaningi Sithole, national chairman of the Zimbabwe African People's Union (ZAPU).

15. Roberto. "Address to Central African Students in the US,"—*Voz do Estudante Angolano*, no. 2, Dec. 1962–Jan. 1963.

16. Interview with author, Léopoldville, August 1963.

17. Gumane and Mahluza, interviews with author, Léopoldville, August 1963. For background on the Congo Alliance, see Marcum, The *Angolan Revolution*, vol. 2, *Exile Politics and Guerilla Warfare*. Cambridge, MA, MIT Press, 1978, pp. 74–78.

18. Marcum Papers, Box 38/4.

19. Chagonga, "Truth about Slavery in Mocambique: Petitions Addressed to The Portuguese Overseas Minister and the Governor General and Their Reply," mimeo, Blantyre, Malawi [1965]. Marcum Papers Box 38/4.

20. Marcum Papers, Box 38/4.

21. Interview with author, Blantyre, February 6, 1965. Chagonga sponsored the candidacies of several students for scholarships to study in the USA, including one who asked whether he would be free to pursue his Catholic faith in the USA and who ultimately became a professor at Howard University in Washington, DC, Luis B. Serapiao.

22. UNAMI, "President Kidnapped," *Voice of the Party*, mimeo, No. 1, Blantyre, Malawi, 1965, Marcum Papers, Box 38/4. Chagonga died in obscurity shortly after Mozambique gained independence, but his experience and zealotry were reflective of a racially traumatized society.

23. Interview with former Malawi foreign minister, Kanyama Chiume, Dar es Salaam, May 16, 1967.

24. UNAR, *O'Brado Rumbeziano*, nos. 1 and 2, Limbe, Malawi, 1969.

25. Circular to Frelimo Militants, "Conversations Frelimo/Udenamo (Gumane)," mimeo, August 17, 1964, Marcum Papers, Box 35/3.

26. Paulo Gumane, "Failure of Unity Talks," from press release in *Combate*, no. 8, 1965, reprinted in Chilcote, *Emerging Nationalism* ..., pp. 479–491.
27. Cabrita, *Mozambique*, p. 38.
28. UDENAMO, *Resolute Combat*, December 1964, Marcum Papers, Box 38/2. The delegations at the meeting were: Frelimo: Mondlane and Simango; UDENAMO-MONOMOTAPA: Gwambe and Mahleyeye; UDENAMO-MOZAMBIQUE: Gumane and Sakupwanya; MANC: Peter Simbi (president) and Mathew Kambezo. A.J.K. Kangwa, "Conclusions of the Committee Set Up on the 24th March, 1965 to Consider Some Common Basis for Unity," Lusaka, mimeo, March 25, 1965.
29. In opposition to the creation of the new movement, the UDENAMO (Gumane) office in Cairo denounced the dissolution of UDENAMO and insisted that the old movement would persist under new leadership. It did not. Nonetheless, from Cairo, Narciso Namburete Mbule, Secretary for External Affairs of UDENAMO, openly opposed the creation of COREMO. Ironically, the motto on Mbule's stationery read: "In Unity Lies Our Freedom. *A Uniao e a Nossa Liberdade.*"
30. Interview with author, September 15, 1965.
31. John de St. Jorre, "Forgotten War," *London Observer*, October 25, 1966.
32. *Times of Zambia*, February 16, 1966.
33. Letter to author, January 20, 1967.
34. COREMO leadership as reconstructed under Gumane included: Deputy President Amos M. Sumane (soon to defect); Secretary General Joseph B. Chiteji; Deputy Secretary General Alfredo S. Chembene; Treasurer Absolom T. Bahule; Defense and Security Gabriel Machave; Foreign Affairs Mazunzo M. Bobo; and Education and Culture Fanuel Mahluza, the veteran of Mozambican politics.
35. De St. Jorre, "Forgotten War."
36. Richard Gibson, *International News and Report*, London, April 1967.
37. Cabrita, *Mozambique*, p. 40.
38. *Rhodesia Herald*, (Salisbury), June 12, 1968.

CHAPTER 5

OAU, UN, and USA

Pan-African Illusion

In the early 1960s many observers believed that collective Pan-African suasion would provide a short cut to independence for Portugal's colonies. The expectation was that collective African action could relieve MANU, UDENAMO, and later Mondlane's Frelimo from the daunting prospect of a long, costly political struggle. In February 1962, Crosby S. Noye wrote in a dispatch from Accra for a Washington, D.C., daily paper, "A violent and possibly decisive showdown over Portugal's African possessions is brewing ominously today." He reported that Pan-Africanists were serious about finishing the task of freeing Africa's last colonial holdouts. Did this mean that the drama of Portuguese Africa would follow the precedent of Goa and lead to a painful but essentially bloodless Portuguese acceptance of the inevitable? That was one of the bases for Eduardo Mondlane's optimism as he monitored matters from Syracuse.

At the United Nations, Guinea's delegate, Diallo Telli, warned that if Portugal continued to ignore its responsibilities, independent African states would have to consider concerted military action in Angola. More concretely, Morocco's Minister for African Affairs, Abdelkrim El Khatib, speaking to a New Delhi seminar on Portuguese colonies called for an Afro-Asian summit meeting to draw up a timetable for the decolonization of Lisbon's African territories. If the timetable was ignored by Lisbon, then an African expeditionary force would form under the command of the "Casablanca powers": Guinea, Ghana, Mali, Morocco,

© The Author(s) 2018
J.A. Marcum, *Conceiving Mozambique*, African Histories
and Modernities, https://doi.org/10.1007/978-3-319-65987-9_5

73

Egypt, and Algeria. And, in fact, at an early 1962 Marrakesh gathering the Casablancans decided to set up a permanent headquarters in Accra under an Egyptian commander, Marshal Fawzi. "The groundwork for a serious organization [was] clearly being laid."[1]

Guinea-Bissau was the presumed initial target. This diminutive colony on Africa's west coast was of negligible economic value, had no potential for significant Portuguese settlement, and consisted of a maze of islands, marshes, and forests difficult for a European expeditionary force to defend. Moreover, the Portuguese confronted a well-organized guerrilla insurgency led by a talented Cape Verdean military leader, Amilcar Cabral. Logic suggested that Portugal might not wish to waste its limited resources in a fight to preserve colonial rule over such a place. On the other hand, military supply lines were relatively short—Guinea-Bissau was a lot closer to Portugal than Goa. And the Portuguese government and military were determined to avoid a repeat of the embarrassing Indian disaster.

Although the "Khatib Plan" appeared to present a genuine threat to Portugal's African empire, even Lisbon's small Guinea garrison of two to three thousand soldiers was not expected to be a pushover. "Sober" experts in Accra believed that "the ambitions of African leaders likely exceeded their reach."[2] CONCP officially endorsed the plan, but the necessary funds, organizational resolve, and military capacity of the Casablanca countries to execute the Khatib Plan were wanting. With its annexation of Goa, India lost interest. The plan stalled and was abandoned.

Even the like-minded CONCP liberation movements themselves failed to carry out their own undertaking to coordinate plans and synchronize action against Portugal. Three years would pass before CONCP leaders scheduled, twice postponed, and finally held another meeting in Dar es Salaam in September 1965 to revive the organization. By this time, the center of Pan-African activity had shifted from Accra to Dar es Salaam and Tanzanian President Julius Nyerere had replaced Kwame Nkrumah as its prime mover. CONCP Secretary General Marcelino dos Santos later attributed the delay in convening CONCP to a lack of finance and to excessive task dispersion. CONCP's information service was based in Algiers, its education unit in Dakar, and its political headquarters in Rabat. This meant that the prescribed twice annual meetings of the heads of CONCP's constituent parties were, he acknowledged, "not working too well."[3]

At the 1965 CONCP meeting, Tanzanian trade union leader Michael Kamaliza resurrected the ghost of the Khatib Plan by calling for African armies under OAU command to move into Angola, Guinea, and Mozambique behind nationalist forces. He claimed this would assure the "effective occupation" of liberated regions. But, once again, the threat of internationalization failed to materialize.

Another Pan-African organization emerged in 1961, the Pan-African Freedom Movement of East, Central and South Africa—PAFMECSA— through which African countries doled out modest funding and "legitimation" to liberation movements. But it lasted only two years. In 1963 it was replaced by an OAU Liberation Committee, based in Dar es Salaam. The city's leading daily predicted at the time: "It's only commonsense that Portugal cannot possibly afford to fight an escalating war on three fronts and the result of a joint action is bound to lead to a speedier liberation for all."[4] Despite such observations, each of the insurgencies in Portuguese Africa continued on a separate course with limited external African support. And Mondlane's hopes for Pan-African deliverance faded.

DASHED HOPES

At about the same time that the students and I were meeting with Mondlane in Syracuse in August 1962, the new Secretary of State, Dean Rusk, was meeting with Premier Salazar in Lisbon. Rusk's objective was to mollify the Portuguese leader, angered by American criticism of his colonial policies. Rusk hoped to pave the way for renewal of the NATO lease on bases in the Azores due to expire at the end of December 1962. According to Richard Mahoney, "The whole premise of the administration's policy was that through pressure by the U.S. on both sides— Portuguese and African—an orderly transition toward independence could be achieved and a full-scale colonial war that might invite Soviet intervention averted."[5] The also had been Mondlane's original premise.

From the outset, however, Portugal manifested stubborn defiance. In January 1962, Salazar denied refueling rights in the Azores for the US Air Force planes carrying UN troops and cargo to the Congo (and, unlike Washington, Portugal supported Katanga secession). Salazar also complained about the anti-colonial activities of George Houser and the ACOA and exacted a promise that the Angolan rebel leader, Holden Roberto, would henceforth not be received at the US Mission to the United Nations. The US Embassy responded to Portuguese pressure by seeking the removal of both Houser and me from the State Department's African advisory committee and the closure of the Lincoln University-based refugee education program that I directed. Kennedy rejected those demands. Salazar made no promise about lease renewal. But Rusk's effort to placate Salazar was an early sign that the influence of liberals such as the US representative to the UN, Adlai Stevenson, was severely limited. And the Cuban missile crisis in October 1962 increased the importance that Rusk and the Pentagon attached to the air transit bases in the Azores.

Chester Bowles was not deterred. In December 1961 Bowles was named as President Kennedy's Special Representative and Adviser on African, Asian, and Latin American Affairs after he had been replaced as Rusk's chief deputy. In June 1962 Bowles failed to attract Kennedy's attention with memos about the Azores. In October he traveled to Africa, and then issued a report that fitted with Mondlane's early optimism about American policy and influence over Portugal. In a lengthy "Report of Mission to Africa, October 15–November 9, 1962," Bowles wrote that "until we find some way to free ourselves from the pressures of Salazar and the Portuguese, our position in much of Africa will remain fragile." Accepting the importance of protecting basing rights in the Azores, he argued that the USA needed to avoid Portuguese "determination to keep us indefinitely 'on the hook' and to use this to modify our African policies." If necessary, Bowles wrote, the Azores base issue should be referred to the NATO Council, given their "primary role" for the defense of Western Europe. They should be considered a "NATO responsibility," and "[o]nce Salazar is confronted with a united NATO front," it would be "difficult to see how he could maintain his present position." Bowles observed that it fell on the American government "to free Portugal of her present paranoia and help her to become a viable and effective member of the European society of nations." He recognized the difficulty that a small colonial power with huge overseas holdings that had long fended off the designs of stronger colonial contenders such as Britain and France would have in divesting itself of its overseas possessions. But he contended the Portuguese were "faced with a bitter choice: continued stubborn refusal to abandon their empire with the consequent drain on Portugal's meager resources while earning the

increasing contempt of all free peoples, on the one hand, or a humili-
ating withdrawal under pressure on the other." Bowles suggested the
USA might "be able to break the present impasse" by offering Lisbon
an alternative and he recommended that, in cooperation with its NATO
allies, Washington should propose:

> (1) that Portugal agree to grant self-government and self-determination to
> Mozambique and Angola within a brief period (say five years), and (2) that
> the Atlantic Community provide a sizeable sum to ease whatever financial
> burden may be involved in the adjustment (this is a face saver since the
> colonies are now a net liability), and simultaneously to provide the capital
> required to modernize the Portuguese economy.

Bowles noted that Portugal had not qualified for the aid given to other
European countries under the Marshall Plan, and argued that the NATO
allies should "help establish Portugal as a modern industrial nation and
a respected member of the Atlantic Community." Bowles also suggested
that "President de Gaulle, who has just emerged from a costly experience
in Africa [the Algerian war], might agree to act as an intermediary."

Bowles did not expect immediate acceptance by Salazar. But he predicted that the threat of financial disaster and isolation would create
healthy political pressures within Portugal itself" and that Lisbon

> would be confronted with a clear dramatic choice: either blindly to cling to
> a colonial concept which is doomed, or to recognize the dynamics of our
> modern world by joining a partnership of their friends and allies from the
> rapid economic and political modernization of Portuguese society, while
> disengaging themselves from an African situation which is becoming an
> increasing embarrassment.

Much as American financial aid after the Second World War had set in
motion the process of European integration, so Bowles argued that aid
to Portugal could be used to free it from imperial delusion and open the
way to economic prosperity.

But Bowles's advice fell on deaf ears. His role as Kennedy's Special
Representative proved to be nothing more than a face-saving advisory
role and he was eventually appointed for a second stint as ambassador to
India. The policy tide in Washington was turning in favor of Cold War

78   J.A. MARCUM

priorities. Richard Mahoney, author of a trenchant review of Kennedy's African policies, explained:

> Had it not been for the sudden chill in U.S.–Soviet relations during that summer of 1962, Kennedy might well have sided with Bowles and the other liberals [notably Stevenson, Williams and Harlan Cleveland ...] Not long after the Bowles memo, however, the CIA sent an urgent report to the President. There was "something new and different about Soviet operations in Cuba. (Aerial discovery of the nuclear missiles emplacements would come later, in October.) Worse yet for the liberal position, Berlin which had traumatized the Kennedy administration during its first year, was heating up again giving the Pentagon added leverage on all policy fronts." In the view of the military, the Azores were "irreplaceable" in the event of the need for a transatlantic undertaking on the order of the Berlin airlift of 1948.[6]

In 1963 there were several American efforts to persuade the Portuguese to confront reality. In August, Under Secretary of State George Ball offered Salazar an aid package, but it elicited only disdain. He was told Portugal was "not for sale." Ball cabled back to Washington that the USA had been under the misapprehension Portugal was ruled by a single autocrat. It was, he said, ruled by a triumvirate: "Salazar, Vasco de Gama and Prince Henry the Navigator. The Portuguese were living in another century."[7]

Salazar lived in a time warp. He had ruled Portugal for thirty years with the calm of an ascetic headmaster. The former economics instructor "lived the life of a cloistered bachelor among his books and papers and behind an iron curtain of protocol [...] unfailingly courteous, completely unmovable." His dress and office décor were "strictly nineteenth century–the buttoned-up shoes, the blanketed lap, the crimson velvet Louis XIX chairs. Salazar saw his mission in the light of papal encyclicals from the nineteenth century: the stern pastor of the Portuguese flock." And he rejected any notion of change in the glacial pace of Portugal's vaunted 400-year effort to create lusophone societies in Africa in return for American financial assistance.[8] As of early 1963, US–Portuguese relations were stuck in mutual recrimination, a *dialogue des sourds*.

An American policy shift was in full swing by mid-1963, and a polished, patriarchal American diplomat, Dean Acheson, was at the heart of it. His biographer, Douglas Brinkley, summed up Acheson's role: "[H]e was antipathetic to the European colonies struggling to become independent states." Moreover, he was "downright belligerent to Americans who supported these aspirations." This attitude of white, Western superiority on the part of the former Secretary of State became more pronounced in his post-secretarial years. His pivotal role in obtaining US rights to the Azores bases and his dealings with Salazar during the NATO conference of 1952 [had] resulted in a "deep respect for Salazar's competence," despite the fact that Salazar's government was propped up by a pampered military, ubiquitous secret police, corrupt judges, and draconian laws.[9] By the summer of 1962, as the tide was turning in Washington, Acheson, joined by "Europeanists" in the State Department—Secretary of State Rusk and Under Secretary Ball, who had replaced Bowles—and the Pentagon, argued that the strategic indispensability of the Azores bases made it a *necessity* not to alienate Salazar. In a meeting with President Kennedy on April 2, 1962, Acheson resonated with Salazar's resentment of American support for Angolan nationalists. He condemned American "smuggling of Angolese students" out of the country and educating them in at Lincoln College [*sic*] outside Philadelphia, a predominantly black school, with the "most extreme nationalist views." Moreover, Acheson, confusing my role at Lincoln, falsely accused the president of the college of having "secretly and illegally entered Angola and on his return [...] engaged in violent anti-Portuguese propaganda."[10] The reference was unmistakably to the journey by me (not the president of Lincoln University) and George Houser into guerrilla-occupied territory in Angola. Acheson's acerbic criticism of Adlai Stevenson and warnings about the potential loss of the Azores impacted Kennedy's thinking. As a "devoted and loyal ally," Portugal would like nothing better than to extend the Azores agreement, Acheson told Kennedy. "But if you are going to continue opposing what they are doing in Angola, nobody can get an extension in the Azores, 'I can't—nobody can.'"[11]

Lincoln University was the alma mater of Thurgood Marshall and Langston Hughes, among other notable African-Americans. The students were refugees who had not been smuggled out of but had fled Portuguese oppression. Reacting with fury against the US government-funded Lincoln project, Portuguese Foreign Minister Franco Nogueira declared publicly that he could not but wonder how many more free-spirited Eduardo Mondlanes the refugee program might create. The

80   J.A. MARCUM

program prepared them linguistically in English and placed the students in diverse colleges and universities throughout the USA. In due course, Protestant church and UN scholarship students were added to the mix.

Just how far things had changed was evident in May 1963, when Mondlane visited Washington and warned of military action unless Portugal agreed to negotiate. In order not to offend the Portuguese, Rusk and Ball determined that Mondlane should be ignored. When Deputy Assistant Secretary of State Fredericks was photographed speaking with Mondlane on African Freedom Day at Howard University, the head of State's European Bureau, William R. Tyler, complained to Rusk. The Secretary of State called Fredericks to warn him against such contacts. Fredericks offered to resign, but Rusk backed off.[12]

Government infighting over policy toward Portugal intensified. And when the Azores bases agreement lapsed at the end of December 1962, Portuguese leverage increased. Americans were henceforward allowed to use the facilities only at Salazar's sufferance on a day-to-day basis. However, not all news in Washington was bad for the Mozambican cause. In April, Kennedy appointed Averell Harriman as Under Secretary of State for Political Affairs. In a counter punch to Acheson, Harriman determined that the US was jeopardizing its whole position in Africa by appeasing the Portuguese. To the displeasure but with the forbearance of Dean Rusk, he issued a memorandum calling for broader contact with nationalist leaders of Portuguese Africa and provision of more educational assistance to exiled Africans.[13]

On May 2, 1963, Mondlane summoned me to his hotel in New York. He was disturbed by the incoherence of US policy and by internal pressures within Frelimo to move quickly to military action and develop close ties with China and the Soviet Union. Reluctantly, he was being obliged to schedule visits to both countries in quest of assistance. For its part, Portugal was showing no signs of willingness to negotiate. Mondlane was desperate to break through the no-contact barriers imposed by Dean Rusk and understood that the Attorney General, Robert Kennedy, was the one avenue open.

We spent the evening drafting a memorandum to Robert Kennedy. Mondlane wished to sound an alarm that would be urgent and persuasive but not menacing. Arguing for increased American pressure on Lisbon and for assistance to Frelimo, he predicted the "inevitable collapse" of Portuguese rule.

The needs of the liberation forces are many but none is so great as a change in United States policy toward Portuguese colonialism. Friends of freedom and democracy throughout the world cannot comprehend why the United States does not move to the forefront in the struggle for freedom. It is inconceivable to us that the United States must remain silent and secretive to placate Portugal.

It would be "tragic," he warned, if "indifference and ignorance" along with an assumed need "to assuage Portugal and hold on to the Azores should prevent the United States from supporting the struggle." If the U.S. failed to provide substantial assistance to Frelimo, Mondlane warned, "the nationalist leadership which desires to avoid dependence on the Sino-Soviet bloc will be repudiated."

Shortly thereafter, Fredericks managed to arrange a private meeting with the President's brother. In deference to Dean Rusk's edict, he suggested that Robert Kennedy might wish to meet Mondlane in a neutral place such as the International Club or a private home for dinner. "Bring him to the Attorney General's Office" was Kennedy's response. Their meeting went well. Robert Kennedy was impressed with Mondlane and in a gesture of personal support signed over to him a personal check for $500 that he had received for a speaking engagement.

Fredericks had already arranged a meeting for Mondlane with Harriman at the latter's elegant Georgetown residence. Their conversation lasted two hours. In a memorandum to Rusk, Harriman described the encounter as an "extraordinarily rewarding experience" with an exceptionally well-balanced, educated, serious man" who had given him a different impression of the movement as a result of the talk. "I am sure," he continued, "it would be worth your giving him a half hour of your time." Unmoved, Rusk wrote on the margins of the memorandum, "I do not want to meet him." He did not.[14]

Rationalized as required for intelligence in Cold War competition, modest American government support continued despite the darkening political context. There was a Ford Foundation grant (of $100,000) for the Mozambican education center in Dar es Salaam, the Mozambique Institute, headed by Janet Mondlane. Under subsequent Portuguese pressure against the Ford Motor Company, however, the Foundation promised to consult Lisbon before making any further grants related to Portuguese territories. There were none.[15]

82   J.A. MARCUM

As with other African nationalists, notably Holden Roberto, Mondlane received "personal intelligence-information support," beginning with a contribution of $60,000 from the CIA channeled through the African American Institute (AAI). This support was largely outdistanced in amount and kind by military assistance from the Soviet bloc and China plus the OAU Liberation Committee and a few African states, such as Algeria, where the nucleus of a Frelimo army was being trained.[16]

Last Effort To Negotiate

American policy and Mondlane's assumptions had been based on a mutual expectation that Portugal could be persuaded within a reasonable time frame to accept the principle of self-determination for its colonies. The US view was grounded on the presumption of financial leverage over a small, economically poor ally. Mondlane's was based on the threat of an insurgency like those under way in Guinea-Bissau and Angola.

In October 1963, representatives of nine African states selected by the OAU decided to put Portuguese intentions to the test. Under the auspices of UN Secretary General U Thant, Portuguese representatives led by Foreign Minister Franco Nogueira met with African delegates to discuss the principle of "self-determination" as it applied to Portuguese colonies. With slippery semantics, the Portuguese argued, as always, that their African territories already exercised "self-determination." For Africans, the concept meant "the right of a people to determine the future of their territories including the option of being independent of Portugal." But from the Portuguese perspective, the Organic Law of Overseas Portugal of June 1962 had provided elected provincial authorities with self-governing control over local government.

Mondlane, who did not participate directly in the talks, pointed out to the African representatives that the much-touted local elections were stacked. They guaranteed Portuguese control over local authority. Bearing this out, March 1964 elections to the Mozambique Legislative Council totaled 93,079 qualified to vote out of a population that had grown to about 7 million. This percentage of 1.3% of a potential electorate was not just small: in most districts the number of qualified voters was roughly the same as the number of non-African citizens. In sum, Portuguese settlers plus a few Asians and *mestiços* represented the electorate.

A frustrated Mondlane laid out the rationale for war in UN testimony:

> It was no longer possible to pretend that a peaceful solution by negotiations was possible. The time for condemnation by censure was past unless it was accompanied by a programme of direct action. Resolutions by international organizations would not alleviate the misery of the people, or remove the electrified iron fences built round them or free them from the constant terror of the secret police, the armed police or the Portuguese soldiers, or give them any hope of a better life. The people of Mozambique had become convinced that their oppressors would not leave their land until they took up arms.[17]

Mondlane was in the halls of the UN during the talks. "My function during these conversations," he later explained, "was to expose the veiled attempts by Portugal to hoodwink the African representatives and the people of the world concerning the status of our country." The pretense that Lisbon had already granted self-determination was a semantic game. In fact, the "organic law" they referred to furthered incorporation of Mozambique into Portugal. After reading the law itself, African statesmen saw the point, and suspended the conversations. They insisted that Portugal declare its readiness to grant real self-determination and take immediate steps with representatives of its colonies to implement the modalities of how to turn over the economic, political, and other instruments of independent governance to Africans.[18]

The UN fiasco was a setback for American policy. And for Mondlane, his earlier optimism was extinguished. Portuguese rationality, to the extent that it had existed, along with strong Pan-African diplomatic support and American anti-colonial assistance, had all diminished. Frelimo's soldiers were beginning to return from training in Algeria and Communist countries. They were impatient and restless. Some defected. Pressure mounted. War loomed.

NOTES

1. *Washington Evening Star*, February 12, 1962; *Jeune Afrique*, Paris, January 17, 1962.
2. Ibid.
3. Interview with author, Dar es Salaam, May 20, 1967.
4. *The Standard*, October 4, 1965 and CONCP, La Lutte de Libération Nationale dans les Colonies Portuguais, Algiers Information, 1967.

5. Mahoney, *JFK*, p. 203.
6. Ibid., p. 21.
7. Ibid., p. 241.
8. Ibid., p. 199.
9. Douglas Brinkley, *Dean Acheson: The Cold War Years: 1953–71*. New Haven: Yale Univ. Press, 1992, pp. 303–304.
10. Mahoney, *JFK*, p. 206.
11. Brinkley, *Dean Acheson*, 310–331.
12. Mahoney, *JFK*, pp. 236–237.
13. Ibid.
14. *Foreign Relations of the United States*. 1964–1968, Vol. XXIV, Africa, No. 423, July 1, 1964. Department of State, Washington, D.C.
15. Houser, *No One Can Stop The Rain*, p. 83.
16. Whitney Schneidman, "American Foreign Policy and the Fall of the Portuguese Empire, 1961–1976: A Study in Issue Salience," doctoral dissertation, University of Southern California, January 1965, p. 96.
17. United Nations, General Assembly, Report of the Special Committee on the Situation With Regard to the Implementation of the Declaration on the Granting of Independence to Colonial Countries and People, A/6000/Add 3*, October 11, 1965.
18. Mondlane, "The Crystalization of a Struggle ...".

CHAPTER 6

Mondlane in Dar es Salaam

MONDLANE RETURNS

In mid-1963, Mondlane returned to Dar es Salaam.

Faced with the chaos in Frelimo and restricted options, Mondlane dropped his notion of part-time leadership, hurled himself into the fray, and analyzed the evolving scene in letters to his wife, who was closing down their Syracuse household in preparation for a July 1963 entry into the political life of Dar es Salaam. Despite the increasing challenges, Mondlane was still a confident academic revolutionary. In one letter, he described what "life was like in Dar": getting up in the morning about a quarter to seven; running to the beach about a mile away; dipping "into the nice, balmy water" and swimming; getting out, doing some push-ups and exercises; taking "a shower in the Tanganyika Club of which I am now a member"; dressing and taking "a nice walk back"; then having breakfast about 8:15 and getting ready for work. On some days, Mondlane was picked up 9:00 to go the office; on the other days he stayed in his hotel room "writing, answering letters, suggesting things." He was also occupied with trying to find a house for his family and taking classes in Swahili. Mondlane described his schedule as "open," shifting around as people came to see him and discuss issues.[1]

Mondlane was encouraged by the creation of the OAU at a Heads of State summit in Addis Ababa in late May 1963. He described the conference as "superb!" In his view, "the most important agreement" was

© The Author(s) 2018

85

J.A. Marcum, *Conceiving Mozambique*, African Histories
and Modernities, https://doi.org/10.1007/978-3-319-65987-9_6

86   J.A. MARCUM

the OAU's pledge to support Frelimo's independence efforts. Hope for a Pan-African solution was reborn. Mondlane was also optimistic about the prospects for unity in East Africa. He predicted, "By the end of the year we will have a state called the East African State or the United States of East Africa, whatever name it is going to get. It seems to me that everybody is serious about this and I don't see how they can back out of it." Mondlane added: "It's wonderful! I can see how we in Mozambique could look forward to a thing like that as we develop our political program towards the independence of Mozambique." And he suggested that this development would "give more security to Tanganyika" and make threats from Portugal "quite an empty thing."

Mondlane continued to deride, but also be to put off balance by, the activities of Mabunda, Gumane, Gwambe, and their respective UDENAMO followers, referring to them over and over in his letters. Continuing taunts by Gwambe "slightly upset" party members, and Mondlane wrote to Prime Minister Kenyatta about his concerns and to introduce Simango, who was to register Frelimo in Nairobi and prevent Gwambe from developing roots there. In a parable sent to his wife, Mondlane explained his approach to the perils of loyalty that beset exile politics. He described meeting with someone who had joined the Gwambe group because members of Frelimo's Central Committee had rejected him, because someone had reported that the man was working against the party. Mondlane wrote that this kind of thing happens often:

> Somebody has the idea in his mind that so and so is dangerous and they immediately decide to whisper around and then they blackball somebody that they thought was dangerous without any formal meeting in which they charge him of this and they make quickly a decision to oust him out of the party.

He warned that what happens is that someone ends up being forced to work outside of Frelimo. Mondlane had the man he met with write a letter rejecting Gwambe's group and then allowed him to begin working with the party. After the meeting, the central committee member who had rejected the man protested that he would double-cross them and continue to support Gwambe. Mondlane said he replied:

> I don't care what he will try to do, so long as he does his work with us openly, if he tries to do something underhanded, the people will judge him

for what he is. He will be considered a liar and a cheat and a person that must not be trusted. But if we throw him out of the party the work that he is going to do for Gwambe will be more authentic and more genuine. [...] Throwing him out of the party [...] and out of the country [...] are all feeding small splintering little groups that finally are going to be a nuisance to our organization.[2]

Seemingly oblivious to his own insight, however, Mondlane continued to describe Mabunda and Gumane as the "two people who broke with Frelimo," making it sound volitional, and as people who "concentrated on innuendos and whisperings about my supposed being an agent of American imperialism, which by the end of the [OAU] conference, after seeing how the Nassers, Ben Bellas and Nkrumahs were very warm to me personally, I was beginning to be labeled a stooge of the communists." Labeling Gumane a "child" and Mabunda a "tsotsi," Mondlane dismissed their branch of UDENAMO as weak and funds-strapped, and argued that his protests and pressures on African leaders in Accra and Cairo were succeeding in reducing support for it, at least to a "certain extent." Noting the failure of the two "characters" to influence the OAU conference, he boasted: "I then returned to Dar in the presidential plane with [Julius] Nyerere and [Milton] Obote."[3]

As he acclimatized to the role of revolutionary leader, Mondlane continued to play the role of educator. He confided to his wife that Frelimo was advancing in some quarters, slipping in others, and his job was "to create some order out of confusion and develop the program of the party."[4] He attributed political problems to "the ignorance of a large portion of the population." "As you know, most people are illiterate and they are not quite sure as to what makes what run. So it's my job to try and create a picture in their minds as to what I am doing and why."[5]

Frelimo's detractors were impatient for a speedy move to independence. For this reason, Mondlane emphasized that it was his job to try and develop programs that would give Frelimo's supporters confidence in the party's leaders. But he noted that the party was "definitely short-handed," and needed "support both in terms of personnel and in terms of funds." He noted frankly that the party "can hardly pay our bills for even a small item as a cup of coffee or tea."

Mondlane met with refugees at camps such as Mgulani, refugees "waiting for training and for general educational preparation." He was surprised to find that over eighty percent spoke and understood

Portuguese. When it came to questions, "it was a bit creaky. Very few people wished to raise their hands to ask questions."[6] But drawing on his academic experience, he "teased them with leading questions;" they loosened up, and they went on until the Arnatouglou Community Center closed. Pleased with his ability to communicate and encouraged by members of the Central Committee present, he decided to stage such "fire side chats" on a regular basis. He reported to his wife on his "rousing talk" to a stadium crowd of "about a thousand," mainly Mozambican Maconde at Tanga on the Tanganyika north coast. He observed that the people want "leadership—someone to really show responsibility," and confidently wrote, "I think I'm that person." He concluded his letter to his wife, Janet:

> The rest—well, we'll have to talk when we see each other. There are a lot of plans to make and lots of work. Of course, you remember that this is going to be a year of real hard work. You are going to play a vital part in this and I want you to remember this as you are planning to come here.[7]

Mondlane's return to Dar es Salaam gave Frelimo a new lease of life. With "private" funds from the Ford Foundation, he moved swiftly to establish a school and student hostel, the Mozambique Institute. Frelimo sent increased numbers of students abroad to the USA, Western Europe and Eastern Europe. It also sent several hundred men of military age to Algeria and Eastern bloc countries for training. Portugal's continued refusal to admit the principle of self-determination or to permit even a modest degree of political liberty seemed to leave the nationalists with a grim choice: become permanent exiles or fight.

But, in a less than optimistic appraisal of the situation, a US intelligence report described Mondlane as a "U.S.-educated intellectual who [had] only a tenuous relationship with the Makondes," and predicted it would be "extremely difficult" for Mondlane to build dedicated support among "these largely primitive tribesmen." The report also suggested—in an obvious reference to Mondlane's marriage to a white American—that he had either overlooked or on principle had disregarded local taboos concerning relationships between blacks and whites.[8] There were more troubles ahead.

The War Begins

Mondlane's return to Dar es Salaam in mid-1963 coincided with the beginning of Frelimo's efforts to prepare for an armed struggle inside Mozambique. Frelimo fighters trained in Algeria had begun to return to Tanzania. They were billeted at Kongwa, a Frelimo military camp in southern Tanzania. Eager to plunge into what they had been trained for, they chafed at the failure of Frelimo's Central Committee to launch an immediate attack in deference to a more modulated long-term politico-military strategy. Some defected and looked for jobs in Tanzania.

A small group of Maconde trained by the Chinese in Tanzania crossed the Ruvuma River, attacked Nangololo, and killed a Catholic priest (Father Luther Meeks) and a truck driver. As trainees returning from Algeria and Eastern Europe grew in number, so did the pressure against what the northerners (who constituted the bulk of the guerrilla force) decried as the reticence of the southern leadership in Frelimo's Central Committee, the "*mestiço-assimilado*" group, to commit to the armed liberation of Mozambique. Having large numbers of mostly ill-educated young men trained in the rudiments of guerrilla warfare idle and marking time was a problem of explosive potential. As a result, the military calendar was speeded up.[9]

Officially, Frelimo's armed assault on Portuguese positions in northern Mozambique began on September 25, 1964.[10] Small squads of guerrillas attacked across the Ruvuma River boundary from bases in Tanzania. The war that Mondlane had sought to avoid, the war with its military and civilian casualties, physical destruction, and political radicalization, was under way. The Portuguese had long been alerted to the probability of such raids, and there was no repetition of the panic or explosion of violence that had occurred three years previously in Angola. Despite claims of major military victories by Frelimo versus concessions of only minor skirmishes by the Portuguese, the fighting incited the flight of some 5000 Maconde refugees across the border from the thinly populated north into Tanzania. Hit-and-run raids in Cabo Delgado and Niassa provinces and as far south as the Nyasaland (Malawi) border inflicted the initial casualties of war. Lisbon officially admitted to modest military casualties during the first half of 1965: 42 (Mozambique), 28 (Angola), and 48 (Guinea-Bissau).[11]

The question was whether, from these modest beginnings, the impact of the liberation forces would become strong enough to wear down Portugal's resolve to hold onto Mozambique, and, if so, how long it would take. In March 1965 an American military observer predicted that the exiled political leaders and insurgent forces would not be up to the challenge. They might have to either hire mercenaries, as Moise Tshombe had done in Katanga, or reconcile themselves to accepting the painful pace of gradual economic, social, and political change set by Portugal. He wrote that the reluctance of Mozambican nationalists to accept outside volunteers or mercenaries underscored an overriding desire to keep a firm hand on the helm of their own destinies, even at the price of a longer struggle.[12]

Mondlane met with Cuba revolutionary leader Che Guevara in February 1965. In a frosty exchange, he declined to accept Cuban military volunteers and subsequently rejected a similar offer from Cuban President Fidel Castro.[13] Cuba denounced Mondlane as hopelessly pro-American. But Frelimo was left to be master of its own fate.

A British observer, Lord Kilbracken, who visited the Mozambique insurgency, had a more optimistic view of Frelimo's prospects. After ten days with Portuguese forces along the shores of Lake Malawi, he reported, "the scale of fighting in this bitter, unsung war has steadily increased since the first minor incidents just a year ago—especially in recent weeks when there has been a strong Frelimo build-up." A former lieutenant commander in Britain's Fleet Air Arm, Lord Kilbracken concluded that in "3000 terrorized square miles" stretching some 20–40 miles inland from the lake shore and running from the Tanzanian to the Malawi border, the Portuguese "are confined to five small isolated garrisons." He described Frelimo as a "tough and elusive enemy" operating in small units, often only half a dozen men, "striking silently by night, withdrawing swiftly into the dense cover, if the Portuguese reply in strength." They mined roads, bridges, and airports. Their patrols were armed with heavy machine guns, mortars, bazookas, and grenades of Chinese and Russian make. Kilbracken suggested that the Portuguese with some 30,000 troops for the whole of Mozambique had put 1200 in the lake area and a like number in the northeast Maconde action zone around Mueda. But, he reported, "Throughout the troubled north the Portuguese are now desperately short of equipment as well as men."[14]

N'Kavandame

Military action in the northeast Maconde region of Cabo Delgado was critical to the war effort. The Maconde were over-represented among the foot soldiers of Frelimo insurgents, while Frelimo officers were predominantly from the relatively more developed south. For better regional balance, in mid-1963 Mondlane had brought a prominent Maconde entrepreneur, Lazaro N'Kavandame, into the movement's leadership ranks. He did this even though the newcomer was distrusted by the movement's growing numbers of Soviet- and Chinese-trained militants.

N'Kavandame, a Catholic Maconde émigré trader and merchant, returned from Tanganyika to Mozambique in the 1950s. He had hoped to bring the trading culture in which he had prospered under British rule to the Maconde of his home country. But he was frustrated by Portuguese obstruction. In 1963 he fled back to Tanganyika and was incorporated into Frelimo as chairman of the Cabo Delgado region. His conception of Mozambique was regional, capitalistic, and Maconde-centered.

On June 2, 1965, N'Kavandame testified at the UN alongside Mondlane before a "Special Committee" on the Implementation of Independence for Colonial Countries and Peoples.[15] N'Kavandame reported on the tortured history of his efforts to establish agricultural cooperatives in the area of Cabo Delgado. According to him, he had faced Portuguese blockage at every turn. In 1957 he had presented a petition to Portuguese authorities asking for "permission to institute instruction to eliminate illiteracy and improve methods of cultivation, in the hope that by producing better work results the constant whippings, imprisonments and fines would cease." He had tried to impress upon the government that "the farm labourer's monthly pay of 60 escudos (2 US dollars) was holly [sic] inadequate for subsistence. The head tax alone amounted to 120 escudos a year." Eventually, he obtained authorization to set up an educational program in his district and to establish a farming cooperative, "on the understanding that so long as each peasant family produced its quota of cotton it could cultivate as much land as it wished."

A local Portuguese administrator sought to discourage the venture by arguing that the only way to make lazy and illiterate blacks work was the whip. Nonetheless, the cooperative launched with a small membership of 500. "Sorghum, groundnuts and maize [were] cultivated in addition to the fixed four hectares of cotton per peasant farmer." A special fund was raised to purchase equipment and develop marketing. However, the success of the venture led suspicious local authorities to conclude that there was secret funding behind these efforts. The Portuguese tried to suborn N'Kavandame by offering him a well-paid position in the SAGAL concessionary cotton company. He declined.

By 1958 the cooperative had grown to more than 1000 members and by mid-1959 to 1500. Then, a government ban was imposed. It required that all African Mozambicans work for a Portuguese-run company. The government also began to harass the cooperative's members by sending out visiting inspection teams, ordering the destruction of fruit trees on the farms on the ground that they were detrimental to the production of good cotton, making the planting of crops other than cotton illegal, and arresting cooperative members for failing to fulfill the official cotton quota. "Thus," N'Kavandame declared, "it was obvious to everyone that the Portuguese Government had no real interest in the welfare of the African people and, indeed, was opposed to freedom for the black man and betterment of his living conditions."[16]

N'Kavandame had persuaded cooperative members to build roads to ease the transport of produce to market centers. He was arrested for having done so without government approval and spent two years in jail. During that time the cooperative was dissolved, and others within its leadership were arrested. Under house arrest after his release from prison in 1961, N'Kavandamev accepted a government proposal that he establish a small, 25-member cooperative. Over the next two years "he worked within those constraints to plant rice, sesame, potatoes, castor oil plants and maize." People of the Mueda region greeted the delivery of a tractor purchased with cooperative funds with a feast, and N'Kavandame used the occasion to "explain to the people the significance of the tractor purchase." Now there could be "no grounds for the charges of laziness and by organizing among themselves and learning better ways of farming" they had found "all that was needed for prosperity." Local authorities took exception to the assertiveness of his speech.

N'Kavandame was interrogated about Frelimo, concerning which he professed no knowledge or involvement. However, increasingly fearful Portuguese authorities in the Mueda area once again overreacted and by repressing N'Kavandame's initiatives created the conditions they most dreaded. N'Kavandame fled into the forest where he "consulted" with "people's leaders" and concluded that "the Makonde people, alone, could not succeed in getting rid of the enemy and that [they] must link forces with Mozambicans elsewhere in the country. Contact [was] therefore made with the Frelimo liberation movement."[17]

According to one scholar, for N'Kavandame, Frelimo was simply a way to achieve what he had been denied by the Portuguese: a modernized agricultural system for the Maconde like that which he had experienced in British Tanganyika. The difference between this Maconde perspective and that of the majority Frelimo leadership was later portrayed by Frelimo as a division between "bourgeois" and "revolutionary" wings within Frelimo. Cahen characterized it as a social gap between "two very different petty bourgeois milieux: a rural modern merchant elite [versus] an urban bureaucratic petit bourgeois elite of military Frelimo leadership." This social gap combined itself with, and was exacerbated by, the fact that the merchant milieu was ethnically Maconde, from the far north of Mozambique and under the influence of British colonial free capitalism, whereas the military bureaucratic one was "ethnically Changane and *assimilado* or *mestiços*, from the capital city and other towns of southern Mozambique." There a tiny African elite was not made up of merchants but instead had "small bureaucratic and service jobs."[18]

As Mondlane had recognized, as the war began in northern Mozambique, N'Kavandame was an important asset for Frelimo. But over time, his uneasy relationship within Frelimo soured. His views and values were inimical to an increasingly radicalized and socialist-oriented southern leadership.

EDUCATION AND WAR

Frelimo's exclusive access to northern Mozambique from Tanzania continued to give it a great advantage over any competitors. It also enjoyed a monopoly of OAU financial support. Though Mondlane would complain that some arms provided by the OAU Liberation Committee and Soviet Union were diverted to Biafran separatists or to Tanzania's own armed forces, Dar es Salaam remained steadfast in its support. Defectors and critics who multiplied over time found themselves marginalized to Kenya and beyond. Their cacophony of anti-Frelimo rhetoric, exacerbated by PIDE infiltrators and exile behavior, grew and revealed weaknesses within the movement yet simultaneously became less and less relevant to the ultimate military outcome. Of course, there were other

94   J.A. MARCUM

borders. And as Frelimo's war spread slowly southward, the role of competing movements based in Malawi and Zambia assumed enhanced significance and became sources of African student candidates for the US scholarship program.

With the outbreak and spread of insurgency, the central focus of nationalist activities shifted to the war zones in the north. However, the top Frelimo leadership remained in Dar es Salaam where Eduardo Mondlane's passion for education continued in evidence. The extent to which he remained an academic was illustrated by an anecdote recounted in *The Teeth May Smile but the Heart Does Not Forget*, by Andrew Rice.[19] Rice wrote of a young student at the University of Dar es Salaam who "was able to endear himself to the founder of the Mozambican rebel group (Frelimo)." The rebel leader put the enthusiastic student to work as an errand boy and propagandist. "As a reward, over the Christmas holidays in 1968, he sent [that student] and a few [others] to visit Frelimo's bases in the mountainous north of Mozambique, where the guerrillas were battling the country's Portuguese rulers." On their experiential education tour, they crossed the Ruvuma in small boats and hiked to a rebel camp, where they spent three weeks as guests of "Commander Notre." They trained, sang rebel songs, met "comely female fighters," and observed that "rebel officers slept in the same kinds of huts, on the same crude beds of underbrush, as frontline soldiers." They sat in on tactical military briefings in which Notre sat at the head of an "earthen mound shaped like Mozambique and outlined his plan of attack." On Christmas "they attended an ideological lecture where the commander compared the rebels' sacrifices to the one that Jesus made on the cross."

Returned to Dar es Salaam, the student turned his observations into a senior thesis. Deeply impressed and energized by his "study abroad" experience, the student had become committed to a Franz Fanon view of the world and wrote of the value of liberation violence to kill off the plagues of tribalism and superstition and create a "new peasant" and "purified society" without crime and immorality. In 1986, at the head of a rebel National Resistance Army, that student, Yoweri Kaguta Museveni, became the president of Uganda.[20]

In the 1960s, Dar es Salaam was a magnet attracting followers of Julius Nyerere's idealism and socialist experimentation. The Liberation Committee of the OAU headquartered there, and its influence extended as far afield as the South Pacific, where it inspired anti-colonial liberation movements in New Caledonia and Western Papua. During visits in 1965 and 1967, as the war developed inside Mozambique, I was able to observe Frelimo pursuing educational operations in exile parallel to those of the war.

The Mondlane family lived in what was by American standards a modest home in the Oyster Bay area of Dar es Salaam. One evening in February 1965 after Bill Sutherland, a legendary African-American supporter of African liberation, dropped by to deliver a bathroom scale to the somewhat sparse and chaotic household, we went off to dinner at a Mahlaza street hotel along with the young commander, Filipe Magaia, who had recently undergone military training in Algeria. During the course of a spirited meal, Mondlane commented that running an army was costing Frelimo around $10,000 a month. He wondered how Holden Roberto was managing to finance his forces in Angola. Then, succumbing to middle-class conditioning, he called the waiter over to the table and returned his steak, complaining that it had not been properly cooked.

It was in and from Dar es Salaam that Mondlane's educational vision for Mozambique was undergoing a kind of pre-testing. Under its director, Janet Mondlane, the Mozambique Institute (IM) had grown and taken on multi-institutional form. Headquartered in Dar es Salaam, it expanded to include a secondary school in Bagamoyo, a women and children's center in Tunduru, southern Tanzania, and a hospital at the southern port of Mtwara. Conditions at Bagamoyo were made to emulate conditions found in the Mozambique bush, from water pumps to oil lamps, and from open cooking fires to outdoor privies, all ready for displacement into the Mozambican bush. Janet Mondlane developed new sources of finance in Scandinavia, to replace Ford Foundation assistance lost because of Portuguese protests.

In a 1967 brochure Janet Mondlane described the Institute's aims and achievements and beseeched Western donors to make contributions, using pictures of unfinished structures awaiting funds for completion. The brochure highlighted the way in which the Institute was designing an educational system for an independent Mozambique.

> It is usually necessary to write our own textbooks and it is not far from the truth to say that the secretaries of the Institute serve as in a publishing house. Since all classes are conducted in the Portuguese medium, the textbooks as well as the outside reading material must be in Portuguese too.

We are determined to find and translate materials into Portuguese that are of vital interest to the students. In this regard, "it is our determination to keep abreast of the developments of new math and modern science, as well as to develop an accurate and readable history and geography of Mozambique." The brochure continued:

> As important as any academic subject or creative art is training and experience in the responsibilities of self-government. An active Student Council works within the Institute whose members are elected by their respective classes. Each counselor must listen to the voices of the constituency, offer social and cultural activities to the student body, and advise the school administration on student problems.[21]

As is turned out, unanticipated "student problems" would soon erupt and engulf the Institute.

BACK TO SYRACUSE

In August 1966 Eduardo Mondlane returned to Syracuse to participate in a university conference on "African Development." His optimism of four years earlier had shriveled. Hopes for Portuguese rationality, American consistency, Pan-African support, and internal movement unity had each collapsed in the brief period since he had won the Frelimo presidency in a landslide vote. Now, everywhere he turned, there was trouble. Within and without Frelimo, sharply differing conceptions of what an independent Mozambique should be had surfaced and sharpened. And above all, war—the war that Mondlane had so hoped to avoid, the WAR—had become the central, complex, and cruel dynamic of the independence struggle.

In a somber speech on August 3, 1966, at Syracuse's Maxwell School, Mondlane began by acknowledging the severity of the blow to Frelimo strategy caused by Portuguese intelligence operations in Lourenco Marques in December 1965–January 1966. Frelimo cells were broken, and hundreds arrested. All civic associations suspected of ties with Frelimo, notably the Centro Associativo dos Negros de Mocambique, were smashed. Leading cultural/intellectual figures, including Luis Bernardo Honwana, Jose Craveirinha, Rui Nogar, Malgantane Valente Ngwenya, and Domingos Arouca, were detained. The crackdown deprived Frelimo of urban leadership that could challenge Portuguese rule from inside. In Mondlane's view, only organized and popularly led opposition from inside could force the Portuguese to negotiate. But now Frelimo was left without an urban underground and was dependent instead upon guerrilla warfare led by troops trained by Algerian, Russian, and Chinese militaries. Guerrilla fighters constituted nearly the sole means for realizing Frelimo's independence goals. PIDE had deprived Mondlane of his role as galvanizer of southern intellectual resistance. As a result of the Milas and N'Kavandame affairs, his personal influence had declined. Mondlane was neither a military strategist nor a guerrilla commander.

As of September 1964, Frelimo had some 250 trained personnel with which to launch a long-term guerrilla war (in contrast to the one-shot Angola uprising of 1961). By July 1966, Mondlane claimed that figure had reached 7000, growing at a monthly increase of 100–150 at an additional monthly cost of $35,000. Sustained guerrilla warfare Algeria-style had become the Frelimo model of choice. But how long would it take to induce a capitulatory De Gaulle-like 1958 "Je vous ai compris" response? Mondlane could only speculate.[22]

In keeping with Mondlane's now pessimistic expectations, Portugal remained steadfastly impervious to rational behavior. Confronted with Portugal's enduring obduracy, Mondlane argued that Frelimo diplomacy still remained an important avenue for bringing its cause before the world: this held true for the OAU, Afro-Asian region, and even hostile countries such as the USA, where it remained the responsibility of enlightened individuals to speak out.

With the assassination of President Kennedy and the escalation of the Vietnam War came an end to sympathy for the African cause in Washington. It had evaporated. There was even growing conjecture that American intervention on Portugal's behalf might morph into an escalating sequence of technical assistance … from advisors, to foot soldiers and to full military engagement … a Vietnam-style slide into direct support of Portuguese rule in Mozambique. Therefore, Mondlane argued, he was obliged to use every opportunity available to urge Washington not to see Mozambique as a Cold War opportunity for CIA adventure.

Mondlane was especially alarmed by an official tour of Mozambique by a former US Deputy Secretary of Defense, Roswell Gilpatrick. Gilpatrick visited Angola and Mozambique in 1964 and enthused about Portuguese progress in housing, education, employment, and public health. Portugal was achieving this, he argued, despite negative interference from hostile neighboring states. Gilpatrick recommended mutual concessions in a new policy of "mutual example." The USA should remove restrictions on Lisbon's purchase of military spare parts and equipment; in return, Portugal should allow LORAN-C (radio navigation) sites to be established with full access to the Azores. Under Gilpatrick's plan the USA would refrain from UN actions inimical to Portugal if Portugal would *continue* its dialogue with African states. (In fact, African states had already cut off any dialogue.) In early 1965 the Johnson administration decided to sell Portugal twenty B-26 warplanes. Seven were delivered before the sale was determined to be illegal. To Mondlane, the Gilpatrick approach suggested that the USA was now prone to a step-by-step intervention in Mozambique ... just as it was extricating itself from the bitter pain of Vietnam.[23]

At the conclusion of his 1965 Syracuse speech, Mondlane noted that the State Department scholarship program for African refugee students faced an annual battle with the State Department's European Bureau and Europe-oriented officials in the White House and Pentagon who wanted to close it down. Consequently, Frelimo was redoubling efforts to increase student placements in the Soviet bloc, India, and Scandinavia while continuing to work through private Western connections such as the World Council of Churches and the American Catholic Church.[24]

NOTES

1. Letter to Janet Mondlane, Marcum Papers, Box 34/7
2. "Report by Janet Mondlane," typescript, Summer 1963, Syracuse, N.Y. Marcum Papers Box, Box 34/7. For an analysis of the perceptual and behavioral problems of exile politics see Marcum, "The Exile Condition and Revolutionary Effectiveness: Southern African Liberation Movements," Christian P. Potholm and Richard Dale, eds., *Southern Africa in Perspective: Essays in Regional Politics*, New York: The Free Press, 1972, pp. 262–275.
3. Letter to Janet Mondlane, Marcum Papers, Box 34/7
4. Ibid.
5. Ibid.
6. Ibid.
7. Ibid.
8. Cabrita, *Mozambique*, p. 19.
9. George Chilambe, "The Struggle in Mozambique," *East African Journal*, Nairobi, July, 1966, p. 6.

10. "Proclamation to the Mozambican People," *Mozambique Revolution*, New York edition, vol. 1, no. 4, 1964.
11. *New York Times*, August 7, 1965.
12. Col. Donald H. Humphries, "The East African Liberation Movement," *Adelphi Papers*, no. 16, London, Institute for Strategic Studies, March 1965.
13. Cabrito, *Mozambique*, p. 45.
14. *The Chronicle* (Bulawayo) September 29, 1965.
15. Marcum Papers, Box 38/8.
16. Ibid.
17. Ibid.
18. Cahen, "The Muede Case ..."
19. Andrew Rice, *The Teeth May Smile but the Heart Does Not Forget*, Henry Holt, New York, 2009, p. 97.
20. Yoweri K. Museveni, "Fanon's Theory on Violence: Its Verification in Liberated Mozambique," in Nathan Shamuyarira (ed.), *Essays on the Liberation of Southern Africa*, Dar es Salaam, Tanzania Publishing House, 1971, pp. 1–24.
21. Report by Janet Mondlane, Marcum Papers, Box 34/7
22. Author's notes, Syracuse conference, August 3, 1966.
23. For details of the Gilpatrick report and its significance see Schneidman, "American Foreign Policy ..." pp. 155–157, 227.
24. Author's notes, Syracuse, August 3, 1966. At this time, in a move to calm critics in Lisbon and Washington and preserve the Lincoln scholarship program, I resigned as its director.

CHAPTER 7

New Contenders

GWENJERE

Nineteen sixty-six was proving a sobering year for Frelimo. It marked a transition from a phase in which the party was led by civilian nationalists and dominated by the vicissitudes of exile politics to a phase in which the war took precedence and military leaders began to gain sway. In addition to Portugal's dismantling of Frelimo's Lourenco Marques underground lamented by Mondlane, the movement suffered other sanguinary losses. Frelimo's Secretary for Internal Organization inside Mozambique, Jaime Rivaz Sigauke, a member of its central and military committees, was lured into a trap by Portuguese agents and murdered on July 14 near Lusaka, Zambia. One observer wrote that this incident was a "salutary lesson for Frelimo," but also "a measure of how seriously [the Portuguese were] taking it these days; the movement evidently now warrants [...] political killings by Portuguese agents in foreign countries."[1] Fatefully, the warning did not lead to reinforced security measures for Frelimo's president.

Frelimo's top military commander, 29-year-old Filipe Samuel Magaia, was shot and killed on a mission in Niassa province. His death would become a source of bitter controversy within Frelimo and an overall game changer. In 1966, reflecting the ascendancy of the military among Frelimo decision makers, the Central Committee instituted key changes in its educational and military policies. Mondlane had left these

© The Author(s) 2018
J.A. Marcum, *Conceiving Mozambique*, African Histories
and Modernities, https://doi.org/10.1007/978-3-319-65987-9_7

101

102   J.A. MARCUM

unaddressed in his Syracuse address. But he engaged US-based students in intense private discussion about them. Central was a new requirement that obliged all students to participate in the armed struggle. At the same time, reorganization of the military was assuring that it would be controlled by what critics called the southern *mestiço-assimilado* wing of the movement.

Such were the issues and dynamics within Frelimo in June 1967 when a 40-year-old priest, Father Mateos Gwenjere, and a contingent of his seminary students arrived in Dar es Salaam from Beira. After a regular training session at Frelimo's Nachingwea camp in southern Tanzania, Gwenjere volunteered for military service inside Mozambique. But his intellectual demeanor captured Mondlane's attention. He plucked Gwenjere from the group and thrust him into a senior political role. Believing that a joint Catholic and Protestant presentation at the UN would serve to promote Frelimo's case against Portugal, Mondlane sent Gwenjere along with vice-president Rev. Uria Simango to testify before the Fourth Committee of the UN General Assembly in New York. Not only that, according to Joao Cabrita, but "Mondlane arranged for the priest to meet the Kennedy brothers [*sic!*] in Washington."[2] (President Kennedy had been assassinated four years earlier, in 1963).

Presbyterian pastor Rev. Simango introduced Gwenjere to the UN Committee as a fellow Christian who, like himself, had sought refuge in the safety and freedom of Tanzania. Embittered by the humiliations of working in what he described to the Committee as a racist Salazar Catholic Church that deviated from the "universality" of the Roman Church, Gwenjere proceeded to cite incident after incident of racial discrimination by church authorities in Mozambique. He recounted events dramatizing the cruelty of the religious order: church women beaten and incarcerated because their husbands who worked in South African mines had failed to pay their head tax; use of *palmatoria* mallets to beat hands to bloody pulp as punishment for trivial offenses; expulsion of foreign Catholic missionaries guilty of pursuing humane policies; bagging and setting fire to Africans suspected of being Frelimo sympathizers; and license for poor white settlers, or *colonados,* to impose themselves on African women.

In words reminiscent of Adelino Gwambe and Balthazar Chagonga, Gwenjere set forth the racial theory that drove him:

The Portuguese Government encouraged and promised rewards to those [whites] who were able to procreate three or four mulattos. The intention was to make a second Brazil out of Mozambique; it was said that with more mulattos in the country the Portuguese would not be forced to leave Mozambique. In fact, the greatest progress being made in Mozambique was the production of mulattos in increasing numbers.[3]

Uria Simango followed with testimony that similarly attacked Portuguese rule, hitting hard on the racial issue. "There was no respect for persons whose skin was black." Although Portugal was itself 40% illiterate and not highly developed, he said, its war effort was supported by German, American, and other Western governments. Asked by the representative of Sierra Leone whether Portuguese rule was "purely a racial one [...] without sympathy among individual Portuguese citizens," Simango replied:

[It was] not a racial conflict as such, although it was known that the Portuguese were committed to the extermination of the black race by various means such as transferring the indigenous population to remote dry areas and giving their fertile land to the white colonados, encouraging the Portuguese soldiers and white colonados to produce as many mulattos as possible, selling many of the indigenous people to work in South African mines and thereby separating them from their families, and forbidding the use of national dialects in the schools. Since Portugal had refused to grant independence by peaceful means and was engaged in the extermination of the indigenous population, the latter had been compelled to resist by the use of armed force. The people bore no animosity towards white people as such, but since [the African people] represented a majority of about 7 million as against a white minority of less than 100,000, they refused to be ruled by the latter.[4]

Gwenjere and Simango bonded during their trip to the USA. They met with Mozambican students in New York, at Lincoln University, and elsewhere during their visit and stoked critical sentiment about the Frelimo leadership. They listened sympathetically to student arguments about their need to continue their studies rather than accept military service. Simango described to Gwenjere the extent of discontent among northern and central Mozambique militants due to what he perceived as a military power grab by the southern "mulatto-*assimilado*" group in the

104 J.A. MARCUM

wake of the death in 1966 of the military Commander Felipe Magaia. The Magaia factor loomed large.

MAGAIA

Born in 1937, Magaia was a Macua, a large northern ethnic group that had been most resistant to Frelimo proselytizing. His credentials were those of a former leader of the Nucleo dos Estudantes Secondarios Africanos de Mocambique (NESAM), and "one of the prime movers of nationalist groups who had worked secretly in Mozambique." Imprisoned several times (including for most of 1961), Magaia fled to Tanzania in February 1962. There he became one of the founders of Frelimo, underwent military training in Algeria, and became the commander of Frelimo forces in Mozambique.[5]

According to Frelimo, Magaia "fell while commanding a guerrilla unit." However, an inquiry by Frelimo representatives from the Songea district purported to show that he had been killed by one of his own men with the connivance of at least two others. During interrogation, the assassin allegedly confessed that he had acted on orders received from Nachingwea, the key military encampment near the Mozambique border commanded by Samora Machel.

At Dar es Salaam in October 1965, the visiting head of Frelimo's affiliated student organization heard "murmurs from some fighters," including Filipe Magaia, that the political leadership was "detached" and "did not heed the advice of its fighting men and women inside the country. Magaia felt that the political cadre had little stomach for the guerilla war and that party communiqués were unhelpful to his fighters." A "very modest guy," he was preoccupied by a concern for their safety. Some of the "pronouncements of the politicos" were dangerous as they detailed the conquests of the Frelimo fighters, pinpointing the locations of some of their bases, thus inviting sure retaliation or bombardments by the Portuguese air force and army. "One could sense that [Magaia] was somewhat distanced from the political leadership in Dar." As a result, he urged the visiting president of the Uniao Nacional dos Estudantes Mocambicanos (UNEMO), Joao Nhambiu, to return from his studies abroad as soon as possible and exert corrective political influence.

Allegations that Magaia "was shot point blank by Lolonzo Matsola, who was subsequently executed, may appear credible." But rumors spread that Dr. Mondlane and Samora Machel were directly involved in the order to kill Magaia. The UNEMO president was left asking: "Are these just conspiracy theories?"[6]

Simango encouraged the aura of conspiracy surrounding Magaia's death. He pointed out that Magaia's second in command, Raul Casal Ribero, was passed over, and instead Machel was named successor. Presumed supporters of Magaia were reportedly removed from their military posts by Machel and, according to some accounts, executed. Northerners such as Augusto Mtuku, a Maconde, logistics chief in Mtwara, were fired, and southerners consolidated military control by turning to leadership trained directly or indirectly by Algerian, Chinese, and Soviet personnel.

The mist of conspiracy spread. Influential Maconde in the Tanzanian government were drawn into the drama. According to one account, within the Frelimo power structure there actually emerged a clandestine dissident group calling itself the Mozambique Revolutionary United People's Party (MRUPP) bent on seizing political power. Headed by Simango, MRUPP allegedly included Filipe Magaia, Raul Casal Ribeiro, Lazaro N'Kavandame, and Manuel da Maia (head of its youth wing), and enjoyed the support of Tanzania's Oscar Kambona among other Tanzanian Maconde leaders.[7]

Whatever may have been the reality of MRUPP's existence, it was clear that cleavage between north and south, between black African populist and *mestiço-assimilado* elites, between entrepreneurs and Marxist socialists, had grown, and Mondlane's ability to hold the movement together and control mounting political opposition to his leadership faced increasing challenge.

On his return to Dar es Salaam from New York, Gwenjere was assigned to a nurses' training facility near the Mozambique Institute. He empathized with students and their complaints about the new requirement of military service and concluded that it was part of the southern strategy to block northerners from leadership roles. Mondlane conjectured that Gwenjere, who had "worked hard for Frelimo" inside Mozambique, had expected and promised to the seminary students he brought with him that they would receive prompt middle-of-term enrollment in the Mozambique Institute. When this proved academically impossible, his protégés denounced him as a "liar."[8]

Embittered, Gwenjere reached out and proselytized among Maconde soldiers and a Maconde Council of Elders. He became intent on replacing Mondlane with Simango. Accordingly, he stirred up defiance among

Institute students who, unlike their portrait in the Institute's literature, had become increasingly radicalized and resentful of the presence of white (i.e., Portuguese and American) teachers. Their rebellious behavior prompted Samora Machel and an associate, Aurelio Manave, to enter the dormitory premises of the Institute in search of the protest ringleaders. The intervening Frelimo leaders roughed up students and ended up being arrested and spending the night in a Kurasini police station. Fearful of being sent to the Nachingwea military camp, students fled the Institute. White faculty members were sent to Algeria for their safety, and Frelimo temporarily closed the facility. Ultimately, most of the students found refuge in Kenya, where they joined the ranks of a growing anti-Frelimo community.

Despite the internal mayhem, Simango chose not to act immediately. Against Gwenjere's advice, he decided to await a special Congress in 1968 to wrest Frelimo leadership from Eduardo Mondlane, Samora Machel, and Marcelino dos Santos—the southern *mestiço-assimilado* leaders.

NOTES

1. John de St. Jorre, "Forgotten War," *The Observer*, London, October 25, 1966.
2. Cabrita, *Mozambique*, p. 53.
3. Marcum Papers, Box 35/7–8.
4. Ibid.
5. Ibid.
6. Joao Nhambiu, letters to author, July 25 and September 22, 2012, Marcum Papers, Box 37/4.
7. The existence of MRUPP was alleged in a May 10, 1995, Maputo interview with Manuel da Maia, in Cabrita, *Mozambique*, p. 47.
8. Testimony before a Tanzanian commission of inquiry into the Institute's troubles, April 2, 1968, Marcum Papers, Box 34/7.

CHAPTER 8

Students vs. Soldiers

Nhambu and UNEMO

Education was at the heart of Mozambique's political awakening. It was a crucial, complex, and controversial part of the struggles within Frelimo. Mondlane had long viewed education as the most urgent challenge confronting his illiterate country. As of 1950, illiteracy had been 97.6%, with vocational training limited to settler-supportive fields: carpenters, tailors, metalworkers, and assistants to white craftsmen. Africans who managed to enroll in rudimentary education programs provided by Catholic missions mostly failed to pass the system and were left bereft of job qualifications. By 1960, illiteracy had dropped to an official 90.4%. Yet by the time of Portugal's departure over 89% of the African population remained illiterate while 7000 resident whites were enrolled in higher education. The literacy rate inclusive of non-Africans was approximately 93%. As of 1974, the lethargy of Portugal's centuries-old "civilizing mission" had left Mozambique with the educational legacy of a ravenous black hole. "Not one single [African] doctor, economist, agronomist or engineer had been trained." There were only 100 trained secondary teachers for a country of seven million.[1] Would the vacuum be filled by "group think" indoctrination? Or would it be filled by a massive infusion of liberal education?

Control over educational development became a struggle within the struggle, a war for Mozambican minds. In late 1968 Mondlane spoke

© The Author(s) 2018
J.A. Marcum, *Conceiving Mozambique*, African Histories and Modernities, https://doi.org/10.1007/978-3-319-65987-9_8

107

108 J.A. MARCUM

to a conference organized by the Frelimo Department of Education and Culture on "the function of education in revolution." He stressed that even the Frelimo army, the "vanguard of the national liberation struggle," required enough math and science to handle chemical materials and blow up bridges. He went on to explain that Frelimo had been forced to put a "Rejuvenation" program for liberated areas on hold because of the lack of trained personnel. The creation of an integrated Department of Commerce, Cooperatives and Industry had to be delayed while Frelimo concentrated on forging the machine tool of education: teacher training.

It is difficult "to communicate to an illiterate population," Mondlane complained, adding that "all Mozambican people who want national independence have the moral obligation to contribute directly to the struggle." Teachers and students must focus on those "basic elements" that will carry us to national independence "as soon as possible."In so highlighting the educational frailty of the Frelimo organization, Mondlane exposed Frelimo's central political nervous system. Did "moral obligation" require "political uniformity?" A bitter internal struggle over the nature and control of education seemed slated to shape the formative character of a country of millions of minds bereft of previous instruction (Fig. 8.1).[2]

By the 1960s international political pressures had so mounted on Portugal that it began allowing a tiny trickle of African students into its secondary schools and universities. Within those institutions police surveillance was omnipresent. But so, too, was an exposure to the unhinging questioning prompted by exposure to academia. It increasingly took hold of students' minds. Feeding on shared colonial grievance, they ventured to challenge the status quo. This led to the breakaway of young talent from the confines of Portuguese control. With their escape to Western Europe, an important student equation entered the Mozambique drama. One of the leaders of this escape was Joao Jamisse Nhambiu, from Inhambane.

Like Mondlane, Nhambiu climbed the narrow ladder of Protestant mission education and spent time in Lisbon, Portugal's capital. As a premedical student he lived in Lisbon's predominantly Protestant hostel, the O Lar dos Estudantes (LAR). In June 1960 he joined protesters at the Lisbon airport in shouting *Monangambee* as the police flew a former resident of the O Lar hostel, Angolan physician and poet Dr. Agostinho Neto, to political prison in the Cape Verde Islands. From that point

Fig. 8.1 John Marcum, Kwame Nkrumah, and others at the 1958 All-Africa People's Conference in Accra, Ghana

forward, Nhambiu, the recipient of a Methodist Crusade Scholarship arranged by the newly resident Methodist Bishop for Mozambique, Ralph E. Dodge,[3] was subjected to police surveillance, harassment, and interrogation. Like Mondlane before him, he decided to cut short his Lisbon residence and, instead, prompted a "Flight before the Fight" for Joaquim Chissano, Pascoal Mocumbi, and himself.

Born in 1936 at Maxixe, near the southern coastal city of Inhambane, Nhambiu, the son of a Methodist pastor, capped Catholic rudimentary education with home schooling given by an older brother trained at the Methodist mission school of Cambine. As a teenager, after passing the third grade elementary test, he worked as a Methodist catechist to earn money for secondary school in Lourenco Marques. This led to a church scholarship and brought him into his "first confrontation with the Portuguese colonial system." The system, he would write, "was not

110   J.A. MARCUM

directed at me or at any of my friends individually, but was aimed at a whole nation of black people whom the Portuguese identified legally as *indigenas*." It included not just the government but "the farmer, the architect, the storekeeper [...] the entire white population in my country."

As it happened, a Portuguese local Catholic priest who had set up a rudimentary school in Mafuane, the village of Nhambiu's service, resented and reacted negatively to his presence. The priest closed the school and had Nhambiu arrested. As he described it, Nhambiu was arrested "for usurping the rights of the Catholic Church which alone can teach the Africans to read, write and to pray." The priest evidently concluded that, as long as Nhambiu was in the community, children would not attend the priest's "catechists who devoted more time to production of cotton for the church than to the enlightenment of the youngsters." At first, Nhambiu thought his arrest was a mistake. He "had a validated permit from the official Administrator of the area to teach those matters pertaining to religion, one of the few matters in which the Africans had freedom of choice." But, he later wrote, he was surprised, when he placed before the Administrator and the complainant/priest and the latter acted both as accuser and judge. The priest said that Nhambiu "was a hindrance to a positive Catholic action" and an obstacle to "effective colonization of the people in that community because [he] was disposing the African population favorably toward the foreigners [because he] was doing some good for the people who knew [Nhambiu] was employed by a foreign mission." The solidarity the people of the community showed to Nhiambiu when the government harassed him "awakened [Nhambiu] to a new sense of suffering" and he "began to realize that the Portuguese nation was not against [him] as an individual but as a member of the colonized community." While he was living in the village, Nhambiu allowed young villagers to spend nights in his room "to escape the nightly searches of their homes by the government authorities [looking] for the forced labour commonly known in Mozambique as shibalo."[4]

Nhambiu learned that the cards were stacked against all Africans, "assimilated" or not. In July 1957 he became aware that a pre-nationalist "African consciousness" had begun to suffuse his community. He was on vacation from school in Lourenco Marques where he had enrolled with a Methodist scholarship to pursue his secondary education. Enrolled at the Instituto Portugal, he endured incessant colonial indoctrination about how the Portuguese "recognize no racial differences"—witness the "harmonious miscegenation" of their former colony, Brazil. But his daily experiences taught him differently. For example, on one Sunday afternoon, he went to hear the local municipal orchestra perform. He went early to secure a place close to the performance and sat down on a public bench. When two Portuguese couples came toward the bench, he moved to one end of the bench to make space for them to sit down. Instead, he was ordered to vacate the bench, and when he did not do so immediately, the police were called and he was taken to jail. He described what happened next:

> When the two policemen who accompanied me arrived at the gate of the jail, they asked me to produce [my] *cadernata indigena* (a pass required for all Africans to carry always) which I failed to do since under the 1954 Overseas Indigenous Code I was classed as non-indigena by virtue of having finished two years of a High School education. [...] I had papers attesting that the [...] government considered me an *assimilado* which implied [...] that I was to be accorded the privileges and rights of a Portuguese citizen. The myth had just fallen to the ground. The chief of the police was urgently summoned to solve this old Portuguese riddle, whereby some Africans are given papers which grant them more rights than [...] other Africans. [...] In fact, it is impossible to distinguish those Africans with papers in their pockets from those that do not possess them.

The chief of police released Nhambiu, and he was undeterred by the experience.[5] Good grades and summer breaks working with an American Methodist surgeon in Maxixe earned him a Methodist scholarship in Lisbon. Before his departure, a Lourenco Marques taxi driver tried to persuade him to give up his plans for a medical career and serve a greater number of people through politics. His medical goal had been inspired by the model of a Maxixe surgeon, Dr. Simpson, who performed a plethora of operations and saved lives without the aid of X-rays or any other diagnostic tools. It was only after Nhambiu's arrival in Lisbon in 1960 and his encounters with the ubiquitous police that the friendship and the counsel of another Angolan student, Pedro Filipe, caused him to alter his career target. Filipe introduced Nhambiu to a Latin treatise on Spartacus, the rebel slave who challenged the power of Rome. Somehow the Portuguese Classic University of Lisbon had failed to see the irony of requiring that first-year legal students read a text on a slave rebellion.

112   J.A. MARCUM

Felipe also introduced Nhambiu to the poetry of Agostinho Neto, in which the Angolan physician implored colonial students to see themselves as the "awaited" who should return to "liberate the motherland."

Nhambiu took and passed the pre-law exam, switched to legal studies, then watched as Angolan and other colonial students made plans to flee the country assisted by missionaries of the World Council of Churches, the Comité Inter-Mouvement auprès des Évacués (CIMADE), and other organizations. He was reluctant to leave, as a lone Mozambican, for the unknown space of Western Europe. But when Felipe informed him that he might ask some trusted friends to join the odyssey, he went straightaway to the government's Casa dos Estudantes do Imperio hostel and persuaded two friends from student days in Lourenco Marques, Joaquim Chissano and Pascoal Mocumbi, to join in what would become known as the "Flight before the Fight." In late June 1961 a "young American idealist, Kimball Jones," led the Nhambiu group of three, plus an apolitical Joanna Simeoa seeking to join her Angolan boyfriend, across the border, a night in a Spanish jail, and a trek on through Spain to Sèvres, France.

There, a year before the creation of Frelimo, the three caucused and created an umbrella student association, the Uniao Nacional dos Estudantes Mocambicanos (UNEMO). They formed a provisional UNEMO) executive committee, with Chissano as president. Chissano was to study in Poitiers, France, stay in touch with CONCP, and seek to travel to Tanganyika to see what students might contribute to shaping events among splintered groups. Mocumbi, the youngest of the three and a protégé of Andre David Clerq (Mondlane's former mentor) became general secretary and also went to Poitiers (he would later study medicine in Lausanne under a Swiss Presbyterian scholarship) with responsibility for reaching out to recruit students in Portugal and Mozambique. Nhambiu became vice-president, invited Marcelino dos Santos to Paris from Rabat for consultations, met Mondlane when he came to talk with students about educational options and politics, and in 1961 accepted a scholarship in the Lincoln University program in the USA and enrolled in political science at Temple University in Philadelphia (Fig. 8.2).

The three UNEMO) founders forged a structure designed to coordinate action within the highly dispersed ranks of a growing exile student community. They sought to avoid the divisions along political lines that

Fig. 8.2 John Marcum with African students at Lincoln University for Crossroads Africa Meeting in 1960

plagued their Angolan counterparts. They organized UNEMO sectionally by country of enrollment, pledged to fight against discrimination based on political, religious, or racial differences and to fight against all forms of exploitation. They undertook to promote economic and cultural development for those who had been the most exploited. A year later, they hailed the creation of an all-encompassing Frelimo in Dar es Salaam and integrated UNEMO into it, stressing "close cooperation with its Department of Culture and Information." UNEMO's Nhambiu and Alberto Jentimane were the two Mozambican students among those

114 J.A. MARCUM

who met with Mondlane at Syracuse in August 1962, in the wake of his electoral triumph in Dar es Salaam.

UNEMO focused on promoting mass literacy and preparing literate refugees for study abroad. It launched a journal, *Alvor II* (a reprise of NESAM's banned *Alvor*), engaged to sponsor a series of sectional seminars on national Mozambican issues, and, in collaboration with Frelimo, established worldwide contact with other national student unions in quest of scholarships.[6]

At the same time, UNEMO resisted pressure from Marcelino dos Santos's CONCP-generated student organization, the Uniao Geral dos Estudantes da Africa Negra sub Dominacao Colonial Portuguesa (UGEAN), to abandon its separate existence. UGEAN argued that UNEMO should merge with it as the representative of students from all the Portuguese colonies. Amilcar Cabral, of Guinea-Bissau, among others, lobbied for such a merger. However, UGEAN was linked to only one of Angola's competing independence movements, the Movimento Popular de Libertacao Angola, whereas UNEMO sought to avoid getting caught up in political divisions and wished to unite Mozambique students within one single organization. Seeking a compromise, it pledged to collaborate with UGEAN and authorized Mozambican students to join it as individuals. But UGEAN (which was formed months after UNEMO) denounced their position as "prejudicious" to transnational unity. In September 1961 UGEAN held a Congress with only one Mozambican participant (Jose Carlos Horta) whom UNEMO held to be "out of touch" with Mozambique realities. As a result, the Congress passed resolutions on Angola, Guinea-Bissau, Algeria, and Bizerte (Tunisia), but nothing on Mozambique.[7] For Nhambiu and his two associates their 1961 flight from Portugal and their creation of UNEMO represented a commitment to an education breakthrough for an education-deprived country. As Nhambiu wrote in a 1963 UNEMO manifesto, despite government claims to have abrogated the Statutes of Indigenous Persons of 1954, reform remained an empty gesture without implementation:

> "African children [still] must attend the rudimentary Catholic schools instead of Official Elementary schools which are reserved for the settlers' children and the so-called *assimilados*. The Indigenous tax (*Imposto indigena*) [...] has been increased in order to support the so-called

8 STUDENTS VS. SOLDIERS   115

pacification forces now stationed on the northern border of our country. The various exporting commercial companies (SIAM, CAM, etc.) continue to operate with the cheap forced labor supplied by the government authorities as *stipulated* by Decree no. 16199 of December 6, 1928 in the Native *Codigo do Trabalho dos Indigenas nas Colonias de Africa.* "Indeed, increase in the number of settlers, the majority of [whom] are illiterate, has dislodged many Africans from the fertile soil which is then granted to the settlers, as in the case of *Colonato* of Guija and Limpopo Valley." And a much touted government decision to create a Mozambican university will serve only a small elite and will leave unmet the critical need for quality primary and secondary education for the vast majority of Mozambicans.[8]

In late 1965, Mondlane addressed the Second Congress of UNEMO in Dar es Salaam. He traced its origins back to NESAM, created in 1949 under its first president, Herberto Matsolo. Mondlane had joined NESAM after his expulsion from the University of Witwatersrand and lauded it as a police-battered precursor to UNEMO and to Mozambique's struggle for independence. Mondlane went on to stress the need for Mozambican students to act as ambassadors within their host countries of study, thereby generating support for the course of the independence struggle, and urged UNEMO to prepare a list of preferred courses of study to serve as a "guide for our students." He thus underscored his continuing commitment to UNEMO's educational role and concluded by addressing the virtue of voluntary student service to "national liberation" and reaffirming his belief in education as the key to the country's future.[9]

By 1965 in the USA a sizeable cohort of UNEMO students was publishing a *Mozambican Student Bulletin.* Nhambiu graduated with honors from Temple that year, then enrolled in an M.A. program in international relations at the University of Pennsylvania. There he endured the pro-Portuguese stance of Professor Robert Strausz-Hupé and received a Masters degree in May 1966. In early 1965 Mondlane visited Philadelphia and invited Nhambiu to accompany him to Lincoln University, where he was scheduled to lecture. On their return trip, Mondlane revealed that he had made plans for himself and Joseph Chicuarra Massinga to pursue doctoral studies with Professor Jean-Paul Chatelanat at the Institut Universitaire des Hautes Études Internationales in Geneva. But in March 1965, Mondlane wrote to Nhambiu from Dar es Salaam:

I am sorry that Brother Rebelo did not do what I asked him to in connexion with [the matter of your further studies in Europe] when he came to New York for the UN General Assembly, for I had given him instructions to contact you and Brother Massinga to help you prepare your applications for the scholarships to the Institute of International Studies in Geneva. I had even given him application forms and prospectuses for that purpose. In view of the letter you have written to me [12 February 1965] I can presume that he did not do what I had asked him to.[10]

Mondlane followed with detailed instructions on how to apply for admission and for scholarships from the Carnegie Endowment's European Center in Geneva. Despite Rebelo's failure to deliver, Nhambiu and Massinga used their respective university libraries to access the requisite forms and both were admitted to Geneva for the fall of 1966. However, during his library search Nhambiu discovered a postgraduate program in The Hague lasting just one year. While attending the second Congress of UNEMO and the meeting of CONCP, he had "heard murmurs from some fighters including from the late Filipe Magaia" that Frelimo had a "detached leadership in Dar which did not heed the advice of its fighting men and women inside the country." Nhambiu reasoned "that a one year stay in Holland would provide a transition from an easy life in the US for my wife while en route to the hardships that [awaited] us in Dar." But while Nhiambiu was in The Hague, a political crisis broke within Frelimo.

In the early spring of 1967 Nhambiu received a terse letter from Mondlane "ordering me to return to Dar immediately, four months before the end of my planned stay (known to Mondlane) and without an explanation as to what had led to this apparent change of heart." Nhambiu learned later that Massinga had received a similar summons. Mondlane's letter arrived shortly after UNEMO-US had issued a denunciation of Mondlane's leadership. Nhambiu had "planned to go to Dar at the end of June 1967 and had already sent some personal items there. Lo and behold, my items were returned to The Hague even before I could respond to Mondlane's letter. I was bewildered."[11] The surprising and disorienting mixed messages added to rumors surrounding Magaia's death, urgent expressions of a desire by Mocumbi to leave Frelimo to take up medical studies in Lausanne, dos Santos's insistence on censoring Nhambiu's prepared speech for the 1965 CONCP conference, Frelimo's "severance of ties with students in the west," and a personal sense that Mondlane may have disapproved of his choice of The Hague over Geneva for his graduate work. All these unsettling issues factored into his response.

In July 1967, Nhambiu completed his Diploma in National Development at The Hague Institute of Social Studies and returned to Philadelphia, where he entered the Ph.D. program in International Relations at the University of Pennsylvania. He was lost to Mozambique. What was going on?

FRELIMO'S HARDENING EDUCATIONAL POLICIES

By October 1966, Frelimo's rhetoric and policies concerning students had hardened dramatically. The Central Committee announced new policies that abandoned voluntary student service and redefined the relationship of students to the movement and its military struggle. Hardline socialist doctrine prevailed. The socialist core included Marcelino dos Santos, Samora Machel, Joaquim Chissano, Jorge Rebelo, Mateus Mutembe, Armando Guebuza, Sergio Vieria, and Francisco Sumbane. They portrayed Eduardo Mondlane as their intellectual leader. Education secretary Armando Emilio Guebuza set out new rules officially designed to address inequity between a privileged class of students and a patriotic class of soldiers slogging it out in the Mozambique bush. In January 1967, Guebuza elaborated on the decision, indicating that Mozambique Institute students would henceforth undergo military training at Nachingwea during school holidays and that those who failed their classes twice in the same year would automatically be inducted into the Frelimo army. Students studying abroad were told that they should not register for a next higher course of study without first interrupting their studies for at least one year to participate directly in another task of liberation. Institute students, who came primarily from north and central Mozambique reacted by comparing Nachingwea to a Portuguese prison colony in Sao Tome.

For students and military trainees sent under contract by Frelimo to Eastern Europe, the Soviet Union, or China, student obligations were fixed from the start. In the words of Vladimir Shubin, the Soviets incurred responsibility to see that even students with an inadequate educational background were "successfully" trained. The nature of this responsibility became clear to him in January 1967, when he accompanied a group of military trainees to Simferopol, in the Crimea. Some "were reading [elementary] ABC books in Portuguese." Many were wearing just T-shirts in the winter cold. Appropriate clothing had to be found and all had to be guaranteed good educational "results." No one was to "fail." Shubin acknowledged: "sometimes, in particular at the Lumumba University in Moscow, political considerations and the wish to please overcame the scientific assessment and even persons with inadequate school training could receive degrees."[12] For the students, be they military, technical, or university level, their contractual obligation to Frelimo was clear and complete. For them, the policies announced by Guebuza represented no change.

For students at the Mozambique Institute, as noted earlier, the circumstances were different. Egged on by Mateos Gwenjere, who was bent upon replacing Mondlane with Simango, the students rebelled and suffered the consequences: the Institute's (temporary) closure. These largely Maconde secondary school students rejected the edict that they "take three months military training and give the balance of the year to serve inside the country as teachers, nurses, administrators [...] or soldiers." All but about 20 ultimately made their way to Kenya.[13] A special OAU investigation into the event concluded that the student revolt was the "direct consequence" of interference in the affairs of the Institute by Father Gwenjere.

Frelimo's Central Committee agreed and blamed the revolt on Gwenjere's racism and support for elitism among students who had come to see themselves as destined to govern Mozambique after independence.[14] In the view of Edward Hawley, who was working among political refugees in Nairobi at the time, the racial cleavage exacerbated by Gwenjere was compounded by another problem that had developed despite Frelimo's efforts to overcome it. This was the disparity in lifestyles between Frelimo leadership and the rank-and-file.

> The latter were mostly living in camps or in crowded dormitory conditions while the leaders tended to have houses—usually modest despite occasional descriptions of them as mansions in the western press—or to live in cheap hotels. Particularly, in the "diplomatic phase" of the movement they made frequent trips to foreign capitals and to the United Natons headquarters in New York, and when in Dar es Salaam could often be seen in bars and restaurants with visiting officials, diplomats, and newsmen.[15]

In the words of another American observer, Walter Opello:

> When the leadership of Frelimo, which was perceived not only as comprised almost solely of the southern mulatto-*assimilado* group but [as] corrupt as well, asked students to do military service, it was not surprising that they refused. A belief that they were to become "cannon fodder" for a "corrupt" southern leadership was fairly widely held.[16]

On two occasions disaffected and armed young Mozambicans attacked the Frelimo office in Dar es Salaam, forcing its temporary closure. Frelimo's disarray became embarrassingly public. The prime target of the new Frelimo student policies, however, was the contingent of university students thousands of miles away, studying at North American colleges and universities. Admission to student refugee programs sponsored by the State Department, church organizations, and UN was based on merit not on a contract with a sponsoring country or political organization. And not all Mozambican students entered via Frelimo channels. None could be admitted, however politically connected, unless they qualified academically. For example, students admitted from exile in Malawi had either UNAMI or unaffiliated backgrounds. Many were initially motivated by a desire to emulate Mondlane's educational pathway, but few were prepared to accept a service obligation to Frelimo.

Frelimo's effort to conflate educational and military roles was almost universally rejected by students enrolled in American institutions. Why, they asked, are we not allowed to do what Mondlane himself did: move seamlessly from undergraduate to graduate work? On what basis did Frelimo have the right to dictate our futures? Suspicions and alienation concerning the death of Filipe Magaia and military purges that followed, altered personal circumstances including marriage, cynicism about whether they would ever be allowed to return to graduate work after a period of service back in Africa, commitment to current educational goals and, in some cases, the sheer attractiveness of American lifestyle, contributed in varying degrees to their rejectionist position.

The drama that ensued was captured in two documents translated, annotated and published in the American journal *African Historical Studies*, by University of New Hampshire historian Douglas L. Wheeler.[17] The first of the two, purportedly written by Eduardo Mondlane, laid out the rationale for Frelimo's new policy. It was

120   J.A. MARCUM

defensive and dogmatic to a degree that suggested ideological authorship other than Mondlane's—in other words, that of a radicalized Central Committee—yet it focused in part on the cases of two students intimately known to Mondlane, which suggested that it was probably a joint product with input both from Mondlane on historical matters (the first part) and the Central Committee on political dogma.

The Frelimo white paper on education declared that "given the scarcity of means at (Frelimo's) disposal" each and every Mozambican "must place his energies in the service" of the country and "participate directly in the struggle for national liberation." Because of "egotistical tendencies" some students had become hesitant, and this document was meant to "correct weaknesses" and assure the 'integral participation' of all, including those studying abroad. It argued that it was only "because of the struggle" that available training programs existed. Being a student was a "privilege" and with it came "duties" to "the struggle of the masses, mainly composed of illiterates." It was "because Frelimo knows the real motivations of the People and ...[knows how] to organize, unite, to educate the people politically" that Frelimo alone was

> capable of defining strategy and tactics adequate in order to unleash, to develop, to consolidate, to extend and to carry to success the armed struggle for national liberation; Frelimo [therefore] appears as the incarnation of the will and aspirations of the Mozambican masses, the depository of national sovereignty and leadership for the Fatherland.

Consequently, "it is not necessary to be a member of Frelimo for there to be a duty to obey the decisions of Frelimo." Its omniscience was not to be questioned.

The Central Committee informed students in North America that they should not enroll in a postgraduate course "without first interrupting their studies for at least a year to "participate directly" in a "task of national liberation." Exception would be made for students in "physical sciences" in cases where interruption would "destroy previous efforts." In the USA, some students "instigated by imperialists and for purely egotistical reasons and [because of] their corruption, have refused to interrupt their studies. Without Frelimo's permission they have taken up internships, further specialization, and prepared for PhD candidacy." Although Mozambique needs trained leaders, "it only needs leaders who are revolutionary" and not those who will utilize their knowledge "to oppress the people." Frelimo has "comrades who yesterday did not know how to read and who today defeat [a] colonial army led by officers graduated from Military Academies." "Under the direction of Frelimo's Central Committee "our ignorant peasants" with at most primary school diplomas have obtained "results superior to those of companies and the Colonial State with all their engineers, agronomists, laboratory experts, technicians, etc." While Frelimo "cherishes its students, leaders and revolutionary intellectuals [...] they can get more of an education in the revolution than in the university." The Frelimo paper attacked Western educational systems and hence the very universities that Mondlane had previously urged upon Christian missions. It declared:

> The standard of living of the students, even though limited, is far and away better than that of most of the inhabitants of our land, and, besides, the material opportunities open to students after graduation are enormous: it is evident that the revolution cannot compete in salaries with imperialism or with the international companies, especially since presently there are neither salaries nor minimum comforts which are the norm in any University. On the other hand, the education provided by Portuguese high schools, seminaries, and technical schools, by imperialist teaching establishments, by the cooperation of information media and at the disposal of imperialism is used to inculcate in students, in the leadership and intellectuals, the dangerous idea that they are superior to the masses and that they are entitled to a privileged social and material situation. These are the germs planted in the mind which open the door to many desertions and treacheries, not only in our country but also in all the countries dominated by imperialism. Only our national faith, our revolutionary convictions, practice in the struggle, and communion with the masses permit us to meet the challenge of this situation.

The report denounced the idea that students are "future leaders" as "imperialist propaganda of corruption" that was trying "to make our students into accomplices of imperialism through the exploitation of the blood and sweat of the People."[18] The majority of students, Frelimo asserted, would act in a disciplined manner, sacrificing personal benefit to "serve the masses and the revolution by means of [their] acquired knowledge" and eschew "petty and criminal ambitions [drawing] from the knowledge, sacrifices and blood of the People."[19]

In what Wheeler described as a "bitter polemic," a largely "personal, rebuttal and angry attack on Mondlane," accusing him of betraying the revolution, was issued by the executive committee of UNEMO-US.[20] In nine mimeographed pages, the UNEMO-US paper hopscotched in

122   J.A. MARCUM

bitter, disjointed prose from praise for Patrice Lumumba and his promotion of Pan-African Unity and "one party states," to expressions of dismay at the "mysterious disappearance of our most sincere patriot, Filipe S. Magaia," and railed against what it saw as the threat of "severe punishment," even the "death penalty," for the allegedly "egocentric" failure to support Frelimo on its terms. Implying continued loyalty to the movement, they focused their wrath on Mondlane, a "failed leader" who should "retire" to the classroom. For student refugees in Kenya and in North American institutions the enthusiasm with which UNEMO's founders had welcomed the creation of and collaboration with a unified Frelimo had evaporated.

MASSINGA

Illustrative of this change was the case of Joseph Massinga, cited in Frelimo's white paper by Mondlane along with Nhambiu for the help he had given to them but with no mention of his having arranged their graduate work in Europe. In a dissertation that chronicled the early years of Frelimo, Massinga, with a secondary education at the Munhuana Catholic Mission, had escaped Mozambique in 1962 via Swaziland to Tanzania. With Mondlane's assistance he obtained a scholarship to study in the USA and received a B.A. from Manhattan College and an M.A. from Fordham University. He also served as Frelimo's first representative in New York. In 1964 Mondlane wrote to him:

> Even if I do not write to you often, you must take it for granted that I, as the President of Frelimo, and the Central Committee am very proud of you. All the information we get from Americans and others who come across your work is very flattering to you. You are apparently doing a fine job of representing Mozambique.[21]

Mondlane had previously written to George Houser requesting that he help Massinga and declaring that he trusted Massinga "completely."[22]

But as conflicts grew within Frelimo and attitudes toward the USA hardened, Massinga took up the graduate studies option that Mondlane had proposed and arranged for Nhambiu and himself to enroll in doctoral studies at the Institut universitaire des hautes etudes internationales in Geneva. He received a letter from Mondlane "attacking him bitterly." In a 180-degree turn from his 1964 accolades, Mondlane wrote to Massinga accusing him of pretending to represent Frelimo while "in fact working clandestinely against Frelimo." Massinga denied the charges in an emotional letter to the Central Committee. He insisted that he had tried to persuade the students in the USA to contribute to Frelimo, defended his own educational decisions, and asked:

> Why not be sure that the skills we will need in the future have been developed as far as possible now, rather than to search the world over, as many African countries are still doing, for needed brainpower. Some of us presently in leadership positions have seen the wisdom of this philosophy, evidently, by completing [our] education fully prior to returning to the struggle for freedom.[23]

Influenced by Gwenjere and Simango during their visit to the UN and the USA, Massinga empathized with criticism of Frelimo's new policies on education. In contrast, Sharfudine Khan, Massinga's successor as Frelimo's representative in the USA, later attributed the student crisis to Mondlane's "permissive temperament" and accused Mondlane of permitting Gwenjere to inject racial animosities into it.[24]

Massinga denounced the educational policy paper signed by Mondlane as "the most destructive document Frelimo ever produced." Mondlane traveled to the USA in 1966 and 1967 in efforts to convince students to return when they had finished their first degrees. But to no avail. UNEMO-US broke its exclusive ties to Frelimo, leaving it to be led by pro-Simango students. In Sweden, Czechoslovakia, and Kenya other students followed suit.

Ironically, Mondlane, the liberation leader for whom education was a core value, almost an obsession—witness the Milas and Gwenjere fiascoes—now found himself deserted by the beneficiaries of his educational fervor. A few graduates from American institutions did return and assume posts within Frelimo. For example, Manuel dos Santos and Antonio Boustcha worked in the Frelimo department of finance and treasury. But for the majority of students, whether out of self-interest or a belief that with trained people so scarce it was senseless to risk their being killed amongst the guerrillas, Mondlane had become an "anti-education" leader.

Left stranded with his Swiss doctorate almost in hand, in January 1971 Massinga wrote to me seeking advice on possible job openings in the USA, noting that in Switzerland it was "difficult to get even a window cleaning job." He had sent his wife and son back to Baton Rouge,

124 J.A. MARCUM

Louisiana, the previous March because his scholarship was not enough to cover their expenses. Meanwhile he sought a meeting with Mondlane in Geneva, where the latter "often came." He intended "to convince" Mondlane that the best way of solving the problems facing Frelimo was for him "to quit the leadership of Frelimo, at least for some time."[25] They had had a close relationship, and for Massinga the break was traumatic. A meeting between the two never took place.

Massinga later related to his biographer, Solomon Mondlane, that he and Eduardo had spent hours talking politics after his escape from Mozambique to Dar es Salaam via Swaziland in 1962. Eduardo, he claimed, had even promised to make him prime minister after independence. Even though Massinga reportedly declined in 1963 to leave his studies, escort Eduardo's family from Syracuse to Dar es Salaam, and undertake to resolder the Milas-engendered split within Frelimo, the two remained close, and Mondlane urged him to communicate directly and thereby bypass the communist element in a divided Frelimo.[26] Always the conciliator, Massinga wrote to Paulo Gumane in 1969, after Mondlane's death, urging him to make yet another attempt to heal the breach with Frelimo. But Gumane refused, reasoning that Frelimo leaders were busy "fighting among themselves for power, since they followed different ideologies." In Gumane's view, "the time for democratic and constructive unity had not yet come."[27]

Nevertheless, Massinga continued to seek permission to travel to Dar es Salaam to press his case for political reconciliation. He was initially denied a travel document by the Tanzanian government at the insistence of Frelimo's ideologue and powerbroker, Marcelino dos Santos. What seemed clear from the experiences of Nhambiu and Massinga was that students with US degrees and close ties to Mondlane were no longer welcome in Frelimo. However, in 1973 he was finally accepted back, worked for Frelimo, and for a period of time even served with the military in the Cabo Delgado bush.[28] After independence, Massinga served as director of staff planning in the ministry of foreign affairs. But in 1981 two personal adversaries, pro-Soviet security officials Sergio Vieira and Jacinto Veloso, leveled charges accusing him of links with American intelligence. Massinga was jailed and tortured but finally freed in 1985 and took refuge in Portugal. There he created Amigos de Mocambique, an organization through which he promoted the idea of creating a truth and reconciliation committee to salve the hatred between Frelimo and RENAMO partisans at the end of the civil war and worked to raise

Fig. 8.3 Founding members of UDENAMO, date unknown. Right to left, among others: Seated: Daniel Malhalela, Lopez Tembe, Absalao Bahule, Lourenço Matola and Silverio Nungo; Standing: Eli Ndimene, Joao Munguambe, Diwas, Antonio Murrupa, Adelino Gumane, Urias Simango, Filipe Samuel Magaia and Fernando Mungaka

scholarships for student refugees. His proposal for a truth and reconciliation committee modeled on the South African experience was subsequently implemented in Mozambique, but with only modest success, by his biographer, Solomon Mondlane.

With the advent of a new post-civil-war constitution in 1990 that opened the country to multi-party competition, Massinga returned to Mozambique and in 1993 formed a Partido Nacional Democratico (PANADE), which elected nine members to the Mozambique National Assembly in the first free election. He served as a member of the Assembly from 1994 to 1999 and died after a long illness in 2003 (Fig. 8.3).[29]

Back to the disarray and disaffection that enveloped the ranks of Mozambican students in the USA in the late 1960s and early 1970s. It was manifest in a UNEMO-US attempt to organize a September 1971

Fig. 8.4 Leo Milas (aka Leo Clinton Aldridge, Jr., aka Seifeddine Leo Milas)

conference on "Mozambique: Colonial Experience" in Washington, D.C. A sympathetic Somali graduate student observer described the meeting paid for by Washington University as an "embarrassment." It began late, and, after one paper was given, the meeting was postponed for two more hours in the hope of gaining more attendance. Though UNEMO leaders claimed to have been organizing the conference for six months, there were only four people in the audience when it started and the papers gave the impression of having been written "the night before." Ultimately an audience of some twenty "drifters" showed up. Slated to be a fundraiser for the Mozambique Liberation Movement, the event's principal speaker, Uria Simango, failed to show.[30] Two of six scheduled paper-givers were also "no shows."

Thus, less than a decade after I had taken a group of eager students to meet Mondlane at Syracuse as he was preparing to lead Frelimo, Mozambicans studying in the USA no longer felt or acted like central players in the independence struggle (Fig. 8.4).

Notes

1. Mozambique Embassy, *Mozambique Update*, Washington, D.C., special edition, June 28, 1988.

8 STUDENTS VS. SOLDIERS 127

2. Mondlane, Opening address, Conference of the Department of Education and Culture. "Report and Recommendations," Dar es Salaam, Marcum Papers, Box 36/7.
3. Nhambiu and his cousin, the future Methodist bishop Almeida Penecela, were the first two Mozambicans to receive Methodist General Board of Global Ministry "Crusade Scholarships" at the instance of Bishop Dodge. Dodge had previously opened academic doors for numerous gifted Angolan students, including Agostinho Neto. He now expanded the scope of his educational outreach to Mozambique. Nhambiu praised Dodge for "opening" doors, "requiring that missionaries forego the perks" granted to whites and *mestiços* and move rapidly to transfer church leadership to African Mozambicans. Joao J. Nhambiu, untitled manuscript, Philadelphia, 1962, Marcum Papers, Box 37/4.
4. Marcum Papers, Box 38/5.
5. Joao J. Nhambiu, untitled manuscript, Philadelphia, 1962, Marcum Papers, Box 38/5.
6. NEMO, "Memorandum sur l'UNEMO," mimeo, Rabat, Morocco, June 30, 1963. Marcum Papers 38/5.
7. UGEAN, "Resolutions: Congres Constitutif," Rabat, September 22–26, 1961. Marcum Papers, Box 38/3.
8. Joao J. Nhambiu, "Mozambican Students Manifesto," UNEMO, Philadelphia, November 1, 1963, Marcum Papers, Box 38/5.
9. Mondlane, "O Valor do Estudante na Luta de Libertacao Nacional," Inaugural address, Second Congress of UNEMO, Dar es Salaam, December 29, 1965, Marcum Papers, Box 38/5.
10. Marcum Papers, Box 37/4.
11. Quotations from Nhambiu in the above paragraphs are from letters to the author written in 2012, Marcum Papers, Box 37/4.
12. Shubin, *The Hot Cold War*, p. 129.
13. Edward A. Hawley, "Refugees in Kenya Formerly Associated with Liberation Movements," Nairobi, Joint Services of Kenya, 1971, p. 4.
14. Frelimo, "Os Graves Acontecimentos de 1968 e as divergencias Ideologicas," Dar es Salaam, mimeo, [1969], Marcum Papers, Box 35/3.
15. Hawley, "Refugees in Kenya ..." p. 3.
16. Opello, "Internal War in Mozambique ..." p. 223.
17. Douglas L. Wheeler, "A Document for the History of African Nationalism: A Frelimo 'White Paper by Dr. Eduardo C. Mondlane (1920–1969)" Frelimo, "A Brief Account of the Situation of the Mozambican Students Abroad and of Their Participation in the Struggle for National Liberation," Dar es Salaam, December 1967, translated from the Portuguese and annotated by Wheeler, African *Historical Studies*, vol. II, 2 (1969).

18. Ibid.
19. Ibid.
20. Wheeler, "A Document for the History of African Nationalism: The UNEMO 'White Paper' of 1968. A Student Reply to Eduardo Mondlane's 1967 Paper," translated with annotations by Wheeler, *African Historical Studies*, III: 3, 1970. The rebuttal, was signed by Marcos Namashulua (president), Joao H. Wafinda (vice-president), Mario J. de Azevedo (secretary general), Gilberto Waya (treasurer), Carlos Anselmo (publicity secretary), and Alberto Jama (auditor).
21. Massinga, "United Nations and Decolonization ..." p. 298.
22. Marcum Papers, Box 36/5.
23. "Letter to the Central Committee of Frelimo," December 13, 1967, in Massinga, "United Nations and Decolonization ..." p. 300.
24. Interview with author, New York, June 16, 1970.
25. Massinga, "United Nations and Decolonization ..." p. 301.
26. Solomon Mondlane, *The Life and Walks of Dr. Jose C. Massinga* (Lyttleton Manor, SA: MP Books, 2003).
27. Marcum Papers, Box 36/5.
28. Massinga, "United Nations and Decolonization ..." p. 302.
29. Solomon Mondlane, "The Life and Walks of Dr. Jose C. Massinga ....".
30. Observations by Said Yusuf Abdi, Atlanta, Ga., October 4, 1971.

CHAPTER 9

Mondlane's Assasination

In July 1968 Mondlane outmaneuvered his opponents by scheduling a second Frelimo Congress in a remote northern-forested region of Niassa province. He eluded opponents left behind in Dar es Salaam and Cabo Delgado, where he would have been vulnerable to pressure from Maconde challengers. N'Kavandame boycotted the Congress. Simango attended and was re-elected vice-president at Mondlane's insistence, but he lacked a Nyanja ethnic support base inside a lightly populated area that could facilitate a successful bid for power. The Portuguese discovered the locus of the Congress just as it ended and were able to bomb the area, but only after the conclave had disbanded. The public relations coup was significant.

Re-elected to the Frelimo presidency, on the surface, Mondlane's political leadership appeared strong. It was not. In November 1968, just before Mondlane set off for Nairobi ostensibly to meet with Kenya's President, Jomo Kenyatta, a popular Dar es Salaam weekly, *The Nationalist*, attacked him as an agent of American imperialism. The timing of his Kenya trip coincided with a Nairobi conference organized by the African American Institute (AAI). Whether the timing was coincidental or not, Mondlane vehemently denied that he was in Nairobi to attend the American conference.[1] But he did acknowledge that he had attended a "private" hotel gathering of influential Americans that included the editor of *Newsweek* and Wayne Fredericks. Recalling the

© The Author(s) 2018   129
J.A. Marcum, *Conceiving Mozambique*, African Histories
and Modernities, https://doi.org/10.1007/978-3-319-65987-9_9

130   J.A. MARCUM

meeting, Fredericks later commented that Mondlane appeared "tense and preoccupied" with Frelimo's internal difficulties.[2]

It was the last time Fredericks would see Mondlane. Initially warm, if wary, American diplomatic contact with the Mozambique independence movement was now frozen. It was history. Fredericks had persistently advocated for Mondlane within and without the government and many times expressed personal regret that he had been politically blocked in the State Department from mustering support for Mondlane and his cause. Mondlane, in turn, had come to express angry frustration with American policy. His bitterness spilled onto the pages of the periodical *War/Peace Report*: "In view of the attitude of the American government toward my people dying, if I were to continue to admire the United States for its democratic ideals the way I used to, I would have to be judged mentally deranged."[3]

Mondlane's focus on education had backfired. Growing numbers of young Mozambicans were receiving military training and ideological indoctrination from the Soviets and Chinese. Students, mostly Maconde, at the Mozambique Institute had rebelled and fled. Those studying in the USA were rejecting Frelimo's calls to forgo advanced degrees and return to serve under the direction of a Marxist-leaning Central Committee.

Mozambique's education deficit was huge and could be addressed only over a period of years of peaceful change (not by impulsive personal award to educational status, as in the cases of Milas and Gwenjere). By 1968 education had been subordinated to the priorities of war and revolution. Educational development had meant one thing in a context of prospective political reform. It had come to mean something altogether different in conditions that Mondlane had warned against, namely, war and dependency on Sino-Soviet military support, and armed conflict forced by Portugal's rejection of political reform and American concessions to Portuguese pressure.

One of the most immediate circumstances confronting Mondlane in late 1968 was a regional rebellion led by N'Kavandame, the Maconde entrepreneur Mondlane had brought into the movement to help solidify Maconde support for Frelimo in the Cabo Delgado region. On March 2, 1968, Mondlane praised N'Kavandame in London for sparking the revival of agricultural cooperatives in Cabo Delgado that had been crushed by colonial authorities. "N'Kavandame," he said, "is back helping our people reorganize their economic life and at the same time

9 MONDLANE'S ASSASINATION   131

directing political and military programs aimed at securing their political independence."[4] Despite harassment by the Portuguese forces, peasants were increasing the production and even the exportation of cashews, sesame seeds, groundnuts, castor oil, other crops and small livestock. As the Central Committee came increasingly under socialist/military domination, however, N'Kavandame's penchant for private agricultural enterprise made him a political deviant. In a fashion similar to what would happen to another senior leader, Silverio Nungo, after being praised by Mondlane at the Second Party Congress, N'Kavandame's fate was sealed. The conflict came to a head when the Central Committee undertook to reorganize and centralize Frelimo structures inside Mozambique following Samora Machel's rise as military commander in the wake of Filipe Magaia's death.

In an August 1968 meeting in Mtwara, which was prompted by N'Kavandame's complaints about Frelimo political interference in his provincial realm, Mondlane listened as local Cabo Delgado leaders vented their grievances. They cited executions of military and civilian leaders whose loyalty had come under question by Frelimo officials. Frelimo had attributed these deaths to Portuguese action. N'Kavandame rebutted Mondlane's efforts to regain his support by hurling a vitriolic rebuke. He then issued orders for border committees to bar Frelimo military units from entering the province.

Members of Tanzania's governing Tanganyika African National Union (TANU) party were present at the meeting in Mtwara. N'Kavandame's boldness may have been encouraged by a belief that, given Tanzania's support for Biafran secession in Nigeria, Tanzania would be tolerant of Cabo Delgado separatism in Mozambique. But the Tanzanians maintained their support for Mondlane.

Defying N'Kavandame's ban, in December 1968 Frelimo's deputy chief of operations, Paulo Kankhomba, entered the province with a mandate from the Central Committee to reorganize Cabo Delgado administration and place it under centralized Frelimo control. He was ambushed and killed by local Maconde militants.

When the Mtwara meeting was held, a US State Department memorandum had commented:

> Mondlane is probably in trouble. His often lofty and almost patrician manner has lost him support of some younger and more radical members of the party. Unless he condescends to palaver in the traditional African

132   J.A. MARCUM

manner with his followers and thrashes out their problems—and his—he may be in danger of losing Frelimo's leadership or, at least, of seriously weakening his position.[5]

Following the disastrous Mtwara face-off, Gwenjere pressed for new presidential elections. To this end, he summoned Frelimo "delegates," mostly Maconde, from Cabo Delgado, Mtwara, Zanzibar, and Pemba, to Dar es Salaam. The elections were to be held at the beginning of January 1969. Gwenjere believed that, thanks to sympathetic police connections, he would have the support of Tanzanian officials, including Minister of State Lawi Sijaona and Second Vice-President Rashidi Kawawa. But Mondlane struck first. He persuaded the Tanzanian authorities to place Gwenjere under house arrest.

On January 3, Frelimo's Executive Committee suspended N'Kavandame from his position as provincial secretary. Mondlane followed with a letter that read:

> I am sorry I have to transmit the decision of the Executive Committee to you in this manner because, as you know, I have had great regard for you for a long time. But your actions during the last six months which culminated in the assassination of Comrade Kankhomba, have convinced me as well as [the Executive Committee] that for one reason or another, Mzee Lazaro has become an enemy of Frelimo.[6]

A Frelimo press release belittled the significance of the loss of N'Kavandame by stating he had masterminded commercial counter-revolutionary activities from Tanzania and not been inside Mozambique since 1967. It also suggested N'Kavandame had not had a military role in Cabo Delgado, the province through which he dramatically defected in order to avoid trial for murder.[7]

Mondlane appeared to have prevailed. But had he? Frelimo's Marxist hard core used the N'Kavandame drama to flex its power and further isolate Mondlane.

At this point Frelimo issued another major policy paper that was as important as its earlier policy paper on education. The mimeographed document, "Os Graves Acontecimentos de 1968 e as Divergencias Ideologicas ao Nivel da Direccao," reviewed the Gwenjere and N'Kavandame episodes and drew two conclusions. First, Frelimo's struggle had reached an advanced phase that required a strong "concentration

9 MONDLANE'S ASSASINATION   133

of power" based in a politico-military structure able to transform it into a true guerrilla movement. Second, Frelimo had to adhere to a uniform ideology free from contradictory capitalist exploitation of man by man and dedicated to mobilizing all sectors of society in eradicating tribalism, regionalism, racism, egoism, and ambition through centralized indoctrination. Frelimo demanded total engagement, total mobilization of all sectors of Mozambican society in a struggle of the oppressed that would eliminate all "exploitation of man by man." *A Frelimo Vencera.*

This was the situation on February 3, 1969, less than a month after the firing of N'Kavandame, when Mondlane decided to pick up his mail at the studio he used at former AAI employee Betty King's house in Oyster Bay. There he was able to read, write, and think like an academic. A new book package had arrived that morning. He tore it open. An explosion killed him instantly.

In spite of previous evidence of increasing Portuguese willingness to resort to desperate means, including the assassination of Sigauke and a steady series of personal threats against him, Mondlane had not taken enhanced security precautions. He had no security guard. An assassin could have walked up and shot him in the studio. And no one screened his mail. Mondlane's professorial commitment to private contemplation and the open lifestyle of a professor had proved fatal.

Who killed him? Subsequent investigations pointed to the likelihood of PIDE collaboration with internal dissidents. Two additional parcel bombs addressed to Marcelino dos Santos and Uria Simango were subsequently intercepted. But the exact motives and identity of Mondlane's assassin(s) would remain an unsolved crime.[8]

Rev. Edward Hawley presided at Mondlane's funeral at the Azania Front Lutheran Church in Dar es Salaam. Hawley had been an assistant pastor at the Congregational Church at Oberlin, where he became a close friend of Mondlane's and presided at his marriage to Janet. Underscoring Mondlane's dual commitment to Christianity and revolution, Hawley intoned:

This strange yet compelling man whom Christians call the Son of God once said, "The Kingdom of God comes by violence, and violent men take it by force." I do not wish to enter here into the long debates that have surrounded this passage, except to say that there have been many who, like Dr. Mondlane, filled with burning love for the oppressed whom Jesus loved, and seeing justice long delayed and the cruel yoke harsh on the

134   J.A. MARCUM

people, have been willing to go against their natures, to become violent men, and to seek to seize the Kingdom by force, trusting in a gracious God to rework the deeds they saw as necessary, into a larger pattern of justice and right.[9]

With the shock of his death came a heightened appreciation of how, even as his political fortunes may have been ebbing, Mondlane had towered over the movement. Tanzania ordered a full state funeral attended by his bereaved wife and children. They were pictured by the world press in photos reminiscent of those of President John Kennedy's stoic family after his assassination. Even political opponents weighed his loss with respect. COREMO's Paulo Gumane regarded Mondlane as the only one who could maintain bridge the differences between two rival ideological leaders in Frelimo: Simango and dos Santos. Gumane wrote that, although Mondlane made mistakes, he "had so much to offer in a free Mozambique of tomorrow."

Frelimo was shaken—paralyzed. With the sudden finality of a parcel bomb blast, the charismatic glue that held its competing elements together dissolved. Yet, after a pause to mourn, these elements, freed from Mondlane's unifying restraint, shifted swiftly into an internal power struggle for control of the movement and of the political character of a future Mozambique.

SIMANGO

As vice-president, Uria Simango seemed slated to succeed Mondlane.

In March, N'Kavandame, fired from the Central Committee and now accused of complicity in Mondlane's murder, was reportedly revealed by Tanzanian police accounts to be the beneficiary of wealth accumulated from the taxation on *sub rosa* trade between Cabo Delgado and Tanzania. He deserted to the Portuguese. He reportedly took with him "three suitcases of secret Frelimo documents." Like Gwenjere, a Catholic, N'Kavandame wore "a rosary and crucifix at all times," defying an increasingly anti-religious Frelimo environment. He vowed to persuade the "fierce, tattooed warriors" of the Maconde, who had been "the vanguard of the guerrilla war" to "give themselves up" in return for "a degree of regional autonomy and Portuguese assistance in agriculture, education and medical care."[10] The Central Committee denounced him as a corrupt traitor. Apparently he had indeed been using at least some of his trade-related assets to equip a militant youth league, influence the Maconde Council of Elders, and prepare for *de facto* Cabo Delgado secession. All of this rendered him a threat to Frelimo aspirations. Frelimo troops moved into the region.

N'Kavandame's well-orchestrated flight prompted Portuguese acclaim in the press and a blizzard of leaflets dropped over the Cabo Delgado area. It also deprived Simango of a vital but discombobulated Maconde constituency that could have helped to solidify his interim authority. In April 1969 a determined Marxist majority in the Central Committee seized the opportunity to wrest the presidency from Simango. He had to settle for chair of a ruling triumvirate with Samora Machel and Marcelino dos Santos.

With N'Kavandame gone, Simango's enemies' next step was to demote Simango's close colleague, the head of the Department of Administration, Silverio Nungu, and send him to Cabo Delgado ostensibly for administrative duties. Once there Nungu soon found himself facing charges of corruption before a "people's court". According to Simango, Nungu was forced to write a confession of financial crime and then beaten until he lost consciousness. The next day he was reportedly hung by the neck and pierced in the stomach with a bayonet. He died on June 18, 1969. This was the same veteran Frelimo leader from Sofala that Mondlane had praised just months earlier at the Second Party Congress:

> Those among us who accompanied the work of the Department of Administration since 1963 and who saw the big achievements that were made to perfect its functioning and efficiency, have the obligation to present their good wishes to 'Mr. Administrator' alias SILVERIO NUNGU, and his 'clerks,' Comrades Kawawa, Lopes, Tembe and others.[11]

Shortly after arriving at the "Provincial Base," Nungu had written cheerily to fellow Central Committee member Samuel Dhlakama:

> My trip was very good. I was well received by all the comrades. Certainly the work which is inside there needs the presence and collaboration of all militants of Frelimo, because the work has greatly developed. The comrades have courageously did [*sic*] and continue to do a lot—the people are conscious. I shall do everything possible to give my contribution too.

He thanked Dhlakama for "*the comb which I consider a great remembrance*" and made a modest additional request of his "comrade and friend" for some soap and two short-sleeved jerseys.[12] Simango attached a copy of Nungu's note to the bombshell document he was about to issue that November.

After Nungu's demise the focus turned to Simango.

Born in Beira (Maropanye District) in 1926, the son of a Protestant minister, Simangu was studying at a theological seminary in Lourenco Marques in 1953 when his father, Timoteo Simango, was arrested in a government crackdown on popular protest in the Beira region. In the wake of a Save River flood, twin incidents shook the colonial administration. At Mashango, on the north bank of the river, protest arose over profiteering through the local administrator's sale of relief materials for personal gain. The issue was pressed by a local *instituto negrofilo*. At Mambone, on the southern bank of the river, an issue was created by an effort by African workers to purchase the European- and *mestiço*-owned land on which they worked. Funds were amassed for this purchase from Mozambican workers from as far away as South Africa. Due to an informer, however, the funds were discovered at the home of an African pastor, Andre Macheva. Consequent arrests and deportations from the two incidents then scattered protesters into imposed *chibalo* (forced labor) from the islands of São Tomé and Ibo to prisons in remote areas of Mozambique. Because of his support for the protesters and clandestine fundraisers, Timoteo Simango, without the benefit of trial, was sent to prison in Marrupa, Niassa, followed by supervised house arrest in Beira.[13] It was guilt by association. After being arrested and interrogated for three days, he was offered a scholarship to study in Portugal as a way of deflecting him from anti-colonial activity. He hesitated, and then declined. He later explained his decision to the Goan intellectual Aquino de Braganca. As a Protestant, he considered that the offer was inspired by a Catholic hierarchy fearful of the penetration by Anglo missionaries into this "Portuguese province." So he decided to remain among "his own," declaring, "My people have need of me." He spoke in a tone that convinced de Braganca that he considered himself to be a "providential man" destined to "save the country."[14]

Simango was ordained in 1956 as a pastor in the Church of Christ, Manica and Sofala. The next year his Beira church undertook to send him to Portugal to work with churches in Carcavelos, Cascais. But

Lisbon denied him entry. Prudently, his church (Swiss Presbyterian) sent him to Rhodesia, instead, to serve within the emigrant Mozambican community and to earn a teaching credential at Mt. Silinda Mission. Influenced by his father's fate, he plunged into émigré Mozambican politics while teaching at the Highfield primary school in Salisbury (now Harare). His political apprenticeship was with Joshua Nkomo's NDP. Unbeknownst to his church, he served as administrative secretary of a clandestine cultural group. In this role he corresponded with officials in Nkrumah's Ghana, using fictitious names such as "Jose da Silva and John Curdy." He also secretly hosted Mozambicans heading to join a newly formed organization in Bulawayo and ultimately became the Salisbury representative of that organization, UDENAMO. Locally he was suspected of dangerous leanings, and his Portuguese-language classes were monitored by PIDE agents active in Rhodesia.

In 1960 Simango joined the UDENAMO exodus to Dar es Salaam, where he became active in the local Lutheran church and chair of an ad hoc committee forged expressly to unite existing movements into a common organization. He concluded that Gwambe wanted to "swallow" UDENAMO's competitors and broke with him. He participated in the creation of Frelimo, and it was he and Lawrence Millanga who drafted the movement's first constitution.[15] In a subtly caustic interpretation of Simango's political ambitions, Aquino de Braganca wrote that Simango supported but had not formally joined UDENAMO because he considered that its presidency was "rightfully his." He now hoped to "eliminate his rival, Adelino Gwambe, and assume the presidency of a new, united independence movement." But Eduardo Mondlane's dramatic entry into the equation obliged him to accept the role of Mondlane's deputy "'while not forgiving him for blocking him from realizing the historic mission that Providence had conferred on him' to quote one of his favorite expressions." All of Simango's subsequent actions within Frelimo, de Braganca asserted, were "dominated by this passion, by this thirst for personal power."[16]

Destined to become a close advisor to Marcelino dos Santos and Samora Machel, de Braganca alleged that Simango never understood

> the strategic conception of the guerrilla defended by the progressive wing of [the] politico-military: a popular long term war for the liquidation of imperialist domination. He did not see that new cadres born out of direct

138   J.A. MARCUM

action have already replaced the generation of nationalist precursors. It was around him that opponents of all sorts regrouped, bypassed by the rapid course of events.

Re-elected vice-president by a reluctant 1968 Congress thanks to Mondlane's insistence on organizational unity, Simango watched as "new politico-military cadres confirmed the progressive theses of Eduardo Mondlane."[17]

Simango's relationship with Mondlane had been uneasy from the start. In late 1962, after losing the election to the presidency, he applied for and received a church scholarship to study in the USA. But he was obliged to ask for a delay when he returned to Dar es Salaam from an African tour and found "three secretaries [had been] expelled [by Milas] from the Party due to their connections with world dangerous elements, subversive activities [...] working to divide the Party and overthrow the President, Dr. Mondlane." The Central Committee determined that their action was "not merely irresponsible but also plotery and traitory to the Nation." He observed that since Frelimo had been founded five top officials had been expelled and he was "the only top official" remaining. (Mondlane was still in Syracuse.) "I am now doing the whole party branch and international correspondence and contacts." Mondlane was expected back by February 15, 1963. Meanwhile, he explained, "Milas will act as his secretary." Confirming that he had completed visa requirements and was ready to leave for the USA on January 25, he expressed his gratitude for the "rare" opportunity presented, noted wryly that he was "not too young to lose days or months of learning," and pleaded for a delay of departure until February 15. But Mondlane did not return to Dar es Salaam until March, and with the political turmoil in Dar es Salaam persisting, Simango was unable to leave for study in the USA. His education became another victim of the Milas scam.[18]

Such was the background of political frustration that blurred Simango's vision following Mondlane's murder in mid-1969. Isolated and resentful, fearful of being given an assignment inside Mozambique, where, like Nungu and Magaia, he would be killed, he wrote a desperate, over-the-top indictment of the Central Committee "progressives." He apparently expected active support from northern soldiers. The support did not materialize. Stunned, yet quick to react, the Central Committee denounced and expelled him. In a hyperbolic salvo entitled "Gloomy

Situation in Frelimo," Simango had hurled charges that shook the movement to its core.

The credibility of his missive was undercut by the fact that he himself had been in a position of authority at the time of crimes he now deplored and by the intemperance and overreach of his prose. As recently as March 1966 he had lauded Frelimo's achievements, the establishment of schools, health facilities, and agricultural and training of Frelimo military within insurgent-controlled areas of northern Mozambique. And he had previously drawn positive attention to the role of anti-colonial Portuguese teaching in the Mozambique Institute and Portuguese doctors working with wounded Frelimo soldiers.[19] Simango was also not uninvolved in the outreach to Frelimo's socialist supporters. For example, in May 1964 he led a Frelimo delegation in quest of help from the Soviet Union and took part in the second Soviet Afro-Asian Solidarity Conference in Baku, Azerbaijan, that same year.[20]

London's *Africa Confidential* described him as a former Presbyterian minister who was "certainly more militantly Socialist [pro-Peking] than Mondlane ever was." Simango explained it this way: "I know my Bible. Christ consistently practiced Socialist principles [...] God always worked to set people free."[21] But this history did not stop Simango from denouncing Portuguese teachers and technicians as potential subversives, declaring that Frelimo was not ready for either an abandonment of bourgeois support or an imposition of socialism, or demanding an end to military assassinations inside Frelimo-held areas of Cabo Delgado, Niassa and Tete.

Bristling with suspicion, Simango claimed that the southern socialists of the Central Committee intended to assassinate him and other dissidents, namely Mariano Masinye and Samuel Dhlakama. In July, he said, the Central Committee group, after receiving a report on Nungu's death "discussed how to proceed with the killing of others, the next person being Simango." To this end, they decided that certain "members of the Presidential Council (top echelon of the Central Committee) [would] go into the country separately to inspect work" in the northern provinces. "If he [Simango] goes, Samora and Marcelino declared, [he] will not return, that will be the end."

Simango went so far as to attack Mondlane's widow, Janet, for hosting "conspiratorial" plans by a "clique of criminals." In summary, he claimed, Frelimo was infested with "very strong feelings of sectarianism,

140   J.A. MARCUM

regionalism and tribalism" and a "spirit of individualism manifest in the frequent utilization of the pronoun 'I' (*eu*)."[22]

Dar es Salaam's *Standard* and *Nationalist* newspapers immediately pronounced Simango's verbal blast as irresponsible and harmful to the cause of the independence struggle. Julius Nyerere personally convened the troika in a fruitless reconciliation effort. And an emergency gathering of Frelimo executives suspended Simango from the Presidential Council, and "categorically" and "totally" rejected the contents of "Gloomy Situation" as "calumnious accusations" that denigrated leaders who are "patriots and revolutionaries"[23] The Tanzanian police removed Simango from Dar es Salaam and deported him and allied dissidents to a camp at Dabalo in central Tanzania. Meeting in May, Frelimo's Central Committee formally expelled him and declared that he should be "subjected to people's justice in Mozambique." But "justice" would be delayed. Simango had already flown to Cairo.

Migual Murupa

Echoing Simango and noting what had happened to Nungu, one of the few Mozambican students in the USA to respond to Mondlane's urgings to return to Dar es Salaam to serve in Frelimo, Miguel Artur Murupa produced a gloomy report of his own. He naively presented it to the Tanzanian government. In it he announced his intention to resign from the movement. Janet Mondlane would later attribute this defection to Murupa's ambition to become foreign secretary, which was foiled by Simango's fall.[24]

Born in 1939 at Pebane, Zambezia province, Murupa attended secondary school at a Catholic Seminary in Zobue, then worked as a proofreader and apprentice at Beira's *Diario de Mocambique*. In February 1962 he left for Tanzania, where his energetic canvassing got him a position as announcer and program officer in the Portuguese language section of the Ghana Broadcasting Corporation in Accra. In 1963 he received a scholarship to study in the USA, where he earned a B.A. in economics and finance from Howard University before returning to Dar es Salaam in 1968. After a standard indoctrination at Nachingwea, his communication skills won him the post of Frelimo assistant foreign secretary and a seat on the Central Committee.

By 1969, however, he had become disaffected by what he saw as a "vicious and dirty struggle for power in the top echelon" of Frelimo.

He deplored the "joy one group is having while the other is mourning the death of a comrade" in a "macabre vicious circle." He found his own situation as a "middle stratum" leader "depressing." If, as a leader with non-conforming views, he refused a probable assignment inside Mozambique, he would be declared an "enemy of the people"—a "sure way of death." If instead he accepted to go inside Mozambique, as one who disagreed with the Gaza "clique," he would "disappear." The world would simply be told that "he died of a hunger strike" (Nungu) or in combat (Magaia).[25]

With access to inside information as a member of the Central Committee, Murupa added detail in his report to the circumstances of Felipe Magaia's death. Murupa alleged that Magaia was the first victim of a Frelimo military "assassination policy." According to Murupa, Magaia was shot on the orders of the Gaza clique while crossing the Chitangamwe River in Niassa Province on October 1, 1966.[26]

In May 1969 the Tanzanian police turned Murupa over to Frelimo and he was sent to an underground prison at the Nachingwea training camp. He botched an early attempt to escape the camp. This prompted Frelimo to send him as a simple combatant into Cabo Delgado. Fearing a Nungu-like fate, he successfully managed a second attempt to escape and turned himself over to a Portuguese military patrol at Sagal on the Maconde plateau on November 6, 1970. On December 9 he held a press conference at Nampula in which he professed his belief in ultimate Portuguese victory.[27] After his defection, Murupa became editor of a Beira weekly, *Voz Africana*, then, in advance of Frelimo's rise to power, escaped to Portugal.

Marcelino Dos Santos

With Simango's demise, the troika that had replaced Mondlane dissolved. Samora Machel became president. Marcelino dos Santos, as a *mestiço*, settled for the vice-presidency. This was normal for dos Santos, who had played a low-profile but central role in Frelimo from its beginning. He wrote and spoke sparingly. He worked hard. He was a dedicated ideologue. By at least one account, dos Santos was encouraged by the Soviets, East Europeans, and Cubans to make a bid for the presidency after Mondlane's death. They were concerned about "growing Chinese revolutionary influence on the rank and file." But "the *mestiço* poet and world traveler lacked a firm power base within the party."[28]

142   J.A. MARCUM

Born in 1929 at Lumbo, on the coast near Mozambique Island, dos Santos came from a politically engaged family. His father was an activist in the Associacao Africana, within which he promoted the cause of unity among Mozambicans arguing for "justice and social equality." Marcelino grew up in Lourenco Marques. In 1947, after completing secondary school, he went to Portugal to continue his education at Lisbon's Instituto Industrial. But social issues not engineering most motivated him. At the Casa dos Estudantes do Imperio, where most colonial students were aggregated, he championed nationalist ideas among his peers, and by 1950 the tense political climate in Lisbon led him and others to flee Portugal and relocate, mostly in Paris.

Enrolling at the Sorbonne and entering the intellectual circle of the left bank journal *Présence Africaine* at 25 bis rue des Écoles, he began expressing himself in poetry, using the pen name Kalungano for publication in Portuguese, and later Lilinho Micaia for his poetry published in the Soviet Union. He was influenced by the writings of the pro-Soviet French historian Richard Bloch and called for a thorough rewriting of Mozambique's history. He was especially keen to see a reconsideration of the pre-assimilationist ferment that followed the First World War, a ferment that preceded the creation of the Associacao Africana's *O'Brado Africano*. There was a great intellectual need, he argued, for serious documentation of the past, a need for historical *"fierte"*.[29]

Dos Santos's introduction to Soviet society came in 1958, when he participated in an Afro-Asian Writers' Conference in Tashkent. Along with Mario de Andrade and Viriato da Cruz of Angola he helped to organize a Movimento Anti-Colonialista (MAC) in Paris, which undertook to unite political exiles from Portuguese Africa to campaign together for independence. Dos Santos applied his organizational energy full force to this pursuit. He was rebuffed as a left -wing *mestiço* when he offered to work with Holden Roberto and his Uniao dos Populacoes de Angola (UPA), after it launched a nationalist uprising in Angola in 1961. But he persisted in his efforts to forge a common front among Portuguese anti-colonial organizations.

In January 1960, at the second All African Peoples' Conference in Tunis, MAC expanded, adding Amilcar Cabral's Guinea-Bissau followers to form a Frente Revolucionaria Africana para a Independencia Nacional (FRAIN) which, at a conference in Casablanca in April 1961, converted itself into a formal coalition of nationalist organizations, the core of which consisted of the Movimento Popular de Libertacao de Angola (MPLA), led by Mario de Andrade, and Cabral's Partido Africano da Independencia da Guine e Cabo Verde (PAIGC). At Casablanca, Andrade was elected president of a joint Consultative Council, and a permanent secretariat was established for the Conferencia das Organizaçoes Nacionalistas das Colónias Portuguesas (CONCP) in Rabat. Dos Santos became secretary general. In that capacity he wrote to the Soviets in January 1962 seeking "an annual subvention of ten thousand sterling pounds." Only later in 1965, at the time of a long-delayed second CONCP gathering in Dar es Salaam, was the request "partly met" with a grant of $8400 dollars.[30]

In July 1961, reacting to Gwambe's public announcement that a UDENAMO force of 70,000 was poised to invade Mozambique, dos Santos flew to Dar es Salaam and into the drama of exile Mozambique politics. A member of the Paris branch of UDENAMO, he quickly distanced himself from Gwambe and undertook to salvage UDENAMO's presence in Dar es Salaam by announcing that a popular uprising inside Mozambique—not an invasion—was imminent (which, like Gwambe's claim, was also not true).[31] Although they had very different views about political strategy and goals, Mondlane was impressed by dos Santos's education and intellect, and appointed him foreign secretary at Frelimo's inaugural conclave in September 1962. Unlike Mondlane, dos Santos was convinced from the start that war would be necessary both to force Portugal's exit and to create a socialist state. In retrospect he put it this way:

> When Frelimo was created we were almost completely convinced that only an armed struggle would allow us to fulfill our aspirations. At our Congress in September 1962 we had no idea when we would start. But we set ourselves a number of tasks: first to consolidate the organization inside the country, the political organization.

At the same time between 250 and 300 men were sent to learn the art of guerilla warfare in Algeria, the minimum number needed to launch an armed struggle.

"It was not possible to determine the level of political consciousness necessary to support armed struggle. We also realized that it was not possible to develop a strong political organization under a fascist system." You might build a clandestine political network "but at a certain level it becomes vulnerable to enemy action." Therefore, dos Santos said, Frelimo concentrated on building a basic military support structure,

144 J.A. MARCUM

providing food, organizing hiding places, and creating a communication system. Finally, the start of the armed struggle in 1964 created conditions necessary for "development of the political organization": military force created proper political force. Those who trained militarily and also acquired "political knowledge" proved the best Frelimo militants, the "true interpreters of Frelimo policy." As the army grew, there was a degree of rivalry with political organizers that preceded them inside the country. Because of their "lower political understanding" district political leaders thought that the armed struggle would be short. And some (such as N'Kavandame) began acting with "wrong conceptions" comporting themselves like traditional chiefs. Frelimo had to depend upon trained politico-military cadres to correct deficiencies.[32]

The necessity of a long guerrilla struggle to make political transformation possible was crucial to dos Santos's thinking. This meant sending as many militants to Soviet bloc countries as possible. According to Valdimir Shubin: "Large scale training for Frelimo fighters was organized in Perevalnoe [Crimea] and other places in spite of many difficulties, especially due to [an] inadequate level of education." Frelimo officials seemed satisfied with the quality of military training, but they

> noted that the Soviets 'wanted to show that they had fulfilled the quotas' and would not admit that some students failed. A similar situation arose in the 'Party school', that is the Institute of Social Sciences, where Mozambicans received political training. 'By definition all those who were coming out were good.'[33]

One consequence of this reality was Frelimo's reliance on political-military cadres brandishing diplomas but possessing only rudimentary knowledge, blind loyalty, and a potential for irrational brutality.

Dos Santos's role in fashioning a post-Mondlane Frelimo was the result of his longstanding commitment to the goal of a socialist state. He wrote:

> [W]e are convinced that the building of a new society in Mozambique demands a full scale war against all those negative aspects, all the vices and corruption which, as we know characterize the colonial society from which we come. This involves [...] strong individual effort, continual self-criticism. The transformation of man himself will only be achieved if each of us understands clearly that genuine liberation means liquidation

of all the inequalities which exist among the many different groups in our country. This can only be accomplished in the present phase of the struggle, if we [achieve a commitment of everyone to] a unity in defense of the interests of the people. And only if each of us commits himself completely to revolutionary action; that is, assumes a complete involvement in the everyday struggle, in real concrete practice—which cannot be done spontaneously or at random but needs to be defined and disciplined. The expulsion of [an undisciplined] Simango was, in this regard, quite a natural phenomenon: the rejection of impure elements which every revolution carries within itself. Revolution […] is a process of rejection of impure elements and assimilation of revolutionary ideas and practices.[34]

As an example of the transformation that dos Santos saw developing in the organization, he cited the role of women, who could now speak and be heard. Women had come to serve as guerrillas, technicians, and members of Frelimo's Central Committee. In the past they had been excluded from such roles and were never to be seen in a council of elders or in other traditional bodies. The role of dos Santos's wife was a case in point. In 1968 dos Santos married a white South African, Pamela Beris. From a Jewish family and a militant in the African National Congress (ANC), she worked full-time in Dar es Salaam as a founding member of the Mozambican Women's Organization (OMM) and served with Frelimo's journalism section.

With Mondlane's moderating influence gone, the defection of N'Kavandame, the expulsion of Simango along with other defections and purges, Frelimo was now free to embrace and add "the scientific theory of dialectical and historical materialism" to its struggle. It could now

show up the capitalist nature of colonial exploitation and the class character of the liberation struggle. Ranged against each other in that struggle are the Portuguese bourgeoisie, working hand in glove with the bourgeoisie of the United States, Britain, Belgium, South Africa and other countries, and [on the other side] the majority of the Mozambique people, primarily the plantation workers, miners, and factory workers, railwaymen and dockers and the peasants.

Dos Santos wrote that, "Our own experience, short as it is, furnishes ample proof" of our ability to "deal telling blows" to imperialism. "Now, after 50 years, the October Revolution which opened a new epoch in the

146   J.A. MARCUM

history of mankind, continues to be the beacon that illuminates the path of oppressed nations to freedom. And its great leader, Lenin, will always live on in the minds of men."[35]

By the time of Mondlane's death, the USA, of course, had bowed out of the picture and was no longer even a bit player. Contrastingly, the Soviets remained seriously engaged—and in competition with the Chinese, who, in 1965, began training Frelimo soldiers at Nachingwea and elsewhere in Tanzania. Dos Santos's ties to the Soviets were especially close. Assessing dos Santos at the OAU conference at Addis Ababa in 1963, Mario de Andrade told an inquiring Soviet delegate, Latyp Maksudov, that Mondlane was an honest man but a "missionary," not a politician. Mondlane, he reportedly said, "doesn't hamper dos Santos's work and here a lot can be done. Dos Santos is working, therefore Frelimo exists and acts." Speaking candidly, dos Santos himself told Maksudov:

> Everybody knows and we know that Frelimo President Eduardo Mondlane is an American, but now there is no [other] man in Mozambique who could lead the struggle and around whom the forces, struggling for independence could unite. Mondlane up to now is the only man—educated, who has connections and influence abroad. After all, he is [black] and not a white or mulatto, as I am. One should not forget also, that Mondlane is able to get money. True, they say he is getting it from the USA government, but this money goes to the struggle [...] We decided from the very beginning to let Mondlane be at the head of the movement, and we shall work inside the movement and guide it. Later (if needed) it would be possible to replace Mondlane.[36]

Faith in dos Santos was echoed in the advice of the Cuban ambassador to Tanzania, Pablo Rivalta, who urged Che Guevara not to work with Mondlane, who was under "American influence." Instead he recommended that the Cuban revolutionary work with dos Santos, in whom he had "utmost trust."[37] Further confirmation of the Soviet commitment to dos Santos came from Paulo Gumane. In 1965 he reported that the Soviet embassy in Cairo had urged him to reconcile with Frelimo and get rid of Mondlane later. Meanwhile, Dos Santos and Simango would send off as many militants to the USSR as possible for a long-term takeover. According to Gumane, the Soviets told him that Eduardo Mondlane was just a disposable "figurehead."[38]

9 MONDLANE'S ASSASINATION 147

The Mondlanes viewed Dos Santos's antipathy toward the USA seriously. In 1966 Janet Mondlane received the copy of a letter to the chair of the Senate Foreign Relations Committee opposing the appointment of Admiral William Tapley Bennett as US Ambassador to Portugal. Admiral Bennett had promoted American intervention to suppress a popular 1965 revolt in the Dominican Republic on the basis of "fragmentary and disputable evidence" of Communist participation in that revolt. The letter argued that

> to appoint someone who has demonstrated such poor judgment to a country [Portugal] that uses the issue of Communism in order to implicate us in colonial wars where we might also find a few Communists—for there is armed insurrection in Portugal's three African colonies—is to risk involving us again in costly misadventures.

On reading it, Mrs. Mondlane responded: "I was so pleased to see it. If you have not already done so, would you send a copy to Marcelino dos Santos, Secretary for Foreign Affairs for Frelimo. Their box number is 15274." She continued: "The struggle grows. Yet, no doubt, it will still continue for some time. If only the United States would take up a position against Portugal on this matter!"[39] Bennett was confirmed and served as ambassador to Portugal from 1966 through 1969. On a visit to Mozambique he reported himself "tremendously impressed" by the "progress and well being of the population and absence of racial discrimination."

Dos Santos firmly controlled public presentation of a "correct" Frelimo image. An example was his response to an initiative by Herbert Shore, one of Mondlane's ardent admirers, who wished to publish a biography of Frelimo's founding president. Shore asked Frelimo to provide him access to relevant documents written by Mondlane. Dos Santos welcomed Shore's decision to write such a book but insisted Shore first agree to "let us read your manuscript, for political approval, before it is published." Dos Santos wrote,

> We hope you understand that this is necessary in order for Frelimo to be able to take the responsibility for and acknowledge anything you might write about Dr. Mondlane regarding his work in the struggle for freedom in Mozambique [...] We are sure [your work] will be of great benefit to our struggle.[40]

148   J.A. MARCUM

Later, Janet Mondlane was reportedly barred from writing a biography of her late husband on the grounds that it might diminish Machel's standing.[41] Similarly, when Joao Nhambiu was scheduled to speak as the official representative of UNEMO at the 1965 meeting of CONCP in Dar es Salaam, dos Santos demanded to review his text in advance. In response to the censorship, Nhambiu tossed his prepared remarks and limited himself to simple greetings on behalf of the student organization.

Eduardo Mondlane's Christian beliefs were incompatible with dos Santos's dialectical materialism. Yet he permitted the ascendancy of dos Santos's Marxist ideology within the movement and in late 1968 publicly hailed the foreign secretary and the "epic quality" of dos Santos's latest poem, "REVOLUTION." The war, Mondlane said, is "generating a popular reaction against Portugal and everything it stands for." And with the movement's efforts to promote literacy at all ranks, soldiers are now reading and absorbing dos Santos's poetry "in their military camps."[42]

SAMORA MACHEL

In 1974 Samora Machel declared:

> The socialist countries, because they have destroyed the system of exploitation, constitute the strategic rear base of the struggle of the oppressed peoples and classes, and hence the natural alliance between us. The Mozambique people and Frelimo will never forget the exemplary internationalist solidarity extended to them.[43]

But some socialist countries were held to be more "exemplary" than others. In the wake of Mondlane's assassination, Frelimo sent two delegations to its socialist benefactors. In July–August 1969, Simango, Joaquim Chissano and Candido Mondlane traveled to Moscow. According to Valdimir Shubin, Simango was welcomed as a member of what was then the ruling triumvirate, "though the Soviets would have preferred to have discussions with Machel, who was regarded as the strongest leader in Frelimo." Shubin added, "Alas, Machel decided to lead a similar delegation to Beijing."[44] Later, Simango supporters tried in vain to dissuade the Soviets from supporting the post-troika leadership of Machel and dos Santos. Seeking to curry favor by impugning leaders associated with Mondlane, Simango told the Soviet embassy in Dar es Salaam that after Mondlane's assassination "an American diplomat visited

9 MONDLANE'S ASSASINATION   149

its Headquarters to find out who would receive the US $100,000 annual allocation, destined for the late Frelimo president." But the Soviets gave their support to the new leadership. Shubin wrote:

> No doubt, Samora Machel was an extraordinary figure. Yevsyukov claims that he knew "the peculiarities of Machel's nature and the motives of his actions" well enough to paint a picture of this "natural hero and a simple man": "He was a talented man [...] a person of natural gifts, but he was lacking education possessed, say by Eduardo Mondlane [...] He was resolute and capable of infecting people with his enthusiasm; he knew the crowd and knew how to influence it. He could speak to simple people and surprised experienced diplomats and politicians by his mind."[45]

During the years of armed struggle, relations between the Soviets and Frelimo "developed steadily, though rather slowly and it seemed like their scope did not entirely satisfy the Mozambicans." *Pravda* correspondent Oleg Ignatyev visited "liberated areas in 1971 and large-scale training for Frelimo fighters was organized in Perevalnoe and elsewhere in the USSR." Financial assistance was also substantial. Yet as of 1973 Frelimo "received just US $85,000, much less than the MPLA and PAIGC in tiny Guinea-Bissau."[46] In financial terms support from the OAU's Liberation Committee outstripped that of the Soviet Union. For 1970–71, the OAU committee budgeted $325,000 for Frelimo.[47]

In 1970, taking advantage of Frelimo's disarray in the wake of Mondlane's death, the Portuguese mounted a major military offensive, a desperate effort to reverse Frelimo's military penetration southward into Tete and Manica-Sofala. Operation Gordian Knot, led by Brigadier General Kaulza de Arriaga, hurled a force of as many as 35,000 replete with planes, helicopters, and artillery into a fierce effort to seal off Frelimo's infiltration routes into northern Mozambique and destroy its ability to press southward into Manica-Sofala and Tete. De Arriaga consulted with General Westmoreland for advice from US experience in Vietnam and, like the Americans, inflicted high casualties on the enemy (somewhere between 400 and 600 killed and over a thousand captured). But with Portugal now spending over forty percent of its budget on African wars, including a stubborn, costly military disaster in tiny Guinea-Bissau, the government could not sustain its expensive Mozambique offensive.

150   J.A. MARCUM

By 1972 it moved to a lesser strategy of using small search-and-destroy units, regrouping civilians in fortified villages (*aldeamentos*), increasing use of black African recruits, and supporting traditional chiefs in Niassa, where the historic policy of indirect rule had created vested interest in the colonial status quo. Yet Frelimo guerrillas outflanked Portuguese units and on November 9, 1972, opened a counter-offensive in Tete. Weary of the war and its continuing casualty rolls, discord grew within Portuguese ranks pitting, for example, regular army conscripts against spartan PIDE units. And economic stress grew as the government proved unable to sustain the overstretch of a three-country anti-insurgency.

It was at this point that Chinese aid became especially significant. Enjoying close ties with the Tanzanians, Chinese instructors had been training Frelimo soldiers at bases located in Tanzania since 1965. In September 1971, after a delegation headed by Samora Machel was accorded a rare all-night discussion with Chinese Premier Zhou Enlai, the Mozambicans were informed that a shipload of 10,000 tons of weapons and ammunition was leaving Shanghai for Dar es Salaam. "These supplies helped Frelimo to rebuff the Portuguese offensive and then to launch [its own] general offensive in 1972."[48]

On the Soviet side, Machel made his first visit to Moscow in 1970, when he met with the Chief of the General Staff, Viktor Kulikov. The result was a stream of new supplies: guns, lorries, fuel, food and increased financial support. Until then the Soviets had exercised a "certain restraint towards Frelimo either because Machel was considered pro-Beijing or because he was critical of Moscow."[49]

Machel was known to have warned Oliver Tambo in 1974 to be wary of the South Africa's Communist Party because of its connection with Moscow. "The USSR and CPSU [Communist Party] were not genuine friends of the African people, were racist and were interested in dominating Africa." Shubin attributed this sentiment to a pro-Chinese bias that was strengthened when Machel visited China in February 1975 and was "received virtually as a head of state. The Chinese even sent a private plane to bring him from Dar es Salaam to Beijing, and Mozambicans, always 'protocol-minded', highly appreciated this fact. However, apart from protocol matters, Beijing's political stand perhaps was closer to Machel's thoughts. Yevsyukov believes that Machel's characteristic feature was 'leftist extremism'; more than once he spoke about "commitment and respect to J.V. Stalin. Later, during his trip to the Soviet

9 MONDLANE'S ASSASINATION   151

Republic of Georgia at the head of the Mozambican official delegation, at his request he was provided with Stalin's portrait."[50]

In 1987 I was in Moscow and visited the French embassy. I encountered a group of African students seeking visas to leave the Soviet Union because of racism at Lumumba University and in Soviet society at large. Machel was sensitive to the racial attitudes that emerged in a more public fashion after the fall of the Soviet Union. Not an intellectual/poet like the theoretician dos Santos, Machel was from a rural background and resonated with the earthiness of Maoist political-military doctrine.

Machel was born into a farming family on September 29, 1933, at Madragoa (which is now Chilembe), in the Gaza province. His paternal grandfather had played a major role in what was known as the Maguigane rebellion of 1890. Both maternal grandparents had been deported to the forced labor island of São Tomé, where they died. From an early age he was embittered by Portuguese colonial policies. His father was compelled to grow cotton and paid considerably less for it than what white farmers received. Arbitrary colonial administrators forbade his father to brand his cattle in order to prevent their theft.

Machel attended a Catholic mission school in Zonguene in the Gaza province, where he completed fourth grade and then trained as a nurse at the Miguel Bombarda Hospital in Lourenco Marques, a non-degree conferring option open to Africans. He worked night shift there during the 1950s and was paid less than his white counterparts for the same work. He organized protests against this discrimination. Meanwhile during this period, prime agricultural real estate in the Limpopo area around his family's farm was appropriated for white settlers. He met Mondlane during the latter's visit to Lourenco Marques in 1961 and with the founding of Frelimo escaped via Botswana and the assistance of a serendipitous airlift by ANC officials to Dar es Salaam. He left behind a wife and four children.

Frelimo sent Machel to Algeria for military training in June 1963. On his return in April 1964, he was made head of the movement's Kongwa military camp in Tanzania. Machel played a critical role in military planning and organizing. When Magaia was killed in 1966, Mondlane named him successor. Under Machel's leadership, southerners replaced Maconde and Macua military commanders. He reportedly spent much of his time visiting guerrillas inside the country, and gained a reputation for forceful, effective leadership. Incontrovertibly, Machel and his military steadily consolidated their ascendancy within Frelimo and over ever larger areas of northern Mozambique.

NOTES

1. *The Sunday News*, Nairobi, November 24, 1968.
2. Fredericks interview with Schneidman, "American Foreign Policy..." p. 216.
3. *War/Peace Report*, January 1966, p. 7. As a student he had admired the USA for its sympathy for colonial peoples, its refusal to colonize the Caribbean, and its ethical democratic values, which, unlike communism, "enable the individual to grow." Examples of such expression: Mondlane, "Anti-Colonialism in the United States," in G.H. Curry, *Self-Government Movements in Australia and New Zealand in the Nineteenth Century*, University of Sydney, 1957, pp. 187–201; Mondlane, "Woodrow Wilson and the Idea of Self-Determination in Africa," typescript, Woodrow Wilson Foundation, Maxwell School, Syracuse, N.Y., April 2, 1962.
4. Marcum Papers, Box 36/8.
5. Memorandum by State Department researcher Thomas L. Hughes, August 1968, quoted in Cabrita, *Mozambique*, p. 57.
6. Marcum Papers, Box 36/8.
7. Frelimo, Press Release, Dar es Salaam, April 4, 1969, Marcum Papers, Box 35/3.
8. For analysis of facts and speculation including suspected PIDE involvement see Cabrita, *Mozambique*, pp. 59–62.
9. Hawley, "Refugees in Kenya ..." p. 3.
10. "Mozambique: A Chief Surrenders," *Africa Confidential*, London, no. 8, April 11, 1969, pp. 7–8.
11. Documents of the 2nd Congress, p. 21. Marcum Papers, Box 35/3.
12. Nungu message from Cabo Delgado, presumably translated by Simango and dated May 18, 1969, Marcum Papers, Box 37/8
13. Uria Simango interview with author, Dar es Salaam, May 18, 1967.
14. Aquino de Braganca, "L'itinéraire d'Uria Simango," *Africa*, no. 3, Paris, November 24–December 7, 1969, p. 12.
15. Ibid.
16. Ibid.
17. Ibid.
18. Letter, December 17, 1962 from General Secretary of the United Church Board of World Ministries, John Reuling, offering the scholarship; Uria Simango response seeking delay in implementation, January 30, 1963, Marcum Papers, Box 37/8.
19. "Forcing the Portuguese Out," *Anti-Apartheid News*, London, March, 1966.
20. *The Mizan Newsletter*, London, vol. 6, no. 6, June 1964, p. 30.
21. "Mozambique: A Chief Surrenders," *Africa Confidential*, p. 8.

9 MONDLANE'S ASSASINATION 153

22. Uria T. Simango, "Gloomy Situation in Frelimo," Dar es Salaam, November 3, 1969. Marcum Papers, Box 37/8.
23. Frelimo, "Communique," Dar es Salaam, November 8, 1969, Marcum Papers, Box 35/3.
24. Janet Mondlane, Statement to Tanzanian Police on History of Mozambique Institute, March 6, 1968, Marcum Papers, Box 37/3
25. Miguel Artur Murupa, "Statement: To the Government of the United Republic of Tanzania," typescript, Dar es Salaam, February 7, 1970, Marcum Papers, Box 37/3
26. Ibid.
27. Murupa interview, "Portugal Vencera," in *Noticias de Portugal*, Lisbon, June 3, 1971; see also Murupa, *Portuguese Africa in Perspective: the Making of a Multiracial Nation*, Lisbon, 1973.
28. Richard Gibson, *African Liberation Movements*, Oxford University Press, 1972, p. 283.
29. Interview with author, Dar es Salaam, May 20, 1967.
30. Shubin, *The Hot Cold War*, p. 121.
31. *Remarques Congolaises* (Brussels), November 24, 1961, p. 447.
32. "Off the Cuff: Marcelino dos Santos Talks to Sechaba," *Sechaba* (official organ of South African ANC), Dar es Salaam, October 1970, pp. 14–18.
33. Shubin, *The Hot Cold War*, p. 127.
34. Quoted in Liberation Support Movement, Boubaker Adjali, "Frelimo: Interview with Marcelino dos Santos," Richmond, British Columbia, October 1971, pp. 3, 5, Marcum Papers, Box 35/5.
35. Marcelino dos Santos, "The Revolutionary Perspective in Mozambique," *World Marxist Review: Problems of Peace and Socialism*, Prague, January 1968, pp. 43–44.
36. Shubin, *The Hot Cold War*, p. 122.
37. Cabrita, *Mozambique*, p. 45
38. Interview with author, Dar es Salaam, February 4, 1965.
39. Letter to Senator William Fulbright, May 2, 1966, signed by seven heads of department, including Professor Charles Hamilton (Political Science) at Lincoln University, Pennsylvania: and letter to the author from Janet Mondlane, Dar es Salaam, May 9, 1966. Marcum Papers, Box 37/2.
40. Letter from dos Santos to Shore, June 27, 1969. Marcum Papers, Box 37/7. Herbert Shore never wrote the biography but donated his collection of Mondlane material to the library archives at Oberlin College and the University of Southern California (USC).
41. Cabrita, *Mozambique*, p. 88.
42. Poem by dos Santos quoted by Eduardo Mondlane, "Nationalism and Development in Mozambique," typescript, UCLA conference, Los Angeles, February 27–28, 1968.

43. Liberation Support Movement, *Mozambique: Revolution or Reaction?*, Samora Machel, "The Weapons that Brought Us Victory," September 25, 1974, p. 28, Marcum Papers, Box 35/5.
44. Shubin, *The Hot Cold War*
45. Ibid.
46. Ibid.
47. Africa Contemporary Record, Annual Survey and Documents, 1970–71, London, p. B587.
48. Shubin, *The Hot Cold War*, pp. 128–129
49. Ibid.
50. Ibid.

CHAPTER 10

The Collapse of Portugal

The US Tilt

By early 1969 it was clear that Mondlane's pessimism and premonitions concerning American policy were justified. Hope for an enlightened American policy collapsed with the inauguration of Richard Nixon. The new administration restored a retrograde inner consistency to Luso-American relations. After a decade of idealism, ambivalence, and fudging, the USA (mirroring the opportunism of American private interests, such as those of Gulf Oil in Angola) chose the incumbent colonial regime over its challengers.

In May 1962 Premier Salazar commented bitterly that American policy left Portugal to fight a difficult and costly war in Africa "not without alliances but without allies." But in December 1971, with the successful negotiation of a new Azores base accord, Salazar's successor, Marcello Caetano, could proclaim: "The treaty is a political act in which the solidarity of interests between the two countries is recognized and it's in the name of that solidarity that we put an instrument of action at the disposal of our American friends, who are also now allies."[1]

Shortly after taking office, the staff of President Nixon's National Security Advisor, Henry Kissinger, sought out Portuguese officials and assured them that the policies of the Kennedy/Johnson era had been essentially ditched. Reflecting Cold War preoccupations and racial prejudice, the American government set new ground rules decreeing that

© The Author(s) 2018
J.A. Marcum, *Conceiving Mozambique*, African Histories and Modernities, https://doi.org/10.1007/978-3-319-65987-9_10

155

henceforth there would be absolutely no government contact with African liberation movements or their leaders. In a new National Security Study Memorandum, Kissinger and the White House adopted a policy for southern Africa based on the following assumption:

> The whites are here to stay and the only way that constructive change can come about is through them. There is no hope for the blacks to gain the political rights they seek through violence, which will only lead to chaos and increased opportunities for the communists. We can, by selective relaxation of our stance toward the white regimes, encourage some modifications of their current racial and colonial policies.[2]

The "Azores" package that Caetano wrested from Washington was on the face of it substantial. It extended US base rights in the Azores through 1973 in return for a two-year aid package that included $30 million in agricultural commodities, $5 million in non-military equipment (e.g., road building machinery) and eligibility for up to $400 million in Export-Import Bank financing for infrastructure and other development projects.[3] However, the deal did not free up sales of the arms that Portugal's 140,000 expeditionary forces really needed: combat and transport aircraft, anti-missile artillery, etc. Some 40,000 Portuguese soldiers confronted Soviet SAM missiles and the misery of Guinea-Bissau's malaria- and guerrilla-infested marshes. They needed the equipment appropriate to these challenges, whatever that might mean. Though American support for Caetano was enough to arouse African anger, nothing Washington did or could do would alter the basic fact that Portugal's human capacity for colonial war was draining away. During the 1960s and beyond, the emigration of draft-age Portuguese men to other European countries had reached hundreds of thousands, and discord and fatigue within military ranks were growing.

The onset of the Nixon/Kissinger era coincided with internal upheaval within Frelimo. The relationship between Frelimo and Washington was simplified starkly. "Frelimo would no longer have contact with any American officials. Not only did the United States [now] lack a 'client' within the organization, but neither Frelimo nor Washington saw value in maintaining any ties."[4] The United States, by it own choice, was no longer to be a player in the struggle over the future of an independent Mozambique.

American indifference to the African cause was epitomized by a response that the Assistant Secretary of State for African Affairs, David Newsom, gave to an inquiry I made in October 1971. In the wake of the sale of two Boeing 707s for military transport use despite public pledges of a continued embargo arms sales for use in Africa, I wrote to Newsom asking him to respond to published claims that Portugal had greatly increased imports of US herbicides (defoliants) for use against African insurgents. Newsom replied that herbicides were "not the subject of special licensing arrangements" and "not identified in the U.S. export figures." Consequently, there was "no way of determining" how commercial exports of herbicides "may have fluctuated in recent years." No way? What he left unsaid was that there was no thought of a government inquiry into the matter.

Collapse and Chaos

The Frelimo secretary for information, Jorge Rebelo, spent March of 1967 in Cabo Delgado visiting bush villages. He reported that he saw no Portuguese (African villagers had been regrouped in *aldeamentos*, or armed hamlets). He praised progress in Frelimo's efforts to build local political support and claimed that "liberated areas" had a population of roughly 800,000, most of whom were under nourished, ill-clothed, and in desperate need of education. Rebelo acknowledged a need to arbitrate between ethnic differences, namely disputes about who was or was not fighting well. This required face-to-face mediation to overcome local feuding. Overall, Rebelo underscored Frelimo expectations of a "long, hard fight as we move south."[5] This official Frelimo strategy of building slowly but solidly found expression in official publications: Frelimo "est en train de bâtir la liberté graduellement sans action de l'éclat ou succès dramatiques mais avec un rythme ferme."[6] With the bloody persistence of a guerrilla insurgency, the fight did, in fact, move slowly and ineluctably southward. In July 1970, Prime Minister Salazar died of a heart attack and was replaced by Marcelo Caetano.

Portugal's obduracy continued without change. This was dramatized in an exchange in 1971 between Averell Harriman and the Portuguese ambassador to the USA. As Chair of the Democratic Party's Policy Committee on International Affairs, Harriman endorsed and distributed a blunt and realistic political assessment written by his former State Department colleague, Wayne Fredericks. It declared that a decade after

158   J.A. MARCUM

armed rebellion began in northern Angola, Portugal's military forces were bogged down fighting African insurgents in ever more extensive areas of Angola, Mozambique and Guinea-Bissau. Lisbon was being forced to spend 45% of its budget fighting these distant colonial wars. As a result of the wars' increasing social-political costs, political opposition was growing in Portugal. "Tragically," Fredericks report explained,

> the political policies of the Marcello Caetano government are not serving to extricate Portugal from this debilitating colonial conflict. If, in theory, Africans have access to administrative and political posts in the African territories, only a token handful have actually been elevated into the governmental system. In the absence of compensatory educational programs at the technical and secondary levels designed to promote a significant African participation within the territories' economic and social development, the reality of social and economic deprivation continues to render meaningless official pronouncements about racial equality. Obviously, the yardstick of "individual merit" when applied under circumstances of gross inequality simply serves to perpetuate white domination.

> Even more ominously, new constitutional reforms devolving more authority upon white dominated governments in Luanda and Lourenco Marques threaten to push the African population even farther from genuine participation in the political process. Responding to demands by white settler minorities totaling perhaps half a million persons, Lisbon has pledged to transfer more political power into the hands of precisely those whose interests and attitudes incline them toward a more repressive policy vis-à-vis the disenfranchised African majority.[7]

Portugal's ambassador to Washington, Vasco Vieira Garin, reacted fiercely to Fredericks's analysis in a letter to Harriman on May 6, 1971. Nothing had changed in Lisbon's thinking. Without recognizing a sense of belated urgency or a need for a reasonable time frame to reconcile "individual merit" with the massive educational deficit and illiteracy of the African majority, Ambassador Garin argued:

> Considering that European Portugal is a small country with very limited military resources, and considering the ample military assistance the terrorist organizations receive from the Communist states it would have been impossible to maintain the unity of those vast territories against the will of the populations. It is precisely the resistance of the populations of Angola, Mozambique and Portuguese Guinea against both the subversive

10 THE COLLAPSE OF PORTUGAL   159

campaign from the outside and the frequent territorial border raids that has been the principal reason for the thorough defeat of such attempts in the last ten years.

[...] As the people of these Provinces enjoy full representation in the administrative and legislative bodies, both at the provincial and national levels [...] it is they who shall decide upon their political future, not a handful of discontents or professional agitators operating from some of the neighboring African states.[8]

With delusional self-confidence Lisbon continued to embrace the concept of a multi-continental polity extending from Guinea to Timor. Speaking to the United Nations as late as October 1973, just seven months before a military coup overthrew the Caetano government, Foreign Minister Rui Manuel Patricio predicted that if present trends continued, "the Portuguese nation is heading towards a great Euro-African state, with the black majority in political dominance." Patricio added, "With the Cabora Bassa and [Angolan] Cunene River hydroelectric projects and foreign investment pouring into agriculture and industry, the effect is of incalculable magnitude." He then argued,

Whoever will take the trouble to study the facts in depth will reach the conclusion that in the overall balance of the economic and financial flows the positive balance belongs to the African part and the negative to the European. This is a fact that it is hard for some of our friends and advisers from northern Europe to understand. But how can we pretend that the racists of Scandinavia or members of the Dutch Parliament, saturated by centuries of colonialist mercantilism, would be able to grasp the spirit of a people that created Brazil and gave orientation to what is known as luso-tropical civilization.[9]

Lisbon clung to visions of imperial wealth and power. There was no space for an accommodation with African nationalism.

The expectation of a protracted insurgency was shared among Western observers. Most failed to perceive the signs of fatal Portuguese military fatigue. At a Phelps-Stokes Fund seminar on African–American Relations at Jamestown, Virginia, in March 1974, I argued against the common perception that a military stalemate would be long in breaking.

What was happening within Portugal and its military was of equal importance to the gradual expansion of guerrilla war into wider and

160   J.A. MARCUM

wider areas of Mozambique, Guinea-Bissau, and Angola. General Antonio de Spinola, commander of Portuguese forces in Guinea-Bissau, openly abandoned assimilationist tenets and opted for a "pluricultural solution." He chose a pragmatic policy of cultivating ethnic leadership and tribal councils. At the same time, Lisbon took steps toward a dissimulated disengagement, a policy dubbed "regionalization," reminiscent of the American withdrawal policy of "Vietnamization." By 1974 this had led to substantial progress toward Africanizing the armed forces. That, in turn, meant literacy and job skills for African recruits. And it meant saddling the cost of counter-insurgency more and more on provincial, as distinct from metropolitan, budgets. The financial burden of the colonial wars assumed by the "provinces" increased from 25% in 1967 to 32% in 1971. The metropole was on its way out. In the process it was forging armies that were more and more African armies, in part officered by Africans. And in due course with training that included literacy acquisition, these men would be expecting civilian jobs commensurate with skills gained.

In order to maintain its colonial rule, Lisbon doubled the size of its military and mounted costly programs, regrouping rural populations in *aldeamentos*, built roads, bought planes. It expanded primary education and social services as part of a belated and ultimately futile effort to make a reality of assimilation. All this bore a heavy price tag. Portugal was obliged to reverse earlier dogma and adopt an open door to foreign investment in Angolan oil, diamonds, and iron, and to go beyond extractive enterprise into industrial activity such as production of wood pulp, asphalt, tire manufacturing and the development of hydroelectric power (including a massive Cabora Bassa dam on the Zambezi River). Under Caetano, longstanding policies which had aimed at blocking "neocolonial" endeavors by "capitalist syndicates" to wrest control of Portuguese Africa were reversed.

Another important trend, I argued, was the increasing appearance of socio-political dysfunction in metropolitan Portugal. Counter-insurgency was costing something in the neighborhood of $400 million a year. Maintaining armies of over 150,000 in Africa had meant economic dislocation and postponement of domestic development programs. It had meant stagnancy in domestic agriculture, a high rate of inflation (some 22% in 1973), and massive emigration—a million and a half working outside of Portugal (as against 3.2 million

10 THE COLLAPSE OF PORTUGAL   161

working inside). Portugal's population was not ten million, as most demographic projections assumed but something in the order of 8.4 million. Consequent labor shortages in Portugal had led to the importation of Cape Verdean workers, which, in turn, for the first time, brought racial tensions into Portugal. There had also been a recrudescence of sporadic anti-regime terrorism and sabotage. Increasingly, I pointed out, the situation facing Portugal looked analogous to that which faced France in the late 1950s. The military's needs were insatiable. The generals were increasingly impatient with a civilian government that did not provide all the expensive weaponry they felt they needed. And prospects for military victory appeared ever more dubious in a war-weary country with an ambitious, swollen military establishment. In short, it was hardly a stable situation. I concluded that "a general lack of knowledge about social, political and economic realities in Portugal" and a "curious lack of scholarship" concerning contemporary Portugal contrasted with scholarship relating to France at the time of its ordeal in Algeria. The predictive capability of America and other observers, I asserted, had therefore been severely "handicapped."[10]

Twenty-seven days after I made my presentation, a coup led by young army officers overthrew the government of Marcelo Caetano, who fled to exile in Brazil. Initial shock was followed by chaotic reaction. Secretary of State Kissinger, who had been uninterested in southern Africa, became alarmed over the fearsome prospect of a Communist takeover of a NATO ally and its colonies. For the Soviets and Chinese, the collapse of the old regime in Portugal was a chance to establish a new socialist state. For Portuguese democrats it was a chance to end the colonial wars and promote a confederation of the metropole with autonomous African provinces. For most of the 200,000 white settlers in Mozambique it was a chance to make a Rhodesia-style Unilateral Declaration of Independence (UDI). For anti-Frelimo nationalists it was a chance to forge a politically pluralist state in collaboration with the Portuguese. For Frelimo it was an opportunity to propel their military force of some 10,000 southward and, with the collapse and passivity of the Portuguese military, seize control of the country before other contenders could mobilize and overcome Frelimo's military advantage. Suddenly and unexpectedly Portugal and its African territories moved center stage in the East–West Cold War.

The Scramble

Frelimo had a clear sense of what it wanted: the elimination of all current or prospective political challenges to its claim to exclusive power in Mozambique. Dos Santos explained the rationale for such a monopoly of power to members of a Danish support group who asked him: "Now that you are independent, you are going to create new political parties, aren't you?" His response was:

> That was something that really went beyond our understanding. During the liberation struggle we had continuously worked to achieve unity. Why should we create divisions when we were independent? [...] We managed to end tribalism, regionalism, ethnicism, racism and the divisive problem of religion. We were able to build unity. Why should different groups in the country not be able to build deeper unity? This was even necessary.[11]

Foolish actions by Frelimo's would-be competitors played into Frelimo's ambition. In particular, in a desperate attempt to stave off a single-party outcome, competitors, new and old, became tainted by joining into brief and failed efforts of white groups in Lourenco Marques and Beira to spark a takeover by coup. After that failure, they regrouped outside the country and staked a claim to the right to compete freely in the post-colonial sun. Some of them were seasoned opponents, such as COREMO, and some just sprang to life in the wake of Portuguese collapse.

In the thick of their initiatives was Arthur Xavier Lambo Vilankulu, a Dickinson College (Pennsylvania) graduate who had spent a two-year period broadcasting *A Voz da Frelimo* on Dar es Salaam radio and then, disaffected, led UNEMO-US in support of Simango and became a history professor at Jersey City State College. In a document entitled "My Visit to Mozambique: Impressions after Thirteen Year Absence," he sought private American support for educational and social projects in Mozambique and championed the cause of an ephemeral "movement for unity and reconciliation" (MONIREMO) under an acting chairman, Pedro Mapanguelana Mondlane, a nephew of the fallen Frelimo president.[12] For MONIREMO, "all ethnic and tribal groups" were to be represented "in the spirit of one Mozambique," with membership open to Europeans who choose Mozambique as their homeland. Then, in August 1974, Vilankulu threw his lot in with the leaders of five movements who, meeting in Beira, decided to unite their diverse groups within an umbrella organization known as the Partido de Coligacao de Mocambique (PCN).[13] The PCN argued that "the future of Mozambique should not be compromised by any accord negotiated and reached between the Lisbon Government and any Organization or political group which excludes others, because no organization should claim the right to be the sole legitimate representative of the Mozambican people without the test of democratic process." It called for reconstruction and political mobilization "without intimidation, partiality, dishonesty and excitement of hatred against each other" and a multiracial society with respect for "freedom of expression, traditions and cultural values of various races, social sectors and ethnic groups." It formed a "national executive commission" headed by Uria Simango (president), Paulo Gumane (vice-president), and Basilio Banda (secretary general).[14] It purported to subsume a wide range of participants, extending from Simango-Gwenjere Africanists to Mohamed Hanife-Ahmed Haider with multiracial technical expertise and even inclusive of the Maconde hyperbole of Narciso Mbule.

They were united only by a common anti-Frelimo independence agenda. But on January 9, 1975, Vilankulu was obliged to issue an urgent PCN press release from New York. The militarily impotent PCN had been outpaced by Frelimo. Vilankulu denounced Machel and dos Santos for rejecting PCN's calls for reconciliation and decried the arrest of over 1670 people by a Frelimo transitional government, arrests that included "all eleven of the PCN executive committee." Vilankulu charged that Frelimo leaders had always "avoided elections of any kind," having come to power after Eduardo Mondlane's death by usurping power.

As a PCN spokesman, Vilankulu appealed to the Portuguese to use their waning authority to obtain the release of all political prisoners and "in order to obviate a possible civil war [...] grant independence to the Mozambican people, not to a particular group or organization." There was no single party in Portugal claiming to be the sole representative of the Portuguese people pending the outcome of general elections, so "why," he asked, "should the case be different in Mozambique?"[15] His appeal fell on deaf ears. The USA had long since lost influence within the Mozambique independence struggle. The exhausted Portuguese military refused to enforce government authority. And the young Portuguese officers of the Armed Forces Movement (MFA) were eager to hand over

164   J.A. MARCUM

power as quickly as possible to left-leaning revolutionaries. In negotiations led by Joaquim Chissano, the Portuguese turned power over to Frelimo. Thus, Frelimo was given a free hand to conceive Mozambique as it wished.

REVENGE

"The dejected cast shuffled on to the dusty stage, a bush clearing in southern Tanzania, to confess an array of crimes against the Mozambique revolution." So wrote David Martin of the London *Observer* from the Nachingwea military camp on March 23, 1975. The first Western correspondent to be taken to the camp just 17 miles from the Mozambican border, Martin observed a seven-hour-long trial of 200 men and two women for treason, murder, sabotage, and political deviation. Samora Machel paraded the accused before an audience of some 3000 young men. "There is no revolution without traitors," he exclaimed. "But we will not kill them, we will learn from them." Machel perceived the show trial as an exercise in political education, Martin wrote, "the like of which one would probably not find anywhere else outside China."

"Carefully directing the mounting drama," Machel introduced his cast, leaving big names like Paulo Gumane to the last. In a lengthy handwritten statement, Gumane admitted to receiving money from PIDE, the USA, and Israel and to having received a promise of more funds from an American consular officer in Zambia if he opened an office in Mozambique before Frelimo. Gumane went on to acknowledge that five anti-Frelimo parties had formed a coalition (the PCN) in early August. They joined with "white settler extremists," of the Movimento Mozambique Livre, which seized then lost the Lourenco Marques radio station on September 7, 1974, and called for an insurrection against the joint Frelimo/Portuguese transitional government. When this failed, PCN leaders fled the country "but continued planning a military operation and received financial support from the Smith regime in Rhodesia."

"It was dark when Machel ended the meeting. Armed guerrillas marched the prisoners away, their humiliation complete, and the audience watched in silence. Then Machel led them in singing Frelimo's liberation song."[16] Since they had fled the country after the failure of their

10 THE COLLAPSE OF PORTUGAL 165

attempted coup in Lourenco Marques, how was it that Gumane and others were in Frelimo's hands at Nachingwea? How had they been caught? What was to be their fate?

Frelimo effectively outwitted its opponents, using military pressure and external lobbying to convince Major Melo Antunes and the MFA to agree to a direct transfer of power without the encumbrance of democratic elections. Accordingly, a Lusaka Accord signed on September 7, 1974, in the Zambian capital gave Frelimo a date for independence and, in the interim, de facto license to wipe out all opposition.

From Dar es Salaam, Frelimo set about a methodical round up of past and prospective competitors. With assistance from neighboring states (Malawi, Tanzania, Zambia) and even Portugal, it tricked "traitors" into returning home. Former Mozambique Institute students who had fled to Kenya were encouraged to move back by Frelimo's professions of a readiness to "bury the past," but they were then arrested at airports on arrival. Inside Mozambique, Joanna Simeao of the PCN was arrested by Portuguese police and turned over to Frelimo on her arrival in Beira from Blantyre. Other PCN members in Malawi were collected and sent to "reeducation camps." Simango was located in Kenya, and Frelimo prevailed on the secretary general of the ruling Malawi Congress Party to invite him to participate in an urgent cabinet meeting on Mozambique in Blantyre, where he was handed over to Frelimo. Paulo Gumane and ten other PCN officials were arrested by Malawians and, as with Simango, given over to Frelimo at the Milange border post. "Awaiting them was Joao Honwana, Frelimo security chief for Zambezia. He had the prisoners tied against an army truck's bodywork, their heads upside down, and driven to the Frelimo military camp at Mongue. Simango and Gumane were set aside and flown to Tanzania."[17]

Illustrative of the lengths to which Frelimo was prepared to go was the case of Judas Honwana, who had left Frelimo in the early 1960s and later served as COREMO vice-secretary for information.

> Living in Cairo at the time, he was lured to Tanzania by Marcelino dos Santos. Posing as Simango, dos Santos sent a telegram to Honwana asking him to attend a reconciliatory meeting with Frelimo in Dar es Salaam. The telegram promised his travel expenses would be covered by Frelimo. Upon his arrival in Dar es Salaam, Honwana and his family were arrested and taken to Nachingwea.[18]

166   J.A. MARCUM

The show trial at Nachingwea was orchestrated by Machel's private secretary, Sergio Vieria. It took place in the presence of Tanzanian officials and carefully selected foreign correspondents. Machel assured the assembled that, in conformity with Frelimo's tradition of clemency, it was prepared to accept pleas for "re-education" made by those who confessed. Accordingly, Simango confessed to having been "blinded with ambition."

Gwenjere was a late addition to the list of prisoners. He was tricked by a former colleague into attending a bogus meeting in Mombasa with Tanzanian dissidents said to be planning to overthrow President Nyerere, dissidents who would prevent Frelimo from consolidating power in Mozambique. He too was driven south and delivered at Nachingwea. Only massive protests in Nairobi in October 1976 stopped the UN High Commission for Refugees (UNHCR) and Kenyan government from repatriating most of Kenya's largely anti-Frelimo Mozambique refugee community. The long reach of revenge became clear after independence, when Frelimo persuaded several countries and NGOs to cancel their assistance to any Mozambican students who had refused to return in an effort to make sure that those dissident students "would have a difficult life wherever they lived."[19]

Following the Nachingwea drama some 200 to 300 prisoners in Tanzania were sentenced to re-education and sent back to multiple camps in Mozambique. In 1981 a stark description of what happened to the thousands of "enemies" in those camps was presented by a Catholic priest, Rev. Deacon Daniel Jose Sithole, of the Sao Leonardo Parish of Mussorize, in Manica Province. Entitled "The Mozambique Tragedy," it was written and distributed by Sithole in Nairobi. Arrested "time and again" between 1975 and 1980, accused of being a CIA agent and an informer of international organizations, Sithole's real crime was that of protesting against the killing of hundreds of people in Manica province. A former inmate at the Ruarua re-education camp, he detailed with names, location, and modes of indoctrination, incarceration, and execution the frenzy of arbitrary Frelimo brutality that terrorized much of the country.[20]

The drama then moved from the public show trial of Nachingwea to the secret horror of a re-education camp at M'telela, in the remote northeast bush of Niassa province. There a select group of high-profile "enemies of the revolution" were gathered and placed singly in barrack prison cells. Guards were not allowed to look them in the face—an order carrying severe punishment if violated. The camp commander was Afonso Mambole, well known for his role in the military purges and executions that had followed the death of Magaia.

On June 25, 1977, the "reactionary group" was informed that it was to be flown to Maputo (formerly Lorenco Marques), where it would meet with Machel to discuss rehabilitation and release. A convoy composed of state security (Servico Nacional de Seguranca Popular, or SNASP) and party authorities arrived in the camp, loaded the prisoners onto jeeps, and headed from M'telela, on a dirt road in the direction of the Niassa capital, Lichinga. The details of what happened next were published some eighteen years later by investigative journalists Jose Pinto de Sa and Nelson Saute. During those eighteen years the Frelimo government had refused to provide information on the whereabouts of the prisoners. The convoy stopped along side an off-road ditch that had been bulldozed and partially filled with logs. The prisoners were tied, thrown into the ditch, and sprinkled with gasoline. As the wood ignited, soldiers attached to the convoy chanted revolutionary songs.[21] One can only imagine the horror of the scene, the screams of pain as the prisoners sizzled and burned alive. So what was Frelimo's response to these revelations: regret? Denial? No: silence.

The flames ended the lives of leaders who paid the supreme price for political naivety and failure: Uria Simango, Paulo Gumane, Mateus Gwenjere, Joanna Simeao, Raul Casal Ribeiro, Lazaro N'Kavandame, Paulo Unhei, and Arcanjo Kambeu. For the world outside they simply disappeared.

The order for their slaughter was reportedly given by the National Director of SNASP, Jacinto Veloso, a former Portuguese air force pilot who had defected to Frelimo and whose self-laudatory autobiography, published in 2012, made no mention of the incident—or of any others involving the execution of political foes. He did not acknowledge or challenge the publication of a SNASP order (*Ordem de Accao*, no. 5/80) bearing his signature and ordering the deaths of the seven "counter-revolutionaries," that appeared widely on the internet. The names of Paulo Gumane and N'Kavandame did not even appear in his autobiographical narrative, which diverted blame for security excesses onto the German Democratic Republic. He acknowledged that Frelimo security forces were organized by the East Germans and constituted a "heavy, cumbersome machine" with its own "well armed troops, its own prisons and investigators, and a large logistical and support staff." Veloso further attributed a lack of evidence of wartime collaboration with the

168   J.A. MARCUM

Portuguese (for which many were nevertheless punished) to the latter's decision to burn almost all PIDE archives. As a "general" who was to become wealthy with holdings in the energy and mining sectors of independent Mozambique, Veloso wrote sparsely of his role in the period of one-party Marxist-Leninist rule. He simply acknowledged Cold War "mistakes" that might have been averted had Eduarto Mondlane not been assassinated. With Milas-like finesse, he created his post SNASP persona. Swathed in a heroic narrative that failed to document his family wealth, Veloso's autobiography glided silently over a somber past.[22]

The victors pursued a policy of silence and dissimulation. Given widespread international criticism of Frelimo vengeance, Machel eventually acknowledged excesses but exonerated Frelimo. After an "investigative" visit to the Ruarua re-education camp in 1981, he dissociated himself from its human rights abuses and commented: "it was as if someone had stacked hay in our stomachs [...] we cannot digest that." At a November rally in Maputo he admitted to "systematic violations of legality" and blamed outsiders. He pointed to "crimes, abuses and arbitrariness committed by enemy agents that have infiltrated the Defense and Security Forces" and to the "persistence of values and practices of the colonial-capitalist and tribal-feudal societies."[23] The Frelimo government never informed the families of the fate of those it had executed, and in many cases it led families to believe that the victims were alive, working at some distant place, and would be reunited with their family in due course. The wife of Paulo Gumane, Priscilla, on learning that an Amnesty International delegation had been told that victims' relatives would be contacted if they wrote to the president, sent a letter to Machel's successor as president, Joaquim Chissano. She asked for information about the fate of her husband and asked that he be released if he was still alive. It is not clear that he ever received the letter. She never received an answer. Prophetically, Paulo Gumane had written from Zambia in 1970 claiming that COREMO encountered "hundreds of ex-Frelimo members" seeking protection in the wake of Mondlane's assassination and Simango's expose of Frelimo's "evil deeds." While the Portuguese were losing the war, COREMO was "consolidating its [political] position inside the country," he asserted. But—a huge but—he acknowledged that lacking "material assistance from the OAU Liberation Committee, we are militarily weak."[24] And it was that weakness which ultimately reduced him and his colleagues to ashes.

10 THE COLLAPSE OF PORTUGAL   169

Sergio Vieria would later announce to Mozambican exiles in the USA that the incinerated political prisoners had been killed during a raid on a re-education camp by RENAMO insurgents. But lies and lost memories aside, Machel celebrated the re-education process at Frelimo's Fourth Congress in April 1984 as serving the "enhancement of the human being and his capacity for transformation."[25]

NOTES

1. *Noticias de Portugal*, Lisbon, December 18, 1971.
2. For an account of how "Europeanist" perspectives came to triumph within Washington's bureaucracy and displace "Africanist" advisors and their now roundly disparaged views, see Schneidman, "American Foreign Policy ..." pp. 249–267.
3. The political rationale, process, and results of the negotiation are detailed in Marcum, *The Politics of Indifference: A Case Study in American Foreign Policy*. Mondlane Memorial Lecture, Syracuse University, March 9, 1972.
4. Schneidman, "American Foreign Policy ..." p. 278.
5. Interview with author, May 16, 1967.
6. Frelimo, *A Voz da Revolucao*, Dar es Salaam, September 26, 1966.
7. Fredericks Memo, Marcum Papers, Box 40/4.
8. Ibid.
9. United Nations, General Assembly, Verbatim Record, 2138th meeting, New York, October 3, 1973, pp. 68–69.
10. Marcum, typescript, Phelps Stokes Fund conference, Jamestown, Virginia, March 29, 1974, Marcum Papers.
11. Marcelino dos Santos interview with Tor Sellstrom, 1996, *Mozambique para Todos*, internet blog, April 9, 2012.
12. Vilankulu, mimeo, New York, October 1974, Marcum Papers, Box 39/4
13. Members: Mozambique Revolutionary Council (COREMO), Mozambique United Front (FUMO), National Movement for Peaceful Independence of Mozambique (MONIPAMO), National African Movement for the Unification of Mozambique (MONAUMO) and the Mozambique Common Front (FRECOMO).
14. PCN officials: Arcanjo Kambeu (secretary foreign affairs), Nasser Narciso Mbule (secretary information), Manuel Tristao (organizing secretary), Mateus Gwenjere (national adviser), Joana Simiao (secretary education and culture), Mohamed Hanife (secretary finance), Samuel Simango (secretary youth), and Ahmed Haider (administrative secretary). PCN, Communique No. 1, Beira, August 23, 1974, Marcum Papers, Box 37/5.

170 J.A. MARCUM

15. Arthur Vilanculos, "The Dangers of Independence without Freedom," PCN press release, New York, January 9, 1975. (Vilanculos had added an "os" so that his name matched that of his home community.) Marcum Papers, Box 37/5.
16. David Martin, "How Frelimo Held a 7-Hour Confessional," *The Observer*, London, March 23, 1975.
17. Ibid.
18. Cabrita, *Mozambique*, p. 82.
19. Ibid., p. 84.
20. Daniel Sithole, "The Mozambique Tragedy," mimeo, Nairobi, 1981.
21. As reported in "*Os Campos da Vergonha*" [the camps of shame], Jose Pinto de Sa, "*O dia em que eles foram queimados vivos,*" *Publico Magazine*, no. 277, Lisbon, June 25, 1995.
22. Veloso, Memories at Low Altitude, pp. 76–78.
23. Samora Machel, speech, *Noticias*, Maputo, October 3, 1981, supplement; and Machel, Radio Mozambique, November 5, 1981.
24. Letter to the author, Lusaka, Zambia, April 27, 1970.
25. Cabrita, *Mozambique*, p. 103.

CHAPTER 11

Independent Mozambique

Marxism-Leninism

Despite protestations by Shafardine Khan, Frelimo's representative in the USA, that Frelimo was non-sectarian, uncommitted to any particular ideology, and dedicated to educating people out of the warp of racial hatred bred by the colonial system,[1] Frelimo, from within and without, appeared more and more hard-line socialist; and its socialism was portrayed by Frelimo acolytes abroad as in keeping with the philosophy of Eduardo Mondlane. Mozambique scholars Alan and Barbara Isaacman wrote approvingly in their sweeping history, *Mozambique: From Colonialism to Revolution, 1900–1982:* "The selection of Machel as president and dos Santos as vice-president [after Mondlane's death] marked the final victory for the forces of revolutionary nationalism within Frelimo and set the stage for a more explicit adoption of a socialist agenda."[2] But the extent to which this socialist conception of Mozambique's future was Mondlane's is disputable.

In a proposal in support for a biography of Mondlane, Herbert Shore, Mondlane's close friend from his Oberlin days, observed that, by the time of his assassination, Mondlane had become a genuinely revolutionary thinker committed to building a nation that would seek to "eliminate the exploitation of man by man." Shore described Mondlane as "a profound and compassionate humanist in whom the streams of American democratic thought and African social and cultural traditions mingled

© The Author(s) 2018

J.A. Marcum, *Conceiving Mozambique*, African Histories and Modernities, https://doi.org/10.1007/978-3-319-65987-9_11

171

172   J.A. MARCUM

and flowed," and, like Amilcar Cabral, "an original thinker," who sought "a true social and cultural transformation."[3] But Marxist?

In the aftermath of Mozambican independence, some of Frelimo's academic admirers argued that Mondlane had become increasingly radicalized as the liberation war progressed and identified him as being one with the hard-line, scarcely humanist socialists that took hold of Frelimo. At the time, much writing on the Mozambique struggle focused heavily on class struggle to the neglect of issues such as culture, ethnicity, regionalism, and plain old political ambition. For example, these analyses trashed the work of those who gave importance to ethnic differences. In contrast, in *Ethnic Groups in Conflict*, Donald L. Horowitz wrote:

> Revolting insurgencies, although ostensibly inspired by class ideology, have sometimes derived their impetus from ethnic aspirations and apprehensions instead. The independence movement in Guinea-Bissau was a movement of Balante with no appreciable support among the Fula. The core of Mozambique's anti colonial army was UP-FRP, recruited from the Makonde in the North of the country, while the political leadership of the movement came from the Shangans of the South.[4]

In 1983, a University of Minnesota symposium on "The Class Basis of Nationalist Movements in Angola, Guinea-Bissau and Mozambique" assembled a group of largely like-minded "classicists" who presented a picture of linear progress toward Marxist-Leninist outcomes in all three Portuguese colonies.[5] Their findings matched Frelimo's self-image at the time. Exemplary of this vision was the work of Sonia Kruks of New York's New School for Social Research, "From Nationalism to Marxism: the Ideological History of Frelimo, 1962–1977." She depicted a long, steady, salutary March to a formal embrace of Marxism-Leninism at the 3rd party congress in 1977. A former member of the Faculty of Letters at Eduardo Mondlane University in Maputo, Kruks argued that Frelimo "passed from nationalism to a Marxist party because it learned the truth of Marxism—that is, the predominance of class struggle—from its own experience."[6] Aquino de Braganca, then director of the Eduardo Mondlane University's Centro de Estudos Africanos, supported this linear vision in his paper "Frelimo from Front to Party: Revolutionary Transformations." Consistent with this vision, Samora Machel asserted that Frelimo was eager to adopt a program of global significance, and in his words there was indigenous originality in Frelimo's March to socialism, marked by an ambitious dismantling of "the political, administrative, cultural, financial, economic, educational, juridical and other systems integral to the colonial state." Machel continued:

> Although we can seek inspiration and stimulation from the revolutionary experience of other peoples, we shall build on the foundation of our own originality, basing ourselves on the specific conditions of our country. We shall thus also enrich the revolutionary heritage of humanity, a duty we have been fulfilling over these hard years of struggle.[7]

It was necessary to destroy before one could build.

Was all of this congruent with Mondlane's concept of a post-colonial Mozambique? Sonia Kruks, among others, argued the answer was "yes," citing de Braganca as providing proof. A close advisor to Machel, de Braganca recounted a late 1968 interview with Mondlane in which the latter had told him: "There is an evolution of [our] thought which has taken place during the last six years [...] Frelimo is now, truly, much more socialist, revolutionary and progressive than ever and the present tendency is increasingly in the direction of the Marxist-Leninist type of socialism."[8] But it is not clear whether this was Mondlane's academic appraisal of a historical trend or his personal endorsement of the path toward socialism.

By 1983 Mondlane was no longer alive to speak for himself, but a close friend and confidant, the American Friends Service Committee representative in Dar es Salaam, Bill Sutherland, could do so. In a video interview, Sutherland shared a confidential conversation with Mondlane that had taken place "on his front porch." Mondlane told Sutherland that he realized the "Marxist element" in Frelimo considered him "useful" at the present stage of the revolution but indicated that the Marxists will "try to push me aside as the thing goes on. I don't represent the true Marxist position [...] and I'm ready for that. I know it." I would "not be considered a reliable person to be head of state," so I would be pushed aside. Sutherland concluded: Mondlane "realized that they would probably do that to him."[9] Asked about her husband's ideological beliefs, Janet Mondlane wrote that, in his university days, "Eduardo identified [...] as a Fabian socialist, but "did not commit himself ideologically to socialism or Marxism." She explained:

174   J.A. MARCUM

Given the economic structure under colonialism, he felt that there was no alternative but that the government should take a strong hand in the process of lifting the citizens out of poverty. But there was the other side of the coin that he felt strongly about: people must be free and independent in their workplace, their homes and their thinking, not just in relation to an outside oppression, but an internal dictatorship. [...] If he had lived, I have no doubt that he would have sought to combine these two precepts and try to make them work in harmony.

She also had "no doubt that the history of Mozambique would have been different had Eduardo not been killed. But to say what the scenarios would have been in either case, only the gods could say!"[10]

THE ABYSS AND BEYOND

Portuguese military collapse came much sooner than expected. In early 1974 Frelimo's forces had not penetrated beyond the lightly populated north. In 1976 Bridget Bloom, of London's *Financial Times*, summarized the circumstances facing the new government:

Frelimo has probably had the most difficult inheritance of any newly independent Black government in Africa to date. In April 1974, only a tiny minority (perhaps only half of one per cent) of Mozambique's population of ten million could in any sense be counted as members of Frelimo. The guerrilla army of some 10–15,000 men had then penetrated only to the country's sensitive "waist" between the port of Beira and the Rhodesian border near Umtali, while they only "controlled" territory considerably to the north of Nampula. However good a guerilla force it might have been, the army was not equipped to exercise a political and "peacetime" role over an area, which virtually overnight had increased at least tenfold. Frelimo's political wing, for its part had neither the administrative cadres [there may have been ten college graduates] nor the administrative experience to run such a large and disparate country.[11]

Most of the upwards of 200,000 Portuguese fled along with their administrative skills and economic know-how. Some blacks, including up to 30,000 troops who fought for the Portuguese, sought haplessly to challenge Frelimo's military power. White-ruled Rhodesia and South Africa actively sought to subvert the new government. Right-wing groups made several abortive attempts to seize power. Frelimo's army was adroit at bush warfare, not urban conflict. Unaccustomed temptations of city life defied the new government's warnings about behavior and discipline. "Even before independence it was common to see Frelimo soldiers enter restaurants, eat and drink their fill and leave without paying the bill."[12] As many as 10,000 people were detained and sent to prisons and re-education camps. Frelimo attempted to destroy not reform the structures of the colonial order "so as not to be absorbed, corrupted and destroyed by them." And, though the lack of trained personnel threatened to lead the country into crisis, Frelimo's understanding of Marxist-Leninist doctrine told its leaders that technology was secondary to political class consciousness and that the country would become technically qualified as part of the process of revolution much as the movement had learned how to win the war by the process of fighting it.[13]

Dos Santos put it this way:

> A revolutionary fire destroys the enemy and purifies us. In the process of the struggle the individuals who are on the side of the revolution grow as human beings and this is important because we consider that there cannot be a new society without a new man. This applies to all revolutionary struggle whether it takes the form of violence or not. And so, the revolutionary fire helps us to purify our ranks.

And looking ahead, he argued, the shared experience of the struggle generates "collectivist thinking" and that mindset, even if originally essentially pragmatic, creates conditions "from which it will be difficult to withdraw." The future depends upon the continuity and guidance of a "true revolutionary leadership."[14]

Rigid internal doctrine did not obviate a need for external pragmatism or fudging. The country lived with continued dependency on the jobs of over 100,000 laborers in the mines of South Africa. Yet with *triunfalismo*, Frelimo set out to project its wartime experience into a remake of Mozambique, mobilizing *dinamizadores*, groups of locally selected Frelimo militants, to spur the process. Collectivization of agriculture (Soviet model), nationalization of production and retail enterprise, and state acquisition of church property and schools—a complete by-the-book implantation of Marxist-Leninist principles—was the order of the day. However, Frelimo "bit off more than it could chew." State farms received heavy budget support but accounted for only a fraction of total

176   J.A. MARCUM

output, and none was profitable. Between 1979 and 1981 production on collective farms declined by 50% and by 1982 the state-run industrial sector was operating at only 40% of capacity. Human suffering reached grim levels, with per capital GNP falling to around $140 per year.

By 1985, reality imposed itself. President Machel felt compelled to recognize the debacle publicly. Speaking with disarming candor to a session of the People's Assembly, he acknowledged "mistakes." On the one hand, he exhorted Mozambicans to address the "cumulative effects of years of criminal activity by armed banditry, the devastating effects of natural disasters [floods] and the domestic consequences of a grave international economic crisis." On the other hand, he made no mention of ideology, of Marx, Lenin—or Stalin. Instead he had much to say about individual behavior and moral rectitude. Machel attributed Mozambique's problems in considerable measure to a blind adherence to dogma. He was caustic, biting.

> We remain tied to formalism and general analyses. We do not get down to the facts because we have little contact with reality. This is why we are still facing the contradictory situation of having famine in our country, when there [are] maize, sunflowers and vegetables that are not distributed and rot.

"Though agriculture constitutes the basis of our economy," he said, "we persist in talking about the working class, and relegate the majority of the population, the peasants, to second place."

Arguing for a decentralization of agriculture, he reversed the policy of grouping peasants into state farms (*aldeias communais*), based on the infamous model of Portugal's fortified *aldeamentos*. A once fervent architect of the economic model he now denounced, Machel continued: "Gigantic state companies that have management problems must be scaled down, creating several smaller companies, distributing land to peasants, cooperatives and private farmers, giving land to hungry peasants who are on poor land alongside abandoned, overgrown farms that have water." Still, Machel had not totally given up commitment to top-down central authority. Cotton and cashews were "fundamental weapons for our independence." So cotton "must be grown, compulsorily." Cotton is vital for the textile industry. On the other hand, he said, cashews needed to be marketed by rural traders who would freely exchange them for consumer goods—and transport them to the factories. These traders "must be given support in terms of the means to cultivate and transport produce." (N'Kavandame's ghost applauded.) Machel decried "corruption, bribery and embezzlement of state property," lamented the failure to hold local authorities accountable for their actions, and concluded: "We are still assaulted by tribalism, by regionalism, by racism, by divisions."[15] (Shades of Simango.)

Many of the problems that led to the starvation of as many as 100,000 people in 1983–1984 were rooted in Frelimo's prior actions. The "bandits" Machel referred to as the central threat to the state were the forces of the Resistencia Nacional Mocambicana (RENAMO), which was created by the Rhodesian Special Branch in response to Frelimo's collaboration with Zimbabwean liberation movements in 1976–1977. Beginning in 1979, RENAMO was assisted by the apartheid regime in South Africa. Initially, RENAMO leadership was discredited by its association with Rhodesia, South Africa, and the remnants of Portuguese colonial rule. But, over time, the rural-based movement attracted support from the remnants of Frelimo's old competitors within the nationalist movement as well as peasant communities and other economic groups opposed to Frelimo's disastrous economic policies.

After independence, a Frelimo Central Committeeman, Samuel Dhlakama, persuaded his nineteen-year-old nephew, Afonso Dhlakama, to join Frelimo's army. The younger and now much better -known Dhlakama served for two years in the Beira region but was alienated by what he perceived as communist control of Frelimo. He deserted, joined RENAMO, and climbed aggressively up the guerrilla hierarchy to become, by 1984, the top commander of the RENAMO insurgency.

RENAMO was bolstered by the legacy of the past conflicts detailed above. For example, in September 1985 a RENAMO delegation lobbying in Washington, D.C. included Priscilla Gumane and Fanuel Mahluza. And Luis Serapiao, a refugee student in Malawi who had asked if he would be allowed to be a practicing Catholic if he attended school in the USA and went on to become a professor at Howard University, gravitated from UNEMO dissidence to become RENAMO's official representative in Washington. Presenting itself as anti-communist and a defender of the "tradition, customs and personality" of Mozambique, RENAMO became an increasingly formidable force.[16]

In 1985 Samuel Levy, in a report for the Institute of Current World Affairs, graphically described RENAMO and the war it sparked:

178   J.A. MARCUM

This is a particularly brutal war. The overwhelming majority of the casualties are civilian. Village-burnings and massacres, more of them committed by RENAMO than Frelimo, are common. Mutilations—cutting of legs, ears and breasts—are routinely practiced. RENAMO makes the communal villages established by the government a special target. Residents are first invited to leave their homes and live with the Resistance. [Should they decline,] they are subject to attack. Some people live willingly with the Resistance, which in some areas can provide the food, clothes and security that Frelimo cannot. Others choose life with the *matsangas* [RENAMO slang for guerrillas] out of fear of the consequences should they do otherwise. Still others are kidnapped.[17]

RENAMO's strongest operations were in the center of the country, but it spread its hit-and-run destruction companion throughout Mozambique.

Frelimo was forced to accept that its hopes for the construction of a Marxist-Leninist utopia were not to be realized.

Violence usually begets violence. Accordingly, civil war inflicted a decade and a half of extreme brutality. It decimated Mozambique, killing untold thousands. Meanwhile, the world changed: the Soviet Union collapsed, Machel died in an airplane crash, the USA and Frelimo developed constructive relations, and, finally, after multiple failed international efforts, the Vatican pressed its good offices on the protagonists and led them through a protracted peace process that brought an end to hostilities in 1992.

Chissano

In 2012, 50 years—half a century—after Eduardo Mondlane assumed the presidency of Mozambique's independence movement, Mozambique began reconceiving itself. After ten years of anti-colonial insurgency and sixteen years of civil war followed by twenty years of picking up the pieces, the country was starting over again.

When he signed the Rome Accord of 1992 ending the civil conflict with RENAMO, Machel's successor—President Joaquim Chissano—confronted a ravaged and blighted country with thousands of displaced people and an economy in ruins, with the lowest GDP in the world and a million refugees in neighboring countries needing to be re-integrated. Chissano, an early member of Frelimo who was Mozambique's Vice-President, had not accompanied President Machel, Aquino de Braganca and the planeload of other senior Frelimo officials who were killed when their Russian piloted plane crashed on October 19, 1986, while they were returning to Maputo from a conference in Lusaka. Chissano and Machel had disagreed on such things as the terms of the non-aggression pact with South Africa (the Nkomati Accord of March 1984), a treaty that was meant to eliminate Pretoria's support for RENAMO but which failed to do so fully. At the time, the two were reportedly not on good terms—and Chissano was not on the tragically fated plane.

Chissano was left to take the leadership of Mozambique. He proceeded to guide the country through a fitful period of reform and negotiation that climaxed in the Vatican-brokered peace with RENAMO in 1992. During the reconciliation process a new constitution in 1990 opened the way to a multi-party system, the merger (50–50) of the Frelimo and RENAMO militaries, and a substantial house in Maputo for Dhlakama—one of a number of concessions to RENAMO that Chissano faithfully executed.

Born in the remote southern Gaza village of Malehice in October 1939, Chissano was the first African to attend the Liceu Salazar in Lourenco Marques, became an activist in NESAM, and enrolled as a medical student in Lisbon before escaping to France in 1961 along with Joao Nhambiu and Pascoal Mocumbi, the three founders of UNEMO. He entered Frelimo in 1963, served as Mondlane's secretary and rose quickly in its ranks in Dar es Salaam to become a member of the movement's leadership. Chissano played a crucial role in negotiating the Lusaka Accord of 1974 with Portugal that paved the way for independence and secured Frelimo a monopoly of political power. Less impulsive and radical than Machel, he was comfortable with political compromise, and in 1994 he was elected president of Mozambique in a hard-fought contest with Dhlakama, then re-elected handily in 1999.

To the wonderment of many, Chissano declined to seek a third term—an act of selflessness rare among African heads of state. He is credited with healing and steering the country through difficult years of transition and through severe floods in 2001, and into a period of annual economic growth of seven percent a year. His voluntary renunciation of power earned him international recognition as winner of the first international Achievement in African Leadership Award, which carried with it a personal discretionary grant of five million dollars. He was absent at the time that Kofi Annan announced the award at London's City Hall in June 2012 because he was serving with a United Nations mission

180   J.A. MARCUM

attempting to broker an end to the savagery of the Lord's Resistance Army in Uganda.

A little more than fifty years after their "Flight before the Fight" from Lisbon, Chissano, Mocumbi, and Nhambiu were now witnesses to a new country emerging from the long and painful struggle to free it from enforced isolation and the hold of an exploitive, atavistic empire. Walking in the footsteps of a martyred academic and reluctant revolutionary, Eduardo Mondlane, each had contributed to the enormous potential of today's Mozambique. As president, Chissano had led the country out of the cul-de-sac of economic ruin and brutish civil war. Mocumbi, after years serving Frelimo in administrative roles such as head of information, had left in 1967 to earn a medical degree at the University of Lausanne. He was rescued from subsequent rustication in Nampulo by Chissano and brought into the government, first as minister of health and ultimately prime minister (1994–2004). And Joao Nhambiu, who had led UNEMO until being outflanked by the leftist political-military wing of Frelimo, could now return from the Commonwealth of Pennsylvania with his American grandchildren and introduce them to his family, his birthplace at Maxixe, and the peaceful beaches of Tofo and Ponta da Barra.

GUEBUZA

A mix of irony, ambiguity, and hope gripped Mozambique in 2004 as Chissano was succeeded by Armando Guebuza, a former Frelimo hardliner now become millionaire businessman. Guebuza won an internal contest for power in Frelimo and subsequently the 2004 presidential election. He garnered some 64% of the vote against steadily receding support for his RENAMO opponent, Alonzo Dhlakama. Guebuza succeeded Chissano as president of a changing country. A high birth rate had increased the population to over twenty million, three times what it had been in the early 1960s. Portuguese remained the official language but linguistically, Macua speakers (Emakuwa) still outnumbered Portuguese speakers (22 to 11% respectively). Religion was back full steam. Catholics and Protestants were re-engaged in educational missions, and each accounted for roughly 28% of the population, and Moslems for 18%. Rural agriculture, largely restored to traditional small-scale farming, continued as the mainstay of the economy (with cotton, sisal, and cashew exports). Over 11% of the population suffered from

AIDS. And the center of political and economic gravity remained in the south, primarily in Maputo with its million and a half residents, where the influence of private capital from post-apartheid South Africa plays a major economic role.

Mozambique's new president was born in the Nampula provincial town of Murrupula and joined Frelimo at age 20. A former member of NESAM, like Mondlane and other Frelimo leaders, he gained prominence as a successful military commander. Today, he epitomizes the ambiguity of transitional Mozambique. It was Guebuza who announced the details of Frelimo's controversial 1967 policy requiring students abroad to serve in the independence war. After independence, he organized and bungled an "Operation Production" in the 1980s, through which the government attempted to force the resettlement of thousands of "excess" rural refugees clustered in Maputo and Beira to remote areas of economically inhospitable Niassa province. In 1983 Machel had to intervene to end what had proved an inhumane program. A hard-liner, when Frelimo took power, Guebuza, as a government minister ordered the expulsion of resident Portuguese in what became known as the "24–20 program": twenty four hours to leave with a maximum of 20 kilos of luggage.

Would Guebuza attempt to take Frelimo back to a pre-Chissano order?

In a relatively short time he had already forsaken Marxist principles, amassed a fortune in trading, and became a rich businessman, "Mr. Gue-Business." In contrast, unreconstructed, politically marginalized socialists like Marcelino dos Santos were left to opine wishfully that the "temporary" abandonment of Marxism would be reversed when the country had fully recovered from the devastation of RENAMO insurgency.

Ironically, in 2012 Guebuza found himself welcoming a new wave of Portuguese immigration: skilled but unemployed job seekers from the recession-ridden former metropole. And Mozambique assumed a prominent role as a member of the post-colonial Comunidade dos Países de Língua Portuguesa that brought together Portugal, Brazil, and Portugal's other former colonies.

Ambiguity, irony, and hope surrounded the Guebuza government's approach to a problem common too much of Africa: corruption. In 2007 he presided at a ribbon-cutting ceremony inaugurating a 32 million dollar marble-floored shopping center in Maputo. Opulent, the center was built by a south Asian millionaire, Mohamed Bacher Suleman

182   J.A. MARCUM

("MBS"), noted for hosting Christmas parties for the poor and contributing millions of dollars to Frelimo, and designated a "drug lord" by the American government, which placed him on a list of narcotics traffickers with whom Americans are forbidden to do business. It is speculated that Suleman may never be brought to trial, however, because, in the words of one anti-corruption campaigner, "hearings might expose high-level collaborators in government and politics." The Associated Press (AP) acknowledged claims by Mozambican authorities' that they were investigating how Suleiman amassed his fortune. But an AP investigator noted: "the good life continues at Suleman mall. Diners can enjoy a view of Maputo's port through huge windows over sushi and $40 bottles of South African sparkling wine. A patio outside the cinema is named Guebuza Square."[18]

On May 9, 2012, President Guebuza spoke at Chatham House in London pledging to prospective investors that his government was adopting sound policies of transparency, accountability, and legal structuring in the process of "Harnessing Mozambique's Mineral Wealth." Referring to exciting new geologically confirmed riches in coal and gas, he stressed the importance of respecting local interests in their development and assured his international, entrepreneurial audience that he recognized the need to balance private sector interests with those of Mozambique's long-term goal of "making [the] poor, history." The "right not to be poor," he intoned, was a human right and he predicted that within ten to fifteen years Mozambique, given its steady seven percent growth rate and massive expansion of educational opportunity, should achieve middle power status. Guebuza's studied openness and reassuring words seemed designed to allay Western concerns about both the danger of corruption and Frelimo's Marxist-Leninist past.[19]

Guebuza contrasted what he described as his government's policy of attentiveness to legitimate local interests with the actions of colonial Portugal, which had built a huge dam at Cabora Bassa on the Zambezi River that flooded a vast area and displaced thousands of peasants, who were forced to settle in remote areas of poor soil and inadequate transport. But, six months after his speech, a visiting *New York Times* journalist wrote that the smallholder farmers who constitute the bulk of the country's population were benefiting little from the multi-billion-dollar investments in the country's megaprojects in coal and gas. These projects "rarely create large numbers of jobs or foster local entrepreneurships." The rural poor were being left behind. The government had signed up to be part of the Extractive Industries Transparency Initiative, a program set up by Britain and supported by the World Bank. And under it the government promised to invest in antipoverty programs to assist rural famers. But tax revenues from the projects have proved small because of large tax exemptions.

Underscoring skepticism about the benefits of extractive resource development, the *Times* cited the case of the Brazilian mining company Vale, in Tete province. The company had promised to relocate peasants from the site of its massive Moatize coal reserve development and to provide them with sturdy new bungalows and upgraded public services. Subsistence farmer expectations of huge investments in jobs, houses, and education soared. But in a visit to the relocation center of Cateme some 25 miles from the mine, too far from the mine for jobs, the *Times* reporter found Cateme's subsistence farmers living in crumbling, poorly built, leaky houses. Promised water taps and electricity had never arrived, and their new fields were "dusty and barren [...] coaxing anything from them is hard." As billions of dollars poor into gas and coal (and more recently oil) development, it remains unclear whether such development will raise the standard of living of the population at large or will leave Mozambique stuck in the too common status of a rich African country with an impoverished population.[20]

Politically, some echoes of the insurgency and civil war still reverberate.

Daviz Simango was orphaned with his siblings as a young child when his father, Uria Simango, and other oppositionists were slaughtered and his mother, Celina Simango, the first president of Frelimo's League of Mozambican Women (LIFEMO), was abducted and presumably executed by Frelimo militants. Daviz survived, studied, and earned an engineering degree from Eduardo Mondlane University. Then he sought historical revenge against Frelimo by joining RENAMO. The 1992 peace accord and the arrival of multi-party pluralism allowed Daviz to establish himself as a political leader in Beira, Mozambique's second city, which had been the bailiwick of his father. There he gained a reputation as a strong and effective mayor and in 2009 split with the leadership of a declining RENAMO to create his own breakaway Movimento Democratico de Mocambique (MDM). Thus Daviz established himself and his MDM as a regional challenge to Frelimo, restored the role of a historically important Mozambican political family, and demonstrated a new degree of tolerance for democratic opposition. In 2004, evidencing

184   J.A. MARCUM

a significant degree of press freedom, a local author researched, wrote, and published a revisionist biography of Uria Simango. He launched it at a gathering of several hundred people in Maputo. The publication caused a political stir—one that was not enough, however, to prompt the government to authorize an independent inquiry into the circumstances of the Simangos' deaths.[21]

The lingering tugs of history, tradition, and war can also be seen in local drama within the former heartland of the RENAMO insurgency: the Rhode Island-sized Gorongosa National Park. There, at the southern end of the Great Rift Valley, a protracted contest is unfolding between traditionalist and aspirational values, between RENAMO sympathizers and environmental philanthropists. The traditionalists are led by RENAMO followers protected by a local shaman, or medicine man, known as Samategu. His followers clear cut trees and build settlements on the slopes of Mount Gorongosa, which lies just outside park boundaries. The mountain is the park's main source of water. But suspicious of economic benefits promised by the intruding *muzengu* (white) philanthropists, shaman-led locals threaten to destroy the mountain watershed vital for rejuvenation of the war-ravaged park. Aspirational values, on the other hand, are furthered by the fortune of a zealous American philanthropist. These aspirations enjoy the backing of Maputo authorities and the supportive involvement of the local park's *regulo*, or hereditary chief, Joao Chitengo. Undeterred by local opposition, wealthy philanthropist Greg Carr has chosen to pursue a personal commitment to repopulate the park with wildebeest, antelope, and the many other animals eaten to extinction by hungry soldiers during the civil war. He is intent on building a strong ecosystem and tourist business that will train, employ, and raise the living standards of local people. Reforestation, animal restoration, tourism, local technical support, and indigenous management are all features of the Carr Foundation's efforts to recreate and preserve a major national game park. However, today such efforts must win local acceptability by benefit demonstration, not by the intervention of a central government that seems to find it difficult to impose top-down central power and thereby incorporate the mountain within the park.[22]

Civil society is budding. It is visible in the free-spirited discourse and debate of a Centro de Estudos Mocambicanos e Internacionais (CEMO) chaired by a lively scholar from Quelimane with a doctorate from the University of East Anglia, Manuel de Araujo, a member of the country's emerging intelligentsia. Speaking at a 2008 conference in Luanda on "Democratic and Development Processes in Angola and Southern Africa," Araujo attributed the emergence of Civil Society Organizations (CSOs) and activists in Mozambique to "the democratization process" of the 1990s. From their outset local CSOs have exhibited two characteristics: (1) an "enormous weight" of external financing and technical assistance; and (2) danger from the "increasing discomfort [they have] caused to political power." They remain weak, he acknowledges in "technical, managerial and information capacity." And competing for scarce funding, foreign and domestic, they are prone to "fall into the clutches of party-political clientelism, leaving them unable to adopt a critical posture." Nevertheless, "CSOs have been able to mobilize a significant number of citizens to national causes, raising public awareness on civic and political issues," including those related to rights regarding women, health, land, and religion.[23]

Another example of the CSO phenomena is the Eduardo Mondlane Foundation, which focuses on issues of poverty and generates scholarships for Mozambican students. Led by Janet Mondlane, who remains engaged and committed to the educational and social concerns central to her late husband's life, it is part of a plethora of struggling voluntary organizations that are sprouting throughout the country. The future of the country may be fashioned in large part by the creativity of the civil society idealists, domestic and international, committed to them.

Yet, in the words of one seasoned citizen who experienced the struggle in Mozambique from its beginning, "corruption and nepotism are rampant." The generals and close relatives of the president "serve as the gateways" for any investment in the country's resources: coal, gas, oil, bauxite, and agriculture. The ostentatious emergence of the "wabenze" (wealthy individuals who were characterized by their ownership of Mercedes-Benz automobiles) reflects a huge economic gap between governors and governed. And yet, holding to the original ideals of the independence struggle, the same observer sees "islands of progress." And, he confides: "I welcome the openness allowed in the public arena even when the outcome is preordained."[24]

HOPE

The reconception of Mozambique remains a "work in progress." After a false start dominated by doctrinal simplicity and brutish warfare, Joaquim Chissano took power and set the country on a path

186   J.A. MARCUM

toward a more open and free society. The underlying purpose of this book has been to suggest that an independent and probing review of the history of Mozambique's struggle for independence can further that quest.

Mozambicans can choose to deal with the past in one of two ways. They can ignore it, and deny it, much as Japan has continued to deny the dark chapters of its history (including the Nanjing massacre and Korean Comfort Women), which has created enduring bitterness in China, Korea, and elsewhere in Asia. Or they can confront, acknowledge, and atone for it and seek genuine reconciliation, as Germany has done in dealing with the horrors of the Nazi era, thereby opening the way for Germany's emergence as the leader of a new Europe.

By honestly addressing its past, Mozambique's political leaders can help its citizens to comprehend how a long, harsh colonial rule negatively limited human perceptions and behavior, how centuries of educational deprivation and arbitrary rule inevitably warped views of race and ethnicity, and how the shortcomings of military intolerance and class determinism led to authoritarianism, impoverishment, and unspeakable violence. The search for an unvarnished and compassionate understanding of Mozambique's past will be crucial over time to the construction of a more just and democratic future. Hopefully the narrative of the preceding pages may help to provoke such a liberating process.

It is time for the country to clear the political deck and free young minds from the delimiting outcomes of cruel history. It is time for a new generation of Mozambicans to explore, think, question, challenge, and commit to the long, arduous step-by-step process of ... RECONCEIVING AND BUILDING A NEW MOZAMBIQUE.

Notes

1. Interview with author, New York, June 16, 1970.
2. Alan and Barbara Isaacman, *Mozambique: From Colonialism to Revolution, 1900–1982*, Westview Press, Boulder, Colorado, p. 99.
3. Marcum Papers, Box 37/7.
4. Donald L. Horowitz, *Ethnic Groups in Conflict*, University of California Press, 1985, p. 10.
5. My paper—"Class, Race and Ethnicity: The Angolan Revolution Revisited"—struck a discordant note at the symposium. Instead of

11 INDEPENDENT MOZAMBIQUE   187

focusing on class, it stressed the anachronistic and autocratic nature of Portuguese political culture, and impact of a Portuguese colonial-cultural conditioning and the cruelty of guerrilla war, which "did not permit even the flawed but heuristic exposure to democratic process and compromise experienced by other African territories," such that "Angola entered independence in a state of "fratricidal violence." For example, Mai Palmberg wrote, colonial rule in Angola had."

6. See also Irving Leonard Markowitz, *Studies in Power and Class in Africa*, Oxford University Press, 1987, pp. 240–256.
7. Machel, "Mozambique Revolution or Reaction," p. 12.
8. Aquino de Braganca and Immanuel Wallerstein (eds.), *Quem e o Inmigo?* Lisbon, Initiativas Editorias, 1977, vol. 2, p. 200.
9. Videotaped interview by Prexy Nesbett and Mimi Edmunds, "Bill Sutherland: Non-Violent Warrior of Peace," Brooklyn, New York, July 19, 2003.
10. Janet Mondlane, letter from Maputo, May 13, 2011, Marcum Papers, Box 34/7.
11. Bridget Bloom, "Mozambique," paper at "Conference on Southern Africa," Seven Springs Center, Mount Kisco, New York, April, 1976.
12. Ibid.
13. Samora Machel, *Establishing People's Power to Serve the Masses*, Dar es Salaam, Tanzania Publishing House, 1977.
14. Marcelino dos Santos interviewed by Joe Slovo, "Frelimo Faces the Future," *The African Communist*, no. 55, London, 1973, pp. 23–53.
15. *Agencia de Informacao de Mocambique*, Samora Machel, "Mistakes and Deviations Persist," speech to People's Assembly, December 1985.
16. RENAMO, "Manifesto and Program," mimeo, 1985, Marcum Papers, Box 37/6.
17. Samuel Levy, "Report on the Civil War in Mozambique" for the New Hampshire Institute of Current World Affairs, Maputo, June 28, 1985.
18. Donna Bryson, "Mozambique, a Budding Narco-State?" Associated Press, March 22, 2011.
19. Armando Guebuza, "Harnessing Mozambique's Mineral Wealth," video, Chatham House, London, May 9, 2012.
20. Lydia Polgreen, "As Coal Boosts Mozambique, the Rural Poor are Left Behind," *The New York Times*, November 11, 2012.
21. Barnabe Lucas Ncomo, *Uria Simango: Um Homem, Uma Causa*. Edicoes Novafrica, Maputo, 2004.
22. Philip Gourevitch, "The Monkey and the Fish," *The New Yorker*, December 21, 2009, pp. 98–111.
23. Manuel de Araujo, "Civil Society and Politics in Mozambique," in Progress Report 2004–2009, *Democratic and Development Processes*

in Angola and Southern Africa, editor Nuno Vidal, Luanda, 2008, pp. 44–45. See also Araujo and Raul Meneses Cambote, "Civil Society and Development in Mozambique," in Nuno Vidal with Patrick Chabal, *Southern Africa: Civil Society, Politics and Donor Strategies*, Luanda and Lisbon, Media XXI & Firmamento, 2009, pp. 213–222.

24. Interview with author.

BIBLIOGRAPHY

Archival Sources

The John A. Marcum Papers

Conceiving Mozambique is based primarily on John Marcum's unparalleled access to many of the leaders of FRELIMO, the Mozambique liberation movement. As the leading historian of the Angolan freedom struggle, John A. Marcum (1927–2013) enjoyed instant credibility amongst opponents of Portuguese colonialism elsewhere in Africa.

See his *The Angolan Revolution* 2 vols. (Cambridge: MIT University Press, 1969, 1978). He knew most of the Mozambican leadership in this phase of the Mozambican drama personally, and maintained an active correspondence with them. Through them and his personal network of Mozambican, African, and European and American colleagues he amassed a considerable personal archive of correspondence and publications, as well as typescripts, memoranda, notes, and photographs mostly dating from the late 1950s to the 1980s.

These documents form the primary source of the information contained in this book. They are available today for the consultation of scholars and other researchers in the John A. Marcum Papers. On deposit at the Africa collection of Stanford University Library in Palo Alto, California, the Marcum Papers consist of 55 linear feet of documents in 68 boxes and seven map folders. For more on the Marcum Papers, please consult the following on-line finding aid: https://searchworks.stanford.edu/view/8447318.

© The Editor(s) (if applicable) and The Author(s) 2018
J.A. Marcum, *Conceiving Mozambique*, African Histories
and Modernities, https://doi.org/10.1007/978-3-319-65987-9

190 BIBLIOGRAPHY

Theses and Dissertations

Brendan Jundanian, "The Mozambique Liberation Front" (Mémoire presenté pour le Diplôme de l'Institut, Lausanne, Switzerland, 1970).

Joseph Massinga, "United Nations and Decolonization of Angola, Mozambique and Rhodesia" (Ph.D. diss., Graduate Institute of International Studies, Geneva, Switzerland, 1971) [Marcum Papers, Box 36/3].

Eduardo Mondlane, "Role Conflict, Reference Group and Race" (Ph.D. diss., Northwestern University, 1960).

Walter Opello. Jr., "Internal War in Mozambique: A Social-Psychological Analysis of a Nationalist Revolution" (Ph.D. diss., University of Colorado, 1973).

Witney Schneidman, "American Foreign Policy and the Fall of the Portuguese Empire, 1961–1976: A Study in Issue Salience" (Ph.D. diss., University of Southern California, 1965).

Secondary Sources

Edward Alpers, "To Seek a Better Life: The Implications of Migration from Northern Mozambique to Colonial and Independent Tanzania for Class Formation and Political Behavior in the Struggle to Liberate Mozambique" (paper presented at a conference on Class Basis of Nationalist Movements in Angola, Guinea-Bissau and Mozambique, University of Minnesota, May 25–27, 1983).

Gerald Bender, *Angola Under the Portuguese: The Myth and the Reality* (Berkeley: University of California Press, 1980).

Bridget Bloom, "Mozambique" (paper presented at Conference on Southern Africa, Seven Springs Center, Mount Kisco, New York, April, 1976).

Aquino de Braganca, "L'intinéraire d'Uria Simango," *AfricaAsia* (November 24–December 7, 1969).

Douglas Brinkley, *Dean Acheson: The Cold War Years: 1953–71* (New Haven: Yale University Press, 1992).

Donna Bryson, "Mozambique, a Budding Narco-State?" Associated Press, March 22, 2011.

João M. Cabrita, *Mozambique: the Tortuous Road to Democracy* (London: Palgrave, 1988).

Michel Cahen, "The Mueda Case and Maconde Political Ethnicity," *Centre d'Étude d'Afrique Noire de l'Institut d'Étude Politique de Bordeaux, Africana Studia* 2 (1999): 29–46.

Centro de Estudos, "*Africano, Nao Vamos Esquercr! [sic]*" (Universidade Eduardo Mondlane, Maputo, February 1983).

BIBLIOGRAPHY   191

Jose Balthazar da Costa Chagonga, "Truth about Slavery in Mocambique: Petitions Addressed to the Portuguese Overseas Minister and the Governor General and Their Reply," Blantyre, Malawi 1965 [Marcum Papers Box 38/4].

George Chilambe, "The Struggle in Mozambique,'" *East African Journal* (July 1966).

Manuel de Araujo, "Civil Society and Politics in Mozambique," in Vidal Nuno, ed. *Progress Report 2004–2009, Democratic and Development Processes in Angola and Southern Africa* (Luanda 2008).

Manuel De Araujo and Raul Meneses Cambote, "Civil Society and Development in Mozambique," in Vidal Nuno with Patrick Chabal, *Southern Africa: Civil Society, Politics and Donor Strategies* (Luanda and Lisbon: Media XXI & Firmamento, 2009).

Aquino de Braganca and Immanuel Wallerstein, eds., *Quem e o Inmigo?* 2 vols (Lisbon, Initiativas Editorias, 1977).

Marcelino dos Santos, "The Revolutionary Perspective in Mozambique," *World Marxist Review: Problems of Peace and Socialism* (January 1968).

James Duffy, *Portugal in Africa* (Cambridge, MA: Harvard University Press, 1952).

Richard Gibson, *African Liberation Movements* (Oxford: Oxford University Press, 1972).

Philip Gourevitch, "The Monkey and the Fish," *The New Yorker* (December 21, 2009).

Paulo Gumane, "Failure of Unity Talks," *Combate*, 8 (1965).

Paulo Gumane, "Biography," June 3, 1966 [Marcum Papers Box 34/3].

Hlomulo Jani Chitofo Gwambe, "America the Country Responsible for the Colonial Wars in Africa" Dar es Salaam, October 8, 1962 [Marcum Papers Box 36/1].

Hlomulo Jani Chitofo Gwambe, "My Concise Autobiography," Lusaka, June 13, 1966 [Marcum Papers Box 36/1].

Melville Herskovits, *The Human Factor in Changing Africa* (New York: Alfred A. Knopf, 1962).

George Houser, "Journey to Rebel Angola," *Africa Today* (March 1962).

George Houser, *No One Can Stop the Rain* (New York: Pilgrim Press, 1989).

George Houser and Herb Shore, *Mozambique: Dream the Size of Freedom* (New York: The Africa Fund, 1975).

Donald Humphries, "The East African Liberation Movement," *Adelphi Papers* 16 (March 1965).

Allen Isaacman, "The Tradition of Resistance in Mozambique," *Africa Today* (July–September 1975).

192 BIBLIOGRAPHY

A. J. K. Kangwa, "Conclusions of the Committee Set Up on the 24th March, 1965 to Consider Some Common Basis for Unity," Lusaka, March 25, 1965 [Marcum Papers Box 35/3].

Max V. Kemling, "A Chronicle of Events in the Life of Methodist Missions: Mozambique," 1962 [Marcum Papers 40/3].

Helen Kitchen, "Conversation with Eduardo Mondlane," *Africa Report* (November 1967).

Levy, Samuel. "Report on the Civil War in Mozambique," New Hampshire Institute of Current World Affairs (June 1985).

David Mabunda, "Special Report on the Present Disturbances within FRELIMO," Dar es Salaam, January 1963 [Marcum Papers 36/3].

David Mabunda and Sakupwanya, "The UDENAMO at the United Nations, November 7, 1963," Cairo, 1963 [Marcum Papers 36/7].

David Mabunda, J. M. "The UDENAMO and Nationalism in Mozambique," May 16, 1966 [Marcum Papers 36/7].

Samora Machel, *Establishing People's Power to Serve the Masses* (Dar es Salaam, Tanzania Publishing House, 1977).

Newt Malyn, *A History of Mozambique* (London: Hurst & Co., 1995).

John Marcum, "The Exile Condition and Revolutionary Effectiveness: Southern African Liberation Movements," in Christian P. Potholm and Richard Dale, eds., *Southern Africa in Perspective: Essays in Regional Politics* (New York: The Free Press, 1972).

John Marcum, "The Politics of Indifference: A Case Study in American Foreign Policy," Mondlane Memorial Lecture, Syracuse University, March 9, 1972.

John Marcum, *The Angolan Revolution*, vol. 2, *Exile Politics and Guerilla Warfare* (Cambridge, Mass., MIT Press, 1978).

Irving Leonard Markovitz, *Studies in Power and Class in Africa* (Oxford: Oxford University Press, 1987).

David Martin, "How Frelimo Held a 7-Hour Confessional," *The Observer* (London), March 23, 1975.

Leo Milas, "O.A.U. Must Probe Frelimo," *Voice of Africa*, (Accra) January 1965.

Leo Milas, "Portugal's African Vietnam," *The Ethiopian Herald*, February 25, 1972.

Eduardo Mondlane, "*O Valor do Estudante na Luta de Libertacao Nacional*," Inaugural address, Second Congress of UNEMO, Dar es Salaam, December 29, 1965 [Marcum Papers Box 38/5].

Eduardo Mondlane, "The Struggle for Independence in Mozambique," *Présence Africaine*, 20 (1963).

Eduardo Mondlane, *The Struggle for Mozambique* (Baltimore: Penguin Books, 1983).

BIBLIOGRAPHY   193

Eduardo Mondlane, "Dissent on Mocambique," in Ronald H. Chilcote, *Emerging Nationalism in Portuguese Africa: Documents* (Stanford: Hoover Institution Press, Stanford University, 1972).

Eduardo Mondlane, "The Struggle for Independence in Mozambique," mimeo, The American Society of African Culture, International Conference on Southern Africa, Howard University, April 11–13, 1963 [Marcum Papers Box 36/7].

Eduardo Mondlane, "Christian Missions Under Test," *Archways*, December 24, 1952.

Eduardo Mondlane and Janet Rae Mondlane, "Education in Portuguese Africa," in Ruth Sloan, ed., *The Educated African* (New York: Praeger, 1962).

Eduardo Mondlane, "African Nationalism and the Christian Way." [Marcum Papers Box 36/7].

Eduardo Mondlane, "Nationalism and Development in Mozambique," paper presented at UCLA conference, Los Angeles, February 27–28, 1968 [Marcum Papers Box 36/7].

Eduardo Mondlane, "Report of the Central Committee," FRELIMO: Documents of the 2nd Congress, Niassa, Mozambique, July 1968 [Marcum Papers Box 38/8].

Eduardo Mondlane, "Memorandum" to the African Liberation Committee of the Heads of State Conference, mimeo, Addis Ababa, Summer, 1963 [Marcum Papers Box 34/7].

Eduardo Mondlane, "Mozambique," in Calvin W. Stillman, *Africa in the Modern World* (Chicago: University of Chicago Press, 1955).

Eduardo Mondlane and David J. M. Mabunda, "The Mozambique Liberation Front (FRELIMO)," no date [Marcum Papers Box 34/7].

Eduardo Mondlane, "The Mozambique Liberation Front: the Crystalization of a Struggle for Freedom," Dar es Salaam, January 1964 [Marcum Papers Box 36/7].

Eduardo Mondlane, "Present Conditions in Mozambique," May 1, 1961 [Box 36/7].

Eduardo Mondlane, "Anti-Colonialism in the United States," in G. H. Curry, *Self-Government Movements in Australia and New Zealand in the Nineteenth Century* (Sydney: University of Sydney, 1957).

Eduardo Mondlane, "Woodrow Wilson and the Idea of Self-Determination in Africa," presented to Woodrow Wilson Foundation at Maxwell School, Syracuse University, N.Y., April 2, 1962.

Janet Mondlane, "Report by Janet Mondlane," Syracuse, N.Y., Summer 1963 [Marcum Papers 34/7].

Janet Mondlane, Statement to Tanzanian Police on History of Mozambique Institute, March 6, 1968 [Marcum Papers Box 37/3].

194 BIBLIOGRAPHY

Solomon Mondlane, *The Life and Walks of Dr. Jose C. Massinga (1930–2010): Moments of Challenge, Stubborness, Brilliance, Patience and Love* (Lyton Manor, South Africa: MP Books, 2003, 2012).

Edwin Munger, "Mozambique: Uneasy Today, Uncertain Tomorrow," *African Field Reports* (Cape Town, C. Struik, 1961).

Barry Munslow, *Mozambique: the Revolution and Its Origins* (New York, Longman, 1983).

Miguel Murupa, "Statement: To the Government of the United Republic of Tanzania," Dar es Salaam, February 7, 1970 [Marcum Papers Box 37/3].

Miguel Murupa, Interview, "Portugal Vencera," *Noticias de Portugal* (June 3, 1971).

Miguel Murupa, *Portuguese Africa in Perspective: the Making of a Multiracial Nation* (Lisbon, 1973).

Yoweri Museveni, "Fanon's Theory on Violence: Its Verification in Liberated Mozambique," in Nathan Shamuyarira (ed.), *Essays on the Liberation of Southern Africa* (Dar es Salaam: Tanzania Publishing House, 1971).

Marcus Namashula et al., "A Document for the History of African Nationalism. The UNEMO 'White Paper' of 1968. A Student Reply to Eduardo Mondlane's 1967 Paper," *African Historical Studies* III (1970).

Barnabe Ncomo, *Uria Simango: Um Homem, Uma Causa* (Maputo: Edicoes Novafrica, 2004).

Enos Ndlovu "We Will Tell Dictator Salazar," *African Mail*, Lusaka, January 31, 1961.

Joao Nhambiu, "Mozambican Students Manifesto," UNEMO, Philadelphia, November 1, 1963 [Box 38/5].

Roland Oliver and J. D. Fage, *A Short History of Africa* (Baltimore: Penguin, 1962).

Lydia Polgreen, "As Coal Boosts Mozambique, the Rural Poor are Left Behind," *New York Times*, November 11, 2012.

Holden Roberto, "Address to Central African Students in the US," *Voz do Estudante Angolano*, no. 2 (Dec. 1962–Jan. 1963).

Vladimir Shubin, *The Hot Cold War: The USSR in Southern Africa* (University of Kwa-Zulu-Natal: Pluto Press, 2008).

Uria T. Simango, "Gloomy Situation in FRELIMO", Dar es Salaam, November 3, 1969 [Marcum Papers, Box 37/8].

Daniel Sithole, "The Mozambique Tragedy," Nairobi, 1981.

Calvin Stillman, *Africa in the Modern World* (Chicago: University of Chicago Press, 1955).

John de. St. Jorre, "Forgotten War," *London Observer*, October 25, 1966.

Jacinto Veloso, *Memories at Low Altitude* (Cape Town: Zed Press, 2012).

BIBLIOGRAPHY **195**

Nuno Vidal with Patrick Chabal, *Southern Africa: Civil Society, Politics and Donor Strategies* (Luanda and Lisbon: Media XXI & Firmamento, 2009).

Anders Wastberg, *Angola and Mozambique: The Case against Portugal* (New York: Roy Publishers, 1963).

Douglas Wheeler, "A Document for the History of African Nationalism: A FRELIMO White Paper by Dr. Eduardo C. Mondlane (1920–1969)," *African Historical Studies* (1969).

A.J. Williams-Myers, "Regional Aspects of a Historical Legacy of Resistance," *Journal of Southern African Affairs* (January 1977).

David Apter, *The Gold Coast in Transition* (Princeton University Press, 1955).

James Coleman, *Nigeria: Background to Nationalism* (University of California Press, 1958).

Political Parties And National Integration In Tropical Africa, with James Coleman (University of California Press, 1964).

Nigerian Political Parties: Power in an Emergent African Nation (Princeton University Press, 1963).

Africa: The Politics of Independence (Vintage Books, 1961).

Political Parties in French-Speaking West Africa (Calendon Press, 1964).

INDEX

A

Acheson, Dean, 78–80, 84
Adoula, Cyrille, 61
Agostinho Neto, 5, 108, 112, 127
Archdeacon, Sarah, 43, 44, 46
Arthur Xavier Lambo Vilankulu, 162, 163, 169
Azores base agreement, 75, 76, 78–81, 98, 155, 156

B

Ball, George, 78–80
Bande, N.K., 65
Bowles, Chester, 76–79

C

Cabral, Amilcar, 5, 74, 114, 142, 143, 172
Caetano, Marcello, 155–161
Chagonga, Jose Balthazar da Costa, 36, 52, 62–65, 70, 102
Chissano, Joaquim, 109, 112, 117, 148, 164, 168, 178–181, 185

CIMADE, 112
COREMO, 65, 67–69, 71, 134, 162, 165, 168, 169

D

Dos Santos, Marcelino, 5, 30, 31, 38, 40, 41, 49, 61, 74, 106, 112, 114, 117, 124, 133–135, 137, 139, 141–148, 151, 153, 162, 163, 165, 169, 171, 175, 181, 187

F

Fredericks, Wayne, 3, 129, 157
FRELIMO, 1, 2, 4, 20, 31, 32, 35–41, 43–53, 55–63, 65–71, 73, 80–83, 85–98, 101–108, 112–114, 116–124, 126–135, 137–141, 143–153, 156, 157, 161–175, 177–183, 187
FUNIPAMO, 56, 63, 69

© The Editor(s) (if applicable) and The Author(s) 2018
J.A. Marcum, *Conceiving Mozambique*, African Histories and Modernities, https://doi.org/10.1007/978-3-319-65987-9

198 INDEX

G

Guebuza, Armando Emilio, 117, 118, 180–182, 187
General Antonio de Spinola, 160
GRAE, 60, 62
Gumane, Paulo, 30, 33, 37, 39–41, 44, 46, 48, 49, 52, 53, 57–62, 66–68, 70, 71, 86, 87, 124, 134, 146, 163–165, 167, 168
Gwambe, Adelino, 21, 22, 31, 48, 68, 102, 137
Gwenjero, Mateos, 102, 118

H

Holden Roberto, 61, 62, 75, 82, 95, 142
Houser, George, 11, 14, 15, 33, 43, 48, 52, 53, 75, 76, 79, 84, 122

K

Kennedy, Robert F, 80, 81
Kenyatta, Jomo, 46, 86, 129

L

Lazaro N'Kavandame, 32, 91–93, 97, 105, 129–135, 145, 167, 177
Lusaka accord, 165, 179

M

Mabunda, David, 28–34
Machel, Samora, 104–106, 131, 135, 137, 141, 148, 150, 151, 154
Maconde, 19–21, 32, 88–91, 93
Magusa, Samuel, 101
Mahoney, Richard, 75, 78
MANU, 21, 31, 35–37, 41, 44, 49, 50
Massinga, Joseph, 44, 45, 47, 52, 53, 115, 122

Mateos, Mmole, 21
Milas, Leo E., 37, 41, 43–51
Moare, Adriano, 10
Mocumbi, Pascoal, 109, 112
Mondlane, Janet, 1–6, 8–13, 15, 85–91, 93, 95–98
MPLA, 61
MRUPP, 105, 106
Mtwara, 131, 132
Mueda myth, 17
Murupa, Miguel, 140, 141, 153
Musevani, Yoweri Kaguta, 94
Mutembe, Mateus, 117

N

Nachingwea, 102, 104, 106, 117, 140, 141, 146, 164–166
NESAM, 5, 14, 104, 114, 115, 179, 181
Nhambiu, Joao Jamisse, 104, 106, 108–117, 122, 124, 127, 148, 179, 180
Nkrumah, Kwame, 3, 26, 27, 30, 31, 57, 62, 74, 87, 109, 137
Nungu, Silverio, 49, 56, 135, 136, 138–141, 152
Nyerere, Julius, 10, 27, 39, 62, 74, 87, 94, 140, 166

O

OAU, 47, 61, 62, 75, 82, 85, 87, 93, 94, 97, 118, 146, 149, 168
Organic law of Overseas Portugal, 82, 83

P

PAC, 59, 62, 69, 70
PAFMECSA, 21, 36, 75
PCN, 163–165, 169, 170

INDEX 199

R
RENAMO, 50, 70, 124, 169, 177–181, 183
Roberto Mondlane, 61, 70, 75, 82, 95, 142
Rusk, Dean, 75, 76, 79, 80, 81

S
Salazar, Antonio, 3, 22
Shubin, Vladimir, 52, 117
Simango, Uria T., 36, 37, 39, 41, 46, 60, 61, 71, 86, 102, 103, 105, 106, 118, 123, 125, 126, 129, 133–141, 145, 146, 148, 152, 153, 162, 163, 165, 167, 168, 183, 184, 187

U
UGEAN, 114
UNAMI, 50, 63, 65, 67, 70, 119
UNEMO, 104, 105, 112–116, 122, 126–128, 148, 177, 179, 180
UNEMO-US, 116, 121, 123, 125, 162
UN Trusteeship Council, 10

Printed in the United States
By Bookmasters